rangers

player by player

1 2 3 4 5 6 7 8 9 10 11

BOB FERRIER, ROBERT McELROY

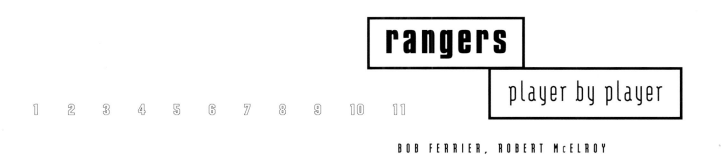

First published in Great Britain by The Crowood Press in 1990

Revised and updated in 1997 and 1998 by Hamlyn
an imprint of Reed International Books Limited,
Michelin House, 81 Fulham Road,
London SW3 6RB
and Auckland, Melbourne, Singapore and Toronto

Publishing Director: **Laura Bamford**
Editors: **Trevor Davies and Tarda Davison-Aitkins**
Design: **Vivek Bhatia**
Design Manager: **Bryan Dunn**
Creative Art Director: **Keith Martin**
Picture research: **Zoe Holtermann**
Production: **Bonnie Ashby**

ISBN 0 600 59495 5

A catalogue record for this book is available from the British Library

Printed in Spain by Graphycem

Picture Acknowledgements:
Colorsport
The Herald, Scottish Media Newspapers Ltd
Syndication International
Sportapics
Allsport

rangers

player by player

1 2 3 4 5 6 7 8 9 10 11

INTRODUCTION

Rangers Football Club is a unique institution. There is nothing quite like it anywhere in the world. On all counts, it is the most successful club in Scotland, and one of the oldest, dating from 1872. Its place in the culture of the nation is as distinctive as that of the Church of Scotland, the Scottish legal system, the Royal and Ancient Golf Club of St Andrews. More than any other element in Scottish life, it represents the Protestant, Unionist, Masonic tradition. It has become institutionalised in defence of these things over the years, and its rivalry with the other prominent Glasgow club, Celtic, with its Roman Catholic and Irish origins, cannot be compared with any other football rivalry anywhere in the world. Real Madrid and Barcelona in Spain; AC Milan and Internazionale in Italy; River Plate and Boca Juniors in Argentina, and Penarol and Nacional in Uruguay – there are classic rivals in the world of football, but nowhere else is the rivalry based on religion, as it is with Rangers and Celtic in Scotland.

The traditions which Rangers have maintained have brought the club the support of 'like-minded men' in astonishing numbers, very many of them organised in a supporters-club network which is world-wide. From Shetland to Southampton, from the islands of Lewis and Harris to Liverpool and Leicester and London and Manchester, there are Rangers supporters' clubs. From Lisburn and Londonderry and Armagh in the North of Ireland, the coaches cross on the ferries to Scotland for every Rangers game. There is a Rangers supporters' club in the British Army of the Rhine, another in Hamburg. There is one in Riyadh in Saudi Arabia, where members gather to listen to match broadcasts. In Australia, New Zealand, South Africa, Canada and the USA there are Rangers supporters clubs. Collectively, these clubs represent a remarkable social organism. The football pool which they sustain generates at least £1 million in income for the football club each year, to be used for virtually anything save the purchase of players.

The club's sustained success on the field, and the massive support available to it, has made it seem arrogant in periods of its history. 'We are Rangers – take it or leave it,' has been the creed. And nowhere has this superiority, this self-confidence been made more evident, than in the huge main grandstand, built in 1929 when the club was dominating the Scottish game as never before. Soaring up to 70 feet in the air, seating 10,000 with standing room for a further 9000, its massive red-brick façade is now a listed building. After 60 years of use, the more public areas of this edifice – stairways, seats, roofs – were creaking, rusting and leaking under the stress of time and in 1990 a repair and even rebuilding programme was initiated. This represented the final transformation of Ibrox from the huge, sweeping 'stadium' with a capacity in six figures, almost all standing, to a modern, sophisticated football ground with a capacity of 50,000, all seated. Let us pray they do not seek to transform the private rooms in the old place – the trophy room, the 'cocktail' room, the offices of manager and secretary which enjoy vintage Art-Deco fittings and furnishings.

The transformation of Ibrox has been achieved under the spur of burgeoning European competition, and of the extension and immense financial power of of international televised sport. Yet no matter how grand, even grandiose, the stadium, no matter the financial investment in salaries and transfer fees, the game as ever ultimately depends on 11 men on the field, week in, week out, season after season. In the history of Rangers, the club has been blessed with outstanding players, outstanding teams. And in honesty, it has had indifferent players, unsuccessful teams. This book is an attempt to record all the players who have played for the club since World War II, more specifically since the start of season 1946–47, to the end of season 1997–98. Our statistics embrace only League Championship, Scottish Cup and League Cup matches, and European competition games. We have ignored friendly matches and those of lesser, local competitions. In a very few instances this includes players who were also at the club before the war. In a couple of cases information is unavailable for international caps won while playing for clubs other than Rangers.

A high proportion of the players listed have played only one game, or a games total in single figures – the wastage at Ibrox has seemed high. But then the wastage in professional football in general is very high, and Rangers probably attract more players, and have first choice of more young players, than any other Scottish club. Many excellent players have been crowded out at Ibrox by simply being there at the wrong time, when there has been a glut of competition for their position, and many have gone on to carve very long and successful careers with other clubs. Examples which come to mind are Alec Scott and Billy Stevenson.

We much appreciate the assistance we have had from Bill Richardson of the Scottish Football Association, David Thomson of the the Scottish Football League, journalists Douglas Baillie and Allan Herron, former Rangers Captain Ian McColl and friends of Rangers, John Dykes, Gordon Scott and the late Sam Johnston. We also acknowledge the invaluable assistance of the 'Rangers Historian' magazine – the definitive club history.

Bob Ferrier, Robert McElroy

LIST OF PLAYERS

ALBERTZ, J.	181	COOPER, NEALE	151	GASCOIGNE, P.	178	KUZNETSOV, O.	157
ALEXANDER, T.	99	COWAN, T.	151	GATTUSO, G.	187		
AMORUSO, L.	190	COX, S.	10	GILLICK, T.	16	LAUDRUP, B.	172
ANDERSEN, ERIK BO	182	CUNNING, B.	40	GINZBURG, B.	153	LIDDELL, C.	34
ANDERSON, S.	63			GORAM, A. L.	162	LINDSAY, J.	25
ARMOUR, D.	108	DALZIEL, G.	118	GORDON, D.	164	LITTLE, ADAM	26
ARNISON, NORMAN	40	DAVIES, B.	122	GOUGH, R.	144	LITTLE JOHN	31
ARNISON, BILLY	19	DAVIS, H.	49	GRANT, B.	63	LOGIE, W.	48
AUSTIN, A.	52	DAWSON, A.	111	GRAY, ANDY	152	LYALL, K.	123
		DENNY, J.	99	GRAY, DAVID	18		
BAILLIE, D.	63	DIBBLE, A.	184	GREIG, J.	70	MACADAM, C.	120
BAIRD, S.	40	DODDS, D.	154	GRIERSON, D.	35	MACDONALD, ALEX	92
BARTRAM, J.	148	DONALDSON, G.	104			MACDONALD, IAIN	95
BAXTER, J.	64	DRINKELL, K.	151	HAGEN, D.	156	MACDONALD, JOHN	120
BEATTIE, S.	135	DUNCAN, G.	53	HAMILTON, J.	105	MACDONALD, KEVIN	153
BECK, T.	80	DUNCANSON, J.	18	HATELEY, M.	160	MACFARLANE, D.	135
BECKETT, W.	31	DUNLOP, R.	31	HENDERSON, MARTIN	108	MACKAY, B.	114
BELL, D.	136	DURIE, G. S.	170	HENDERSON, WILLIE	68	MACKINNON, DAVE	127
BETT, J.	119	DURRANT, I.	134	HERON, B.	94	McCALL, IAN	146
BJORKLUND, J.	182			HOGG, B.	54	McCALL, STUART	165
BLACK, K.	121	ELLIOTT, A.	48	HOUSTON, D.	105	McCALLUM, A.	99
BOLI, B.	175			HUBBARD, J.	27	McCLELLAND, J.	121
BOLLAN, G.	176	FALCO, M.	148	HUISTRA, P.	158	McCLOY, P.	96
BONNYMAN, P.	105	FERGUSON, ALEX	89	HUME, B.	62	McCOIST, A.	132
BOYACK, S.	184	FERGUSON, DEREK	130	HUNTER, DONALD	108	McCOLL, I.	22
BOYD, GORDON	109	FERGUSON, ERIC	128	HUNTER, WILLIE	72	McCULLOCH, W.	30
BOYD, WILLIE	34	FERGUSON, IAIN	130	HURLOCK, T.	158	McDOUGALL, I.	108
BRAND, R.	42	FERGUSON, IAN	150	HYND, R.	75	McEWAN, A.	54
BROWN, BOBBY	8	FERGUSON, BARRY	184			McGINTY, B.	171
BROWN, JOHN	148	FERGUSON, DUNCAN	168	JACKSON, C.	81	McGREGOR, J.	146
BRUCE, A.	126	FINDLAY, W.	25	JARDINE, W.	84	McINNES, D. J.	177
BURNS, H.	131	FITZGERALD, D.	184	JOHANNSON, J.	191	McINTYRE, JIM	121
BUTCHER, T.	138	FLECK, R.	129	JOHANSEN, K.	77	McINTYRE, I.(JOHN)	30
		FORREST, J.	73	JOHNSON, J.	27	McKEAN, B.	110
CALDOW, E.	36	FORSYTH, ALEX	118	JOHNSTON, MAURICE	153	McKENZIE, GEORGE	35
CALDWELL, N.	174	FORSYTH, TOM	104	JOHNSTON, WILLIE	78	McKENZIE, GORDON	35
CASKIE, J.	18	FRAME, J.	27	JOHNSTONE, DEREK	102	McKINNON, RON	66
CHRISTIE, J.	72	FRANCIS, T.	150			McKNIGHT, P.	171
CLARKE, ROBERT	118	FRANKS, A.	63	KENNEDY, ANDY	126	McLAREN, A. J.	174
CLARK, SANDY	126	FRASER, CAMMY	131	KENNEDY, STEWART	109	McLEAN, GEORGE (1)	62
CLELAND, A.	180	FRASER, SCOTT	129	KING, B.	72	McLEAN, GEORGE (2)	62
COHEN, A.	143	FYFE, G.	98	KIRKWOOD, D.	143	McLEAN, TOMMY	106
CONN, A.	94			KITCHENBRAND, D.	44	McMILLAN, HUNTER	35
COOPER, DAVID	116	GARDINER, W.	34				

RANGERS

McMILLAN, IAN.	56	PATERSON, CRAIG	123	SHAW, JOHN	25	WALKER, JIMMY	40
McMINN, K.	135	PATERSON, BILL	55	SHEARER, B.	45	WALKER, NICKY	128
McNEE, C.	26	PATON, W.	26	SHIELDS, G.	169	WALMSLEY, W.	27
McPHEE, B.	94	PAUL, B.	80	SIMPSON, BOBBY	31	WALTERS, M.	147
McPHERSON, DAVID	125	PENMAN, ANDY	88	SIMPSON, BILLY	28	WATKINS, C.	10
McPHERSON, JOHN	27	PENMAN, WILLIE	63	SMITH, ALEC	83	WATSON, CRAIG	72
McSWEGAN, G.	147	PERSSON, O.	88	SMITH, BILLY	52	WATSON, KENNY (1)	95
MARSHALL, D.	26	PETRIC, G.	180	SMITH, DAVE	82	WATSON, KENNY (2)	112
MARTIN, N.	60	PHILLIPS, J.	143	SMITH, GORDON	114	WATSON, BOBBY (1)	80
MASON, J.	105	PORRINI, S.	186	SNELDERS, T.	181	WATSON, BOBBY (2)	99
MATHIESON, W.	76	PRENTICE, J.	30	SORENSEN, ERIC	86	WATSON, STEPHEN	167
MATTHEW, A.	55	PRESSLEY, S.	159	SORENSEN, JORN	76	WEST, C.	136
MAXWELL, A.	167	PROVAN, D.	58	SOUNESS, G.	140	WHITE, W.	95
MELROSE, H.	54	PRYDE, W.	34	SPACKMAN, N.	154	WILKINS, R.	146
MENZIES, R.	35	PRYTZ, R.	124	SPENCER, J.	155	WILLIAMSON, BOBBY	128
MIKHAILICHENKO, A.	166			STANNERS, D.	34	WILLIAMSON, BILLY	19
MILLAR, J.	41	QUEEN. J.	48	STEAD, A.	19	WILLOUGHBY, A.	74
MILLER, ALEX	101			STEELE, J.	112	WILSON, DAVIE	50
MILLER, COLIN	135	RAE	24	STEIN, C.	90	WILSON, SCOTT	184
MILLER, CHARLIE	167	REDFORD, I.	118	STENSAAS, S.	189	WISHART, F.	169
MITCHELL, D.	126	REID, ALEX	72	STERLAND, M.	150	WOOD, W.	76
MOLES, W.	53	REID, BRIAN	159	STEVEN, T.	152	WOODBURN, W.	20
MOORE, C.	171	RIDEOUT, P	164	STEVENS, GARY	149	WOODS, CHRIS	137
MORRIS, E.	105	RITCHIE, B.	46	STEVENS, GREGOR	115	WOODS, JOHNNY	35
MORRISON, B.	52	ROBERTS, G.	142	STEVENSON, W.	55	WOODS, NEIL	143
MORROW, J.	156	ROBERTSON, CHRIS	112	STEWART, J.	122	WRIGHT, S.	176
MUNRO, STUART	129	ROBERTSON, DAVID	159	STRICKLAND, D.	114		
MUNRO, IAIN	112	ROBERTSON, DOUGLAS	123	SYMON, S.	11	YOUNG, GEORGE (I)	12
MURRAY, MAX	40	ROBERTSON, LEE	157			YOUNG, GEORGE (2)	115
MURRAY, NEIL	156	ROBERTSON, SANDY	152	TELFER, W.	53	YOUNG, QUINTON	104
		ROBERTSON, TOM	54	THERN, J.	188		
NEEF, G.	93	RODGER, J.	35	THOMSON, SANDY	48	**THE MANAGERS**	
NEGRI, M.	185	ROZENTAL, S.	183	THOMSON, BILLY	174	ADVOCAAT, DICK	196
NEILLANDS, I.	34	RUSSELL, R.	113	THORNTON, W.	17	GREIG, JOHN	195
NIEMI, A.	191	RUTHERFORD, E.	24	TRAILL, D.	72	SMITH, WALTER	196
NICHOLL, J.	127					SOUNESS, GRAEME	195
NISBET, S.	136	SALENKO, O.	177	URQUHART, B.	114	STRUTH, WILLIAM	192
NIVEN, G.	32	SCOTT, ALEXANDER	38			SYMON, SCOT	192
		SCOTT, ALLY	108	VALENTINE, J.	52	WADDELL, WILLIE	193
O' HARA, A.	105	SCOTT, COLIN	155	VAN VOSSEN, P. J.	183	WALLACE, JOCK	194
ORR, B.	55	SEMPLE, B.	82	VIDMAR, T.	189	WHITE, DAVID	193
		SETTERINGTON, D.	80	VINNICOMBE, C.	154		
PARLANE, DEREK	100	SHARP, R.	108				
PARLANE, JIMMY	19	SHAW, JOCK	11	WADDELL, W.	14		

BOBBY BROWN

1946-56

Bobby Brown was the Adonis, the golden boy who was the first (or last) line of Rangers' famous 'Iron Curtain' defence in the years immediately after the Second World War. From 1946 until 1952, 'Brown, Young and Shaw' was the inevitable start to any Rangers team selection, followed by a variety of wing-halfs – McColl, Symon, Cox, Rae, Watkins – around the centre-half Woodburn.

Tall, slim, blond and athletic, Bobby Brown moved from Falkirk High School to Queen's Park in 1939 and played his first match for them against Celtic at Parkhead in April 1940. The match was drawn, 4–4! Brown served in the Fleet Air Arm during the war and guested for Portsmouth, Plymouth, Chester and Chelsea. In 1945, still an amateur, he became an international player when selected to play against England on 5 February at Villa Park. Young Brown faced a forward line that included Matthews, Lawton and Mortensen, a defence that included Swift, Hardwicke, Franklin and Mercer. The Scots went down 3–2, but 'Boy' Brown played very well.

With the war over, he enrolled at Jordanhill College in Glasgow to train as a PE teacher. He turned professional and joined Rangers on the same day as Sammy Cox arrived from Dundee, and 48 hours later they were both in the team for a Victory Cup match at Airdrie – 3 May 1946. Both players retained their places, and a month later had won both Victory Cup and Glasgow Charity Cup medals. Brown's early days at Ibrox were not all sweetness and light. For one thing, he was succeeding Jerry Dawson, one of Rangers' finest goalkeepers who had been at the club since 1929 and had collected 14 international caps before the war. Dawson was an outstanding goalkeeper and a lively, outgoing personality, and the Ibrox crowd let Brown know what they expected of him. Then as an amateur turning professional, he had negotiated his own signing fee and terms. The fee was spread over a number of seasons and made him the highest-paid player at Ibrox, which was not calculated to delight some of his more senior team-mates.

Bobby qualified and became a PE teacher at Denny High School, remaining a part-time player throughout his time with Rangers. After a few months, he settled into a golden career with the club. He was a signed player for 10 years. In his time, an outstanding Rangers team was challenged persitently and successfully not by Celtic, but by the Hibernian team of Gordon Smith and Lawrie Reilly. Bobby Brown left Rangers for Falkirk in May 1956. The transfer fee was £2200. Within a year he had retired from the game, his heart still with Rangers. In his first six seasons at Ibrox he had missed only one League game, and once played in 179 successive matches. Bobby always took the field with brand-new, shining-white laces in his boots.

He became manager of St Johnstone and led them into the top division, and was Scotland team manager from February 1967 until July 1971.

Games:	296 (plus 6 war time)
Shut-outs:	109 (plus 5 war time)
League Championship:	1946–47, 48–49, 49–50
Scottish Cup:	1947–48, 48–49, 49–50
League Cup:	1946–47, 48–49
Victory Cup:	1945–46
Honours:	3 Scotland caps (plus 8 wartime)
Born:	Dunipace, 19 March 1923

SAMMY COX

1946-55

As beautifully balanced as any footballer who ever played for Rangers and Scotland, Sammy Cox was in a sense a player out of his time. He could well have fitted comfortably into any Brazilian team of the eighties. An Ayrshire boy from Darvel, he played as a teenage amateur during the Second World War with Queen's Park, Third Lanark and Dundee. He joined Rangers as a professional in May 1946, on the same day as goalkeeper Bobby Brown, and like Brown immediately won both Victory Cup and Charity Cup Honours, clearly establishing himself in the team within a year, playing every League match of season 1947-48. He went on to have an outstanding 10-year career at Ibrox, then played a few more seasons with East Fife before emigrating to Canada in 1959.

Cox was essentially a left-sided player, but he played with distinction as either a full-back or in either wing-half position. Indeed, he played an international match against France in Paris in 1948 as an inside-forward. He also captained Scotland against England in the Hampden match of 1954. By the end of the 1940s he was ready to succeed Jock Shaw and became the regular left-back in both Rangers and Scotland teams.

His play was characterised by balance, quickness and a supreme confidence based on his exceptional technical ability. Cox had a sophisticated football brain which, in spite of the fact that he was not quite 5'8" in height and but 150 lb in weight, allowed him to make the most crisp and incisive, but nevertheless, ferocious tackles. His positional and tactical sense led him to base his defensive work on manoeuvring opponents into dead-end locations, and he had particular success against outstanding wingers such as Stanley Matthews and Tom Finney. He was a regular in the Scotland team from 1949 to 1954.

Games:	310 (plus 6 war time)
Goals:	20
League Championship:	1948–49, 49–50, 52–53
Scottish Cup:	1947–48, 48–49, 49–50
League Cup:	1948–49
Victory Cup:	1945–46
Honours:	24 Scotland caps
Born:	Darvel, 13 April 1924

CHARLIE WATKINS

1946-48

Charlie Watkins, a Glasgow boy, was a right-half, a good, honest, right-footer who at 5' 9" was strongly built and always fit. He was already at the club when Ian McColl was signed in 1945, aged eighteen. McColl went straight into the team, but quickly discovered that the professional game required some learning and was bundled into the reserves. Watkins started 1946–47 as the man in possession, but the talented young McColl quickly forced his way into the team and stayed there, going on to have an exceptional Rangers career. Charlie Watkins was hard-working, not over-skilled but a solid club man committed to Rangers. With McColl and Sammy Cox installed as wing-halfs, he was always going to be a reserve, and in September 1948 he moved on to Luton Town. He was a qualified physiotherapist, and later lived in South Africa.

Charlie was one of the very few players who had joined Rangers from the junior St Anthony's club, and was responsible for Rangers signing Don Kitchenbrand.

Games:	13 (plus 49 war time)
Goals:	0 (plus 4 war time)
Southern League Championship:	1945–46
Victory Cup:	1945–46
Born:	Glasgow

SCOT SYMON

1946-47

If ever the talents, the personality, the character of a footballer could be expressed by his performance in one single match, James Scotland ('Scot') Symon would surely have claimed that match was Rangers v Moscow Dynamo, Ibrox, 28 November 1945. A crowd of 90,000 packed the Rangers ground to see the Russian team give a brilliant exhibition of passing skills, speed, finishing power and fitness that had them two up after 25 minutes and threatening to run all over Rangers, a quite bewildered team. Yet in a marvellous second-half recovery, Rangers saved the match at 2–2 and finally dominated the play. It was a recovery greatly inspired by Symon's ferocious tackling, the accuracy of his long-distance passing, and above all by his blazing spirit.

Scot Symon was born in Errol, near Perth, and attended Perth Academy, a rugby-playing school, but he became a junior international footballer with Dundee Violet before turning professional with Dundee FC in 1930. He moved to Portsmouth in 1935, came to Rangers in 1938, and retired in 1947. A powerful build made him an uncompromising wing-half and his tackling was often little short of venomous. He played once for Scotland, against Hungary in 1938, and clearly lost many of his best years to the Second World War. He also played cricket for Scotland and was the only man capped by the country at both sports until Andy Goram played cricket for Scotland against Ireland and the Australia in 1989. Scot Symon retired in 1947 to begin a distinguished managerial career with East Fife, Preston North End and Rangers. (See 'The Managers'.)

Games:	37 (plus 252 war time)
Goals:	3 (plus 11 war time)
League Championship:	1938–39
Scottish Regional League:	1939–40
Southern League Championship:	1940–41, 41–42, 42–43, 43–44, 44–45, 45–46
Southern League Cup:	1940–41, 42–43, 44–45
Summer Cup:	1941–42
Victory Cup:	1945–46
Honours:	1 Scotland cap
Born:	Errol, 9 May 1911

JOCK SHAW

1946-53

John 'Tiger' Shaw will be remembered for his durability. He was a League Championship and Scottish Cup winner in 1950, at the age of 38, and was 42 on retirement. In view of his uncompromising playing style, this was a tribute to his fitness. At 5' 7" Jock was small for a full-back, but his tackling was fast and fearless, bringing him his nickname, and he was a hard-driving captain.

He began with Airdrie in 1933, when they took him from Glasgow junior football and the Benburb club, and he transferred to Rangers in July 1938 for £2000! He played in all four of Scotland's 1947 international matches, but was succeeded by his younger brother David of Hibernian. Following an extensive tour in the summer of 1954 to Canada and the USA, Shaw (and Willie Thornton) retired. He then had a successful association with the club as a trainer and later a groundsman. He played two war-time internationals against England, in 1941 and 1943, and in 'Victory' internationals in 1945 and 1946. Indeed, he and his brother formed the full-back partnership in the 1946 Victory international against England, which Scotland won 1–0. He captained Scotland four times and remained club captain towards his career's end, when George Young was team captain.

Games:	238 (plus 289 war time)
Goals:	3 (plus 3 war time)
League Championship:	1938–39, 46–47, 48–49, 49–50
Scottish Cup:	1947–48, 48–49, 49–50
League Cup:	1946–47, 48–49
Southern League Championship:	1940–41, 41–42, 42–43, 43–44, 44–45, 45–46
Scottish Regional League:	1939–40
Scottish Emergency War Cup:	1939–40
Southern League Cup:	1940–41, 41–42, 42–43, 44–45
Summer Cup:	1941–42
Victory Cup:	1945–46
Honours:	24 Scotland caps (7 wartime)
Born:	Annathill, 29 November 1912

GEORGE YOUNG (1)

1946-57

Dubbed 'Corky' because of the lucky champagne cork he habitually carried, George Lewis Young was a giant in every respect. At 6' 2" and weighing 15 stone, he was a massive man, albeit quite nimble on long, rather spindly legs. A natural centre-half, he played most of his career at right-back, yielding the position to Willie Woodburn, an exceptional player at the heart of a Rangers defence enshrined in club lore as the 'Iron Curtain'. Over six seasons, in 180 League matches, it yielded only 180 goals. When Woodburn was suspended *sine die* in September 1954, Young moved back to centre-half and played out his career there.

He played for Scotland 53 times and played in 34 consecutive matches, records since surpassed by Denis Law and Kenny Dalglish among others. He captained Scotland a record 48 times. As captain he was in a position seldom equalled before and certainly never since in terms of his influence on the team. Because of his close relationship with George Graham (later Sir George), secretary of the Scottish Football Association, Young was left to arrange training sessions, theatre visits, book local transport etc. and was, in effect, a surrogate team manager. The world of football was a good deal less sophisticated in those days and Young carried off all this perfectly well. But there were rumblings of privilege and many players, particularly the Anglo-Scots, were convinced that Young had an undue influence on affairs, team selections included. In consequence, the end of his international career was ironic. He perhaps made the mistake of announcing in advance that his last game would be against Spain in Madrid on 26 May 1957. He was not selected. Perhaps the selectors thought he had been just a shade too presumptuous. He never played for Scotland again.

In movement, George Young was less than a thoroughbred, having a top-heavy look about him, but he was a marvellously effective footballer, dominant in the air and an awesome tackler. One stretch of one of his giant legs allowed him to salvage many an apparently lost cause.

With a casual swing of his right boot he could hit clearances of 60 yards, and this became one of Rangers' most effective attacking gambits. Often these would be directed through the inside-right position, into which centre-forward, Thornton, drifted in anticipation. These clearances, from the deepest defensive positions, would usually catch the opposition completely stretched and exposed. And with the speed and strength of Waddell, the outside-right at the end of these Young clearances, Rangers would be into a counter-attack in a very few seconds. Young's clearances became an important element in attack for that Rangers team. He practised them faithfully in training, and was much more technically skilled than his movement and appearance might have suggested. Young retired in the summer of 1957, and was later manager of Third Lanark for three years. He died in January 1997, aged 74.

Games:	428 (plus 171 war time)
Goals:	31 (plus 27 war time)
League Championship:	1946–47, 48–49, 49–50, 52–53, 55–56, 56–57
Scottish Cup:	1947–48, 48–49, 49–50, 52–53
League Cup:	1946–47, 48–49
Southern League Championship:	1942–43, 43–44, 44–45
Southern League Cup:	1941–42, 42–43, 44–45
Summer Cup:	1941–42
Victory Cup:	1945–46
Honours:	53 Scotland caps (plus 2 war-time)
Born:	Grangemouth, 27 October 1922

WILLIE WADDELL

1946-56

In all the long history of the Rangers club, now well into its second century, no one has made a greater contribution to its development at so many levels than Willie Waddell. From the time he first played for Rangers in a reserve match against Partick Thistle at Firhill, at the age of 15 in 1936, until he retired in the eighties, Waddell had been player, manager, general manager, managing director/vice-chairman, director/consultant and finally an honorary director of the club. All this was over a scarcely interrupted span of some 50 years.

He first went to Ibrox as a schoolboy and manager Struth arranged for him to gain experience with Strathclyde Juniors for a spell. He signed as a professional in May 1938, and played his initial game for the first-team on 9 August at Ibrox against Arsenal. Not only that, he scored the only goal of the match. He established himself that season as Rangers' regular outside-right, playing throughout the war so that when Rangers' first great post-war team of the late-forties fell into place, Waddell, in his mid-twenties, was a seasoned, powerful outside-right.

In action, Willie Waddell was a strangely menacing player. He was strongly built, full in the chest, wide in the shoulder, not over-tall. His upper torso was thrust forward as his stride lengthened and he was alarmingly fast. Exceptional powers of acceleration often brought him pulled thigh muscle injuries. He was particularly skilful in crossing probing balls, many of which found Thornton's head and produced a high proportion of the centre-forward's many goals. Waddell himself was a very powerful finisher. There was intimidation, and huge excitement for the crowds in the very sight of Willie Waddell in full cry, and he was, in addition and in the local vernacular, 'crabbit' and 'carnaptious' with referees, opponents, even team-mates occasionally if they did not conform. To a large extent this attitude persisted throughout his life, and it may have contributed to his later successes.

He was a qualified and talented journalist, working for Glaswegian and national newspapers. He finished playing in the summer of 1956 and a year later became manager of Kilmarnock. He returned to Ibrox in December 1969. (See 'The Managers'.)

Games:	296 (plus 221 war time)
Goals:	56 (plus 221 war time)
League Championship:	1938–39, 46–47, 48–49, 52–53
Scottish Cup:	1948–49, 52–53
Scottish Regional League:	1939–40
Southern League Championship:	1942–43, 43–44, 44–45, 45–46
Scottish Emergency War Cup:	1939–40
Southern League Cup:	1941–42, 42–43, 44–45
Summer Cup:	1941–42
Victory Cup:	1945–46
Honours:	17 Scotland caps (plus 9 wartime)
Born:	Forth, Lanarkshire, 7 March 1921

TORRY GILLICK

1946–50

A superbly skilful 'old-fashioned' type of inside-forward, Torrance ('Torry') Gillick was unique. He was the only player that Rangers' fabled manager, William Struth, welcomed back to Ibrox a second time, after he had left the club. Gillick, from Airdrie, was playing at the age of 15 for Petershill, one of the most prominent of Glasgow's junior clubs. Rangers signed him in 1933 before he was 18 as a winger, and he won a Scottish Cup medal with them in 1935. That same year, rather surprisingly, he was transferred to Everton for £8000, a then-record Everton fee. He played successfully with the Liverpool club until the start of the Second World War, winning five Scotland caps and a Football League Championship medal in 1939 during that time. He was the only Rangers player to win Scottish Cup medals on either side of the Second World War.

He had played for Everton against Rangers at Ibrox in the 1938 Empire Exhibition tournament, then guested for Rangers and Airdrieonians during the war. He was brought back to Ibrox by Struth in 1945, and that year another claim to fame fell to him in the famous Rangers-Moscow Dynamo match. Torry stopped the play to inform the referee that the Russians had 12 players on the field!

Gillick developed into an outstanding forward of impressive ball control and perceptive positional play. In those post-war seasons, in an exceptional Rangers team, he formed a wonderfully effective wing with Willie Waddell, the quality of Gillick's passing being quite superb. From a rather crouching, round-backed posture, he hit and clipped the ball beautifully. He was particularly adept at placing perfectly weighted passes inside the opposing full-back to draw out and maximise Waddell's burning speed and powerful running. He could score goals too – in season 1946–47, for example, he hit 12 in 27 League matches, five in eight League Cup matches. Gillick was heavily set physically, and in motion was certainly not the most beautiful of athletes, but his short strides gave him a crackling burst of speed and acceleration over 10 yards.

He was well-loved, in spite of being disputatious on the field. The Glasgow expression 'greetin' face' might be used to describe him as he moaned at everyone – referees, opponents, even his own players. And he had a rather caustic humour. When opponents would say, 'We're on a £50 bonus,' he'd reply, 'We're getting only a tenner, but then we always win our bonuses, you don't.' And when manager Struth decided that Rangers players, to be properly turned out, must wear bowler hats, the story was that Gillick used to carry his in a brown paper bag until he was within sight of Ibrox, then, reluctantly, put it on his head.

Torry Gillick died, rather prematurely, on 12 December 1971. On that same day, perhaps the most famous of all Rangers players also died. His name was Alan Morton.

Games:	140 (plus 207 war time)
Goals:	62 (plus 124 war time)
League Championship:	1934–35, 1946–47
Scottish Cup:	1934–35, 47–48
League Cup:	1946–47, 48–49
Southern League Championship:	1940–41, 41–42, 42–43, 43–44, 44–45, 45–46
Southern League Cup:	1940–41, 41–42, 42–43, 44–45
Summer Cup:	1941–42
Victory Cup:	1945–46
Everton Football League Championship:	1938–39
Honours:	5 Scotland caps (none with Rangers)
Born:	Airdrie, 19 May 1915

WILLIE THORNTON

1946-54

A prodigy of the generation of Waddell and Woodburn, Willie Thornton of Winchburgh Albion in West Lothian signed for Rangers at the age of 16, in March 1936. As did Waddell, he played his first match for the club in the reserves, against Partick Thistle at Firhill as an outside-right. He became a professional in March 1937 and in season 1937–38 played in 20 matches. In 1938–39 he established himself in the team, played a total of 43 matches, and at the age of 19 won the first of his four Championship medals.

Willie was a stylish, sophisticated and very, very skilful centre-forward, immensely popular with the Rangers fans for the quality of his play and scoring ability, but above all else for his sportsmanship. He was a silky thoroughbred with exceptional talent in the air. One of the most profitable attacking gambits in that powerful Rangers team of the late forties and early-fifties was the Waddell cross to the Thornton head, and a high proportion of Thornton's goals were headed. In the 1949 Scottish Cup semi-final he headed all three goals in Rangers' 3–0 win over East Fife. In the 1950 Scottish Cup Final, also against East Fife in another 3–0

victory, he had headed two goals when a few minutes from time, he headed a third. It was disallowed, to prevent him from becoming the first Rangers player to score a hat-trick in a Scottish Cup Final. Another 46 years passed before Gordon Durie did it in the 1996 final in a 5–1 win over Hearts.

He was the first of the post-war Rangers forwards to top a hundred League goals (109 from 164 matches), his best season being 1948–49 when he had 23 from 29 League games. Rangers won League, League Cup and Scottish Cup that season, the first of their post-war trebles. Perhaps more remarkable was that in his last playing season with the club, 1953–54, he scored eight goals in eight League matches.

Thornton lost precious time during the Second World War, the best part of six years in which he served with the Duke of Atholl's Highlanders and won the Military Medal in the Italian campaign. If there were any criticism of Willie Thornton, even from the bluest-nosed of 'Blue-noses', it might have been that he was too polite, too much of a gentleman to be a vintage Rangers centre-forward. But the length of his career, and its distinction, would reject that. He was Scotland's Player of the Year in 1952, and when he retired in June 1954 he became manager of Dundee FC. He later managed Partick Thistle and became assistant man-ager at Ibrox to Willie Waddell. He was the author of *Blue Heaven*, his guide to the Ibrox Trophy Room and its remarkable contents, and had been host to visitors to the Stadium. On match days he had presided over the Thornton Suite, with its inscription 'One who wore the Light Blue to the honour of himself and the club he served'. Willie Thornton died in Glasgow's Gartnavel Hospital, on 26 August 1991, after a short illness. He was 71.

Games:	303
Goals:	188
League Championship:	1938–39, 46–47, 48–49, 49–50
Scottish Cup:	1947–48, 48–49, 49–50
League Cup:	1946–47, 48–49
Scottish Regional League:	1939–40
Scottish Emergency War Cup:	1939–40
Southern League Cup:	1940–41
Summer Cup:	1941–42
Victory Cup:	1945–46
Honours:	7 Scotland caps (plus 2 unofficial)
Born:	Winchburgh, 3 March 1920

JIMMY DUNCANSON

1946-50

An aggressive striker, the red-haired Duncanson from Dennistoun was a tremendous worker, ranging up and down the field as an inside-left in the manner of his pre-war predecessor, the famous Bob McPhail. Jimmy was quick and combative, and for Rangers fans his greatest single talent may have been his habit of scoring against Celtic – 22 goals in total. One place in history Duncanson could claim was that he was the first Rangers player in the 20th century to score a hat-trick against Celtic, in his case on New Year's Day of 1949, a 4–0 win – before 95,000.

He formed a menacing strike force with Willie Thornton, Duncanson being equally adept in the air. He quite often headed goals from 18 yards. He was a tall, hardy player who occasionally played outside-left. In all, Jimmy Duncanson won a total of 23 medals with the club, a splendid achievement. He moved to St Mirren in November 1950 and to Stranraer in 1953 for a couple of final seasons. He remained a fervent Rangers supporter and in his later days was often seen as a spectator at Ibrox. Jimmy scored Rangers' 4000th League goal against Dundee at Dens Park, on Christmas Day 1947, he scored all three in the 3–1 win. On his death at the age of 77, his obituary notice in the then *Glasgow Herald* read 'On Sunday 1 September 1996 James (Jimmy), ex-player and lifelong supporter of the Rangers Football Club…'

Games:	140 (plus 162 war time)
Goals:	59 (plus 88 war time)
League Championship:	1946–47, 48–49
Scottish Cup:	1947–48, 48–49, 49–50
League Cup:	1946–47, 48–49
Southern League Championship:	1942–43, 43–44, 44–45, 45–46
Southern League Cup:	1942–43
Victory Cup:	1945–46
Honours:	1 Scotland cap (plus 2 war time)
Born:	Glasgow, 13 October 1919

DAVID GRAY

1946-47

A Dundee man, very fit, very quick, small and stocky, David Gray in one sense was looked on as a possible successor at right-back to Dougie Gray, the Aberdeenshire man who played an astonishing and record 940 games for the club from 1925 to 1946. It was a tall order, and David didn't quite make it. A regular during the last season played under wartime regulations, 1945–46, in which he won both League Championship and Charity Cup medals. He played nine League games in 1946–47, but George Young took over the position, and held it.

Games:	12 (plus 27 war time)
Goals:	0
Southern League Championship:	1945–46
Born:	Dundee

JIMMY CASKIE

1946-47

Jimmy Caskie from Possilpark was essentially a pre-war and war-time player. A classic 'Glesca man' – small, bow-legged, tricky – he was a clever player. In war time international matches he played eight times for Scotland while with St Mirren, usually in his favoured position of outside-left, sometimes at outside-right. In one match against England he beat the famous goalkeeper Frank Swift with a sweet left-foot shot. He was an elusive, jinking winger with impish dribbling skills, and against Leslie Compton in particular could be uncontainable. His first appearance for Rangers endeared him to the fans. On 22 May 1940, as a guest player, he scored two goals in Rangers' 5–1 win over Celtic in a Charity Cup semi-final. More than five years passed before Caskie signed for the club, setting off a major diplomatic row with Dynamo Moscow, who clearly felt that Caskie had been transferred from Everton specifically for their match at Ibrox. They refused to play if Caskie was selected for the match on 28 November 1945. Bill Struth relented, perhaps under Foreign Office pressure, and selected Charlie Johnston instead. The match, seen by 95,000, was a memorable 2–2 draw. He had been at Everton with Torry Gillick in 1945, but like Gillick came to Ibrox and they were both in the Rangers forward line which played in a historic match against Benfica in Lisbon in 1948. Rangers played at home on the Saturday, travelled Sunday, played Tuesday, came home Wednesday. The Rangers forward line was Waddell, Gillick, Thornton, Duncanson and Caskie, a quintet valued now in the millions of pounds. Rangers won 3–0. In season 1947–48 Jimmy played fifteen times in all, but with Duncanson and Rutherford and a host of younger players on hand, his time at Ibrox came to an end soon afterwards.

Games:	39 (plus 23 war time)
Goals:	5 (plus 7 war time)
League Championship:	1946–47
Southern League Championship:	1945–46
Victory Cup:	1945–46
Born:	Glasgow

BILLY WILLIAMSON

1946-51

In the annals of the Rangers club, Billy Williamson has a secure, surely unique place. In successive years at Ibrox he played in only two Scottish Cup ties, each time in a final, each time scoring, each time heading his goal, each time on the winning side. In the 1947–48 replay against Morton (seen by a mid-week record crowd of 129,176 at Hampden) he headed the only goal of the match after 115 minutes' play, from an Eddie Rutherford cross. The following year he headed Rangers' second goal in a 4–1 defeat of Clyde. Two games, two winners' medals hard to beat. 'Sailor' Williamson had also scored in Rangers' 4–0 win over Aberdeen in the inaugural League Cup Final in 1946–47. He made his debut for the club on 27 August 1941 in a War Fund Benefit match at Ayr, then subsequently scored on his league debut in a 3–0 win over Airdrie at Ibrox on 13 December 1941. The war intervened and he was not a regular until season 1945–46, when his 14 goals in 25 League games contributed substantially to that season's championship.

Billy was a stocky, barrel-chested inside- or centre-forward, always on hand if either Thornton or Duncanson was injured. He had been a PE instructor in the Royal Navy during the war, a PE school teacher subsequently, and was always tremendously fit, even athletic, often indulging in cartwheels when falling or getting back to his feet. He was transferred to St Mirren on 20 February 1951.

Games:	69 (plus 51 war time)
Goals:	39 (plus 26 war time)
League Championship:	1949–50
Scottish Cup:	1947–48, 48–49
League Cup:	1946–47
Southern League Championship:	1945–46
Born:	Glasgow

BILLY ARNISON

1946-49

Joseph William Arnison – 'Billy' – was one of the first South African footballers to play professionally, and the first of the seven who have played for Rangers.

As a schoolboy Billy progressed from being a goalkeeper to centre-half, wing-half, then inside-forward, in which position he earned representative honours for Eastern transvaal – he was born in Johannesburg. He settled down as a centre-forward. A welder by trade, he left the amateur game for the delights of Scotland, signing for Rangers in April 1946, and on 15 April made his debut at Petershill Park, Springburn, in a 2–1 win over Celtic in a Charity match. He scored the opening goal! Arnison was a bustling centre-forward of some vigour and had an impressive record of 16 goals in his total of 19 games. In his competitive debut five days later, he scored twice in Rangers, 4–1 win over Stenhousemuir at Ochilview Park in a Victory Cup tie. But Willie Thornton, back from war service, took possession of his position and Billy moved to Luton Town on 16 August 1948 in a £7000 transfer. Injury restricted his career and he returned to Johannesburg to work in his father's business. But he often returned to the UK on visits. He died in August 1996, aged 72.

Games:	10 (plus 3 war time)
Goals:	4 (plus 4 war time)
Born:	Johannesburg

ANGUS STEAD

1946-47

Principally a winger, from Shettleston, small and quick, his debut was on 16 August 1945, a home win by 4–2 over Partick Thistle in a League match.

Games:	4 (plus 4 war time)
Goals:	1
Born:	Glasgow

JIMMY PARLANE

1946-55

One of a remarkable footballing family from Rhu in Dunbartonshire, Jimmy at one time had three brothers playing for Dumbarton in the Scottish League. He had three sons, one of whom, Derek, played for Rangers a generation on. Jimmy was a stuffy, hard-working, ball-winning, barrel–chested inside-forward who like so many others had lost prime time to the war and who found it hard to crack into that fine Rangers team of the late forties. He went to Airdrie on loan for a spell and enjoyed it so much that he stayed, signing for them on 8 January 1948. Inside-left to his inside-right in that Airdrie team was young Ian McMillan. Jimmy later played for Dumbarton. He had made his debut on 27 September 1943, in a Glasgow Cup tie at Firhill, Rangers defeated Partick Thistle by 3–0 before 28,000, an indication of the importance of the competition in those days.

Games:	7 (plus 2 war time)
Goals:	3
Born:	Helensburgh

WILLIE WOODBURN

1946-55

Perhaps the most gifted centre-half Rangers have ever had, Willie Woodburn is remembered now mainly for the fact that he was suspended *sine die* on 14 September 1954, and although the suspension was lifted on 23 April 1957 he never again played senior football. Indeed, he had effectively left the club in the summer of 1955.

Woodburn simply had too many brushes with authority, all of these emerging from a burning desire to secure victory for Rangers. Defeat seemed to be a personal affront to Woodburn. He would castigate referees, opponents, and even his own players, never accepting excuses from anyone. In particular he would abuse his goalkeeper, Bobby Brown, for every goal lost, no matter how unstoppable the shot might have been – in short, a very passionate man, Mr Woodburn.

He was enormously talented, beautifully balanced on either side. Fractionally under six feet in height, he was resolute and commanding in the air and extreme in defence, taking no prisoners. In possession he would forage forward, the ball under complete control, elbows out from his sides, meticulous and imaginative in the weight and accuracy of his passing. Woodburn was a player of the highest class, without any question a quality international player, perfectly comparable to his opposite number on the contemporary international scene – Neil Franklin of Stoke City and England. A measure of Woodburn's adaptability was that manager Struth had used him as a right-half, even an inside-right on occasion, but it was as the central figure in that marvellous defence of Brown, Young and Shaw, McColl, Woodburn and Cox that Willie Woodburn was in his proper setting, at the very centre of things. He had gone to Ibrox almost directly from juvenile football with Edinburgh Ashton, signing as a professional in October 1937.

Games:	325 (plus 127 war time)
Goals:	1 (plus 1 war time)
League Championship:	1946–47, 48–49, 49–50, 52–53
Scottish Cup:	1947–48, 48–49, 49–50, 52–53
League Cup:	1946–47, 48–49
Scottish Regional League:	1939–40
Southern League Championship:	1940–41, 45–46
Scottish Emergency War Cup:	1939–40
Southern League Cup:	1940–41, 44–45
Summer Cup:	1940–41
Honours:	24 Scotland caps
Born:	Edinburgh, 8 August 1919

IAN McCOLL (JOHN MILLER McCOLL)
1946–61

Ian McColl vies with, say, John Greig in having the ultimate career, with 13 League and Cup successes in 15 years with Rangers. In addition, there were 14 appearances for Scotland, more than four thoroughly enjoyable years as Scotland team manager, followed by almost three years as manager of Sunderland in the English First Division. Thus a youthful promise was handsomely fulfilled.

Ian was a flinty wing-half from Vale of Leven, in its time a famous forging ground for footballers, and after local school and Boys' Brigade football, was playing with Queen's Park when he was 16 He was signed by Rangers before he was 18 in June 1945, and after half a season or so in the reserves to acclimatise him to the world of the professionals, he was in the 'big' team, with Young behind him, Woodburn to his left, Waddell and Thornton in front – reasonable tutors for a young man. They were accustomed to winning; they were in a winning team, and McColl was quickly infected by the fever.

He was tall, very athletic, a powerful tackler and ball-winner who would fight for every ball and battle throughout the entire match with a hard quality in his play, comparable to the style of one of his predecessors, Scot Symon. Both were very vigorous players who took no prisoners, yet both were gifted in their use of the ball. Manager Struth at times rebuked McColl for 'taking two bites at the cherry', in bringing the ball under instant control. McColl came to realise, rather quickly in that company, that playing for Rangers was rather special, that the expectation was very much higher and the demands more exacting at Ibrox than anywhere else, and he became a perfectionist, a hard-driving taskmaster and an inspirational player and captain of the club.

He took this pragmatic attitude into management with Scotland, and in his later business life. With 16 victories in 27 matches, he is probably the most successful national team manager, but points out that in his time, he could call on Crerand and Law from Manchester United, Brown, Mackay and White from Tottenham Hotspur, and Caldow, Baxter, Henderson and Wilson from Rangers.

Games:	526 (plus 12 war time)
Goals:	14 (plus 1 war time)
League Championship:	1946–47, 48–49, 49–50, 52–53, 55–56, 56–57
Scottish Cup:	1947–48, 48–49, 49–50, 52–53, 59–60
League Cup:	1946–47, 48–49
Honours:	14 Scotland caps
Born:	Alexandria, 7 June 1927

WILLIE RAE

1946-57

A strong, industrious left-side player, mainly in the left-half position, Willie Rae had a decade at Ibrox in which he was in the main a reserve to McColl and Cox, players who could be dispossessed only by injury. He was always a part-time player and became a qualified quantity surveyor, moving to Queen of the South – there were family connections in Dumfries.

Games:	179 (plus 2 war time)
Goals:	7
League Championship:	1946–47, 55–56
Scottish Cup:	1949–50
League Cup:	1946–47
Born:	Glasgow

EDDIE RUTHERFORD

1946-52

A Glasgow boy, Eddie Rutherford emerged during the Second World War when, having signed for Rangers in August 1941, from Mossvale YMCA he guested for Lincoln City and Bradford City. He was a natural outside-right, but with the war over, Willie Waddell firmly in place there and with Jimmy Caskie's career coming to an end, Eddie became the regular outside-left. Slim and quick, Eddie sometimes looked uncomfortable in the position, but he was well served by such wing-halfs as Sammy Cox and Willie Rae and by inside-left Jimmy Duncanson, and was an effective member of the team, particularly dangerous when he cut inside on to his right foot. Eddie, even in temperament, always seemed to enjoy it all. After 10 years with Rangers he was exchanged for Colin Liddell of Hearts on 9 November 1951. He later played for Raith Rovers, then Hamilton Academicals, before retiring in 1956.

Games:	140
Goals:	28
League Championship:	1948–49, 49–50
Scottish Cup:	1947–48, 48–49, 49–50
League Cup:	1946–47, 48–49
Honours:	1 Scotland cap
Born:	Glasgow, 8 February 1921

JOHN LINDSAY

1946-52

John was an elegant, stylish full-back, brought to Ibrox to be the successor to Jock Shaw, to play in the reserves until the time came. It never did. Shaw went on playing into his forty-second year, by which time John Little had appeared from Queen's Park. The few chances Lindsay did have showed that so much reserve football had done nothing for his pace and sharpness. A Bishopbriggs man, John had joined Rangers from Petershill Juniors, aged 19, in June 1943. In eight years at Ibrox, he contrived only one medal, a Glasgow Charity Cup Final 2–0 win over Celtic on 8 May 1948 – 69,500 people saw the match!

In 1951 he went to Everton, had seven years at Goodison Park, where he became vice-captain and helped them to promotion to the First Division. He twice recovered full fitness from leg breaks. In 1958 he moved to Bury for two more seasons, but retired after a surprisingly long career. He remained on Merseyside and as a qualified engineer, he held the position of Chief Maintenance Engineer at Liverpool's Walton Hospital. John died in November 1991, aged 67.

Games:	22 (plus 5 war time)
Goals:	0
Born:	Glasgow

JOHN SHAW

1946-47

John Shaw, reserve goalkeeper signed from Benburb had much the same experience as John Lindsay. He had one season, the last under wartime regulations, as a regular in the first-team 1945–46. It brought him a Southern League Championship medal, and a place in the Southern League Cup final, lost 3–2 to Aberdeen. With Bobby Brown in place at Ibrox, he had only one match, a League Cup tie at Cappielow against Morton, which Rangers won 2–0.

Games:	1 (plus 29 war time)
Shutouts:	1 (plus 8 war time)
Southern League Championship:	1945–46
Born:	Glasgow

WILLIE FINDLAY

1947-54

Willie Findlay was signed from Albion Rovers for £7,500 in the summer of 1947 to succeed Torry Gillick. He was known as 'Banana Findlay' as every pass he played seemed to have a 'bend' on it. He was tall, rather slim, not perhaps a great worker, but a keen and persistent penalty-area player. Willie's sole desire was to score goals, and he had a talent for finding good scoring positions in the penalty area. He scored the first of Rangers' goals in their 3–0 Scottish Cup Final win over East Fife in 1950 with a flying header – in just 30 seconds!

Although he was far from being a physical player, he could snap up defensive blunders without fear. He served Willie Waddell well on the wing, and yet always seemed to be on hand when the Waddell crosses came in. In December 1954 he went back to Albion Rovers. There was no fee involved.

Games:	114
Goals:	65
League Championship:	1949–50
Scottish Cup:	1949–50
Born:	Motherwell

CHRIS McNEE

1946-47

An outside-left from Hamilton Accies, Chris was a bright and clever winger who had lost good years to the war. His debut was on 25 September 1945, in a King George VI Navy benefit match at Ibrox, with Rangers beating Newcastle United 3–2 before 50,000.

Games: 10 (plus 1 war time)
Goals: 3
Born: Glasgow

WILLIE PATON

1947-57

Willie Paton, a contemporary of Willie Findlay, was a rather stronger player, an inside-forward of strength and stamina. From Kirkintilloch Rob Roy with whom he won a Scottish Junior Cup winners' medal, he was well suited to the dictum of the manager, Bill Struth, and indeed that of his successor, Scot Symon – inside-forwards should be the workhorses of the team. Many critics said that if Willie had been less modest, less polite, less of a gentleman, he would have had a more forceful career at Ibrox. On 21 September 1956 he moved to Ayr United for a token £1000 fee.

Games: 164
Goals: 68
League Championship: 1948–49
Scottish Cup: 1952–53
League Cup: 1948–49
Born: Glasgow

DAVID MARSHALL

1946-53

A very skilful inside-forward, signed from St Roch's, one of the most able ball players at the club during his time there, but perhaps a little short of work rate, illustrating that one of the major requirements for success with Rangers is to play flat out in every match, sustaining form and effort through the entire 90 minutes. David was given a free transfer on 2 May 1953.

Games: 20 (plus 56 war time)
Goals: 9 (plus 25 war time)
Born: Glasgow

ADAM LITTLE

1946-51

A fine player who was robbed of vintage years by the War, Adam from Rutherglen was a product of Blantyre Victoria and Queen's Park. He had been with Rangers since 1937, and during the war sometimes featured in a Little-Young-Simon half-back line. He won a wartime cap for Scotland against England at Maine Road, Manchester, in 1943 and probably wished he hadn't – Scotland lost 8–0. He guested for Arsenal during the war, and finally left Rangers for Morton on 3 July 1951 on a free transfer. Adam had qualified as a doctor, and later was in general practice in Scotland.

Games: 6 (plus 169 war time)
Goals: 0 (plus 8 war time)
Southern League Championship: 1941–42, 42–43, 43–44, 44–45
Scottish Emergency War Cup: 1939–40
Southern League Cup: 1941, 42–43, 44–45
Summer Cup: 1941–42
Born: Rutherglen

JOE JOHNSON

1947–52

A physical education teacher from the Renfrew-Paisley area, signed from Arthurlie, Joe was a big, strong, fast, straight-running inside- or outside-left, a good worker but not perhaps the most subtle player Rangers ever had. He was transferred to Falkirk on 8 November 1951 and later went to live in Vancouver, Canada. Joe was known as 'Farmer Joe'.

Games:	36
Goals:	11
League Championship:	1949–50
Born:	Greenock

JOHN McPHERSON

1947–48

A small, stocky inside-forward who came from St Anthony's in June 1947. He played just one first-team game, scoring in a 2–1 win over Clyde on 26 April 1948. He was a grandson of the great Ranger John 'Kitey' McPherson.

Games:	1
Goals:	1
Born:	Glasgow

JIMMY FRAME

1948–52

An outside-right, he joined Rangers from Clydebank Juniors in May 1948. He was a winger, rather small, with close ball control. He played one League game, against Dundee on 28 August 1948, but was freed at the end of season 1951–52, having been on National Service for much of his time at Ibrox. He moved on to Dumbarton.

Games:	1
Goals:	0
Born:	Clydebank

WILLIE WALMSLEY

1948–49

An outside-left from Clydebank Juniors, Willie came in for the odd game but could not sustain any challenge to the wingers Waddell, Caskie and Rutherford and remained a reserve player. His one game was on 19 March 1947, a 4–1 win over Clyde at Ibrox.

Games:	1
Goals:	0
Born:	Kilmarnock

JOHNNY HUBBARD

1949–59

Johnny Hubbard arrived at Ibrox from South Africa in July 1949. He had been recommended to Rangers by the former Hibernian player Alex Prior, who was then a photographer in South Africa and who had described Hubbard as 'the best player in the Union'. In all the years he spent at Ibrox, the South African, who was only 5' 4" tall, never weighed more than 8 st 10 lb. This fragile, elfin figure was far from looking the part, and at first sight the Rangers manager, Bill Struth, had severe reservations about Johnny. Hubbard's skill with the ball, in running, crossing, shooting and above all dribbling, soon convinced him. Johnny was immensely popular with the Ibrox crowd, which dearly loves tricky wingers. Above all, Hubbard is remembered by older Rangers fans as the penalty-kick king. He converted a phenomenal 54 out of 57 penalty-kicks, including 23 successive scores from 1949 until 28 January 1956, when he failed against Davie Walker, the Airdrie goalkeeper. Hubbard did score in the match, however, a 4–0 Rangers win with a hat-trick going to Sammy Baird.

Other goalkeepers who achieved a modest immortality in stopping Hubbard penalty shots were Jimmy Brown of Kilmarnock and Bert Slater of Falkirk. John was transferred to Bury on 16 April 1959 for £6000. He returned to Scotland when he had finished playing and became a recreation officer in the Prestwick area of Ayrshire.

Games:	238
Goals:	106
League Championship:	1952–53, 55–56, 56–57
Scottish Cup:	1952–53
Honours:	1 South Africa cap (v Scotland!)
Born:	Pretoria

BILLY SIMPSON

1950-59

With the Rangers careers of Torry Gillick, Jimmy Duncanson and Billy Williamson drawing to a close at the end of the decade of the forties, the club badly needed to strengthen its inside-forward 'staff'. Many were tried, many found lacking the standards Rangers required. When a Linfield forward was recommended to the club, manager Struth sent Gillick to Belfast to assess him. Gillick reported favourably, and the result was that on 19 October 1950 Struth paid Linfield £11,500 for Billy Simpson. It was a club record fee, but as good a buy, pound for pound, as Struth ever made. Simpson turned out to be one of a handful of players to score a hundred League goals since 1945. He later played with Partick Thistle, under his former Ibrox team-mate, Willie Thornton, and Oxford United. A cruciate ligament injury ended his career, but he settled in Glasgow, and later reminisced about 'signing' talks with manager Bill Struth. They took place not at Ibrox but in Struth's private apartment in Copland Road. The discussion covered 'proper dress sense, decorum, dignity, how Rangers players should in no way tarnish the reputation of the club'. No mention of money. Simpson later worked at the Remington Rand factory, where one of his young apprentices was one Alex Ferguson, then playing for the amateur Queen's Park.

He played all three inside-forward positions at different times with success. Ian McColl, for instance, enjoyed playing behind him when he was at inside-right, saying 'We read each other well,' but Simpson most often played centre-forward. He was not one of the most physical players you could imagine, not powerful in the slightest. And there was not much style about his work, such as Thornton, for example, possessed. But if he lacked polish, Billy had courage to spare. He was above all a goal-scorer, and he would risk injury to reach that ball, adept as he was in picking up chances and half-chances in the goal area.

One thing he did have in common with Willie Thornton, whom he eventually succeeded, was that he was a magnificent header of the ball and would often dive headlong to head crosses other players would not attempt to reach. His first goals for the club came on Christmas Eve 1950, a hat-trick against East Fife. His hundredth league goal was a typical flying header, against Hearts on 26 October 1957. Billy scored four goals no fewer than three times, against Third Lanark on 25 April 1951, against St Mirren on 20 December 1952 and Hibs on 1 November 1958.

His single most important goal for Rangers may well have been with his head against Hearts at Tynecastle on 13 April 1957. It broke the Edinburgh team and set up Rangers' Championship after they had been seven points behind Hearts in the final straight. Billy Simpson was many times an Irish international player. In November 1957, he scored the winning goal for Northern Ireland against England at Wembley (2–3), a rare achievement for an Irishman. He joined Stirling Albion on 3 March 1959.

Games:	239
Goals:	163
League Championship:	1952–53, 55–56, 56–57
Scottish Cup:	1952–53
Honours:	12 Ireland caps
Born:	Belfast

WILLIE McCULLOCH

1949-55 .

From the same junior team, Strathclyde Juniors, Willie was reckoned to be in the same mould as Willie Waddell and an ideal successor in age and style. Alas, it never did happen – McCulloch may have been distracted by his other career as a chartered accountant, for which he trained under Jimmy Simpson, the Rangers club secretary, and also suffered two broken legs. He became an accountant with Alexandra Transport while still playing, and later went to the company's head office in Scarborough, where he worked and sadly died before he was 50.

Games:	68
Goals:	15
Born:	Glasgow

IAN (JOHN) McINTYRE

1949-55

Another schoolboy star outside-right – manager Bill Struth thought he would be something special, but he didn't make the breakthrough. He moved on to Airdrie, but was always a part-time player. He became a very successful artist with Beaverbrook Newspapers.

Games:	2
Goals:	0
Born:	Glasgow

JOHN PRENTICE

1950-56

Transferred from Hearts on 9 March 1950 for £7000, John Prentice was an altogether fine footballer. He was strong and powerful, worked the ball well, particularly with his left foot, and played equally well at left-half or inside-left, where he formed a potent wing partnership with Johnny Hubbard. John was big and fast, and a deep thinker on the game, its problems and its challenges. He was transferred to Falkirk on 18 September 1956 for £2500 and that same season captained Falkirk to a Scottish Cup victory over Kilmarnock. Prentice went on to become a coach, and indeed had a successful spell as manager with Clyde. Jim McLean, former manager, now chairman of Dundee United, claims Prentice as the biggest single influence on his career, saying that everything he knows about coaching he owes to Prentice at Dundee, before moving to Dundee United.

In the sixties John became Scotland's team manager for a few months. Even before his terms had been settled, he went to Canada for a job interview without mentioning this to the SFA selection committee. They thought this was less than discreet, and John was invited to move on.

Games:	142
Goals:	37
League Championship: **Falkirk**	1952–53
Scottish Cup:	1956–57
Born:	Shotts

BOBBY SIMPSON

1950-51

When Bobby Simpson, an inside-right, arrived at Ibrox from the Fife coalfield, he was being compared to Billy Steel! He certainly was the same height, weight, was small and stocky and very, very strong. Alas, Bobby was also rather slow, and never did break through the queue of inside-forwards lining up for places in the Rangers team of the time. He eventually went back to work in the coalfields.

Games:	2
Goals:	2
Born:	Hill o'Beath, Fife

REX DUNLOP

1950-53

A wing-forward, 'Big Rex' played little for Rangers, but remarkably played in the championship decider at Dumfries on the 7 May 1953.

Games:	3
Goals:	0
Born:	Dumfries

WILLIAM BECKETT

1950-51

An outside-left from Renfrew Juniors who played only one game, against Clyde on 10 March 1951. Rangers won 4–0.

Games:	1
Goals:	0
Born:	Dumbarton

JOHN LITTLE

1950-61

Yet another Queen's Park' contribution to the Rangers story. John was born in Calgary in Canada, but came to Scotland as a boy. His first school was rugby-playing, but he started to play football at Queen's Park Senior Secondary, a famous football nursery, and became a schoolboy international player and an amateur inter-national after having joined, inevitably, Queen's Park. He became a professional with Rangers in July 1951 and there have been few better investments on the part of any Rangers management. Johnny Little was the perfect successor to Jock Shaw at left-back. Where the elegance of John Lindsay had failed, the sheer speed, energy and exuberance of Little succeeded with a vengeance and Rangers were secure in the position for a decade, after the long years of the immensely durable Jock Shaw. In fact, there was a substantial likeness in playing styles and attitudes between Shaw and Little. Few wingers could get past Johnny and when they did, he invariably caught them. He was an all-action type with much style and effective distribution and his tackling had much of Shaw's tigerish quality.

Little's charm and even temperament made him one of the best-loved players in the game. He was a qualified PE teacher, and he moved to Morton in the summer of 1962 and eventually taught in a school in Greenock. John Little was the first of several Rangers players who have been capped for Scotland despite having been born outside the country.

Games:	275
Goals:	1
League Championship:	1952–53, 55–56
Scottish Cup:	1952–53, 59–60
Honours:	1 Scotland cap
Born:	Calgary (Canada), 7 July 1930

GEORGE NIVEN

1951-61

In the opening match of season 1952–53, Rangers went to Tynecastle and were trounced 5–0 by Hearts. In the Rangers goal was Bobby Brown. George Niven was his successor, not so dapper, not so striking in appearance as Brown but dependable and courageous. In the 1953 Cup Final, against Aberdeen, he suffered a head injury in going down at the feet of Paddy Buckley after 27 minutes. George Young took his place in goal, but Niven appeared for the second half, his head swathed in bandages, to make a series of magnificent saves which held Aberdeen to a drawn game. Rangers won the replay.

George was on the small side for a goalkeeper, but was thoroughly reliable over a good many seasons at Ibrox. Like most keepers, he had good days and bad days, the worst of them being perhaps the 1957 League Cup Final when Celtic won 7–1, prompting the unsubtle Celtic joke 'What's the time? Seven past Niven.' George had made his debut in fact in the last match of 1951–52, a 1–1 draw with Aberdeen at Pittodrie, and his best season was perhaps 1959–60 when he was outstanding and was selected to play for Scotland against England. Injury in the Scottish Cup semi-final against Celtic caused him to withdraw. It was his only Scottish selection. Billy Ritchie played in that semi-final replay, but Niven was back for the final in a Rangers team which beat Kilmarnock 2–0.

George played his last League match for Rangers against Motherwell at Ibrox on 25 March 1961, a 2–2 draw. His last match for the club was a Charity Cup match against Clyde at Ibrox, which Rangers lost 4–3. George moved on to Partick Thistle in February of the following year. There, he played on with distinction in what was one of Thistle's best-ever teams.

Games:	327
Shut-outs:	106
League Championship:	1952–53, 55–56, 56–57, 58–59, 60–61
Scottish Cup:	1952–53, 59–60
League Cup:	1960–61
Born:	Blairhall

COLIN LIDDELL

1951-55

A Glasgow boy, Colin, described by *The Herald* newspaper in his obituary as '...an enigmatic left winger', was a product of Queen's Park, whom he joined during RAF service in the Second World War. He turned professional in 1946, joining Morton, where he played for three seasons, featuring in the epic Scottish Cup Final and replay of 1948. In 1949 he moved to Hearts for a then-record fee of £10,000. He was exchanged for Eddie Rutherford on 9 November 1951, effectively keeping Johnny Hubbard out of the team for the rest of that season. He was a tall, strong, hard-running outside left with a similarity to his namesake and contemporary at Liverpool, Billy, but without the latter's scoring ability. Colin, a 'graduate' of Albert Senior Secondary School in Springburn, had five years at Ibrox before closing out his career with Morton. He retired in 1956, and spent some time in the East. There he played for a Singapore select, and the Kuala Lumpur club, Belangor. His travels took him to Japan, but he was back in the UK in 1964. He died in Crosshouse Hospital, Kilmarnock, on 24 February 1997.

Games:	52
Goals:	12
Born:	Glasgow

WILLIE PRYDE

1951-56

Willie, from Newburgh Juniors, was a strong, hard-working left-half had his moments of glory in the Scottish Cup Final of 1953 when he replaced injured Sammy Cox against Aberdeen – 1–1 and 1–0 in the replay. He was given a free transfer on 28 April 1956.

Games:	13
Goals:	0
Scottish Cup:	1952–53
Born:	Leuchars, Fife

WILLIE GARDINER

1951-55

Willie, a 6' 3" beanpole from the Dunfermline area, was a prolific centre-forward for Bo'ness United junior team. He was signed in November 1950 – tall, blond, busy and quick – but unfortunately the goals did not come as easily or as often for Rangers as they had in junior football. In contention for the centre-forward position in Willie's time at Ibrox were such names as Thornton, Simpson, Grierson, Paton. He moved to Leicester City on 11 August 1955.

Games:	31
Goals:	19
Born:	Larbert

DUNCAN STANNERS

1951-56

Events and personalities at Ibrox combined to compromise yet another Rangers career. Duncan, 6' 2" tall and a perfectly good centre-half from Dunipace Juniors, was an understudy to Young and Woodburn in the fifties and as a result rarely played in the League team. When Woodburn was suspended, Duncan should have filled the place, but probably found that too many seasons in reserve football had stolen his sharpness. George Young moved to centre-half, Eric Caldow became right-back and Duncan moved on to Stirling Albion on 15 December 1955.

Games:	23
Goals:	0
Born:	Denny

WILLIE BOYD

1951-52

Signed from Ashfield Juniors, Boyd was a close friend of Willie McCulloch. Both were at the club at the same time, and both trained as chartered accountants in the office of Jimmy Simpson, the club secretary. He played twice, as inside-right to Willie Waddell, in March 1952, a 5–1 win at Stirling Albion, and a home win over Morton by 1–0. Neillands followed him, but the regular inside-forwards at the time were Paton and Findlay. He left Rangers for Falkirk.

Games:	2
Goals:	0
Born:	Glasgow

IAN NEILLANDS

1951-56

From Bo'ness United, Ian was a good player not quite up to the demands of being a permanent right-wing partner to Willie Waddell. He joined the club in September 1951 and played three games in March and April of 1952, in what was a barren season for Rangers. All three matches were drawn. Ian was released on 28 April 1956 and signed for Queen of the South.

Games:	7
Goals:	1
Born:	Edinburgh

DEREK GRIERSON

1952-57

Signed from Queen's Park on 5 August 1952, Derek went straight into the team at inside-right and played in every one of the League matches that season, scoring 23 League goals. He was small but strongly built, quick and clever on the ball, a prime striking forward with a highly developed positional strength. He would probably have conceded that he was not over-industrious in the outfield, doing all his work on rather than off the ball, but he was very dangerous in the penalty area, taking up menacing shooting positions as though by instinct. On 10 January 1957 he went to Falkirk in exchange for Bobby Morrison.

Games:	106
Goals:	59
League Championship:	1952–53
Scottish Cup:	1952–53
Falkirk	
Scottish Cup:	1956–57
Born:	Prestonpans

HUNTER McMILLAN

1953-56

Signed from Giffnock Amateurs, P. H. McMillan, cousin of Ian, was a wing-half or inside-forward who joined the club in March 1952 and was freed at the end of the 1955–56 season. He played (scoring Rangers' only goal!) in the 1953 Coronation Cup match against Manchester United 1–2. He later played with Queen of the South and Falkirk and at one time was physiotherapist to the Arbroath club.

Games:	8
Goals:	2
Born:	Glasgow

JOHNNY WOODS

1954-55

A product of Shawlands Academy and Pollok Juniors the red-haired inside-left, Johnny was a very good player who could not sustain his skills. He was freed on 28 April 1956. His only game had been a 1–0 home win over Queen of the South on 26 March 1955.

Games:	1
Goals:	0
Born:	Glasgow

JIM RODGER

1953-55

Outside-right. Tall, leggy, and a schoolmaster. He was freed on 19 May 1955, and won a Scottish Cup medal with St Mirren when they beat Aberdeen 3–1 in the 1959 final. He later became a headmaster in the Western Isles.

Games:	3
Goals:	0
St Mirren	
Scottish Cup:	1958–59
Born:	Cleland

GEORGE McKENZIE

1954-55

George was a right-half or centre-half who was freed on 19 May 1955 despite three winning appearances.

Games:	3
Goals:	0
Born:	Leith

GORDON McKENZIE

1954-55

Gordon was 6' 3" tall, straight as a Guardsman, a lovely man and a fine left-back with a strong left foot. But as George McKenzie suffered from the presence of Ian McColl, so Eric Caldow kept Gordon out of things. Both McKenzies were freed on 19 May 1955.

Games:	9
Goals:	0
Born:	Glasgow

ROSS MENZIES

1954-55

Ross Menzies' only game was an important one, a League Cup quarter-final match which Rangers lost 1–2 at Motherwell. Bobby Cunning made one of his rare appearances for the team in that same match. Ross had been a flight-lieutenant and PE instructor in the RAF, and became manager of Bishopbriggs Sports Centre.

Games:	1
Goals:	0
Born:	Rutherglen

ERIC CALDOW

1953-66

Of all the players who have served the Rangers club, Eric Caldow holds a rare distinction. He has been a member of not one but two of Rangers' greatest teams, the immediate post-war team of the late-forties and early-fifties, and the team of the early-sixties, possibly the best Rangers team of the past 50 years. In his very first match, a League Cup tie against Ayr United at Ibrox in September 1953, Caldow found McColl, Woodburn, Cox and Waddell lining up with him (George Young, his idol, was injured). In his last match at Falkirk in March 1966, the team included Greig, McKinnon, Henderson and Johnston.

Eric Caldow had an outstanding career in which he captained both Rangers and Scotland. He won all the honours. Having played in the earliest European matches, he captained the club in its first European final, the Cup Winners' Cup of 1961 against Florentina. He played 40 times for Scotland, an international tally that would have been greatly increased but for a vicious tackle he suffered from Bobby Smith, the Tottenham Hotspur centre-forward, after only six minutes of the England-Scotland match at Wembley in 1963. Caldow's left leg was broken in three places. Denis Law told him much later that Smith, a very physical player, had boasted to him before the match that Scotland would finish with only ten men!

Six months later Caldow was able to play reserve football, but managed only three League matches that season. His international career, which would surely have taken him close to George Young's Rangers record of 53 caps had it continued, was over. From April 1957 to April 1963 he had missed only two international matches, and had been captain of Scotland for three years. He played a full League season in 1964–65, but the great Rangers team that Scot Symon had put together broke up. His full-back partner Bobby Shearer had been given a free transfer. Ian McMillan moved back to Airdrie, Ralph Brand moved to Manchester City, Jim Baxter to Sunderland. Eric was given a free transfer in April 1966.

Eric Caldow's strength as a full-back lay in his pace. He was very, very quick, and if the best of wingers did get past him, they never could get away from him. He was not a physical player, not over-big at 5' 8" and around 155 lb. In his balance, in the positive nature of his tackling and his adaptability, he was a latter-day Sammy Cox. He played 29 times for Scotland at left-back, 11 times at right-back. His technique was excellent, his tactical thinking in defence that of manoeuvring his winger until the time was exactly right for a crisp tackle. He was a phlegmatic character; nothing seemed to upset Caldow and his captaincy of both Rangers and Scotland was one of example, not of exhortation. In fact, he was never once booked in his long career.

From Cumnock in Ayrshire, Eric had been committed to Rangers from the age of 14 when he was playing in schools and youth-club football. It was said that a local schoolteacher, Alex Sloan, a friend of Rangers director George Brown, recommended him to the club. Rangers farmed the boy out to Muirkirk Juniors for a couple of seasons before calling him to Ibrox in 1952. Within a year he was in the team, and within two years he was established in one of the great Rangers careers. After leaving the club 14 years on, he had a year at Stirling Albion then retired as a player. Ventures in management with Corby Town and Stranraer were not successful. Eric returned to Ibrox in December 1989 to host the new executive facilities with Alec Willoughby.

Games:	407
Goals:	25
League Championship:	1955–56, 56–57, 58–59, 60–61, 62–63
Scottish Cup:	1959–60, 61–62
League Cup:	1960–61, 61–62, 64–65
Honours:	40 Scotland caps
Born:	Cumnock, 14 May 1934

ALEXANDER SILCOCK SCOTT

1954-63

In all the long line of brilliant Rangers wingers, Alex Scott must have an honoured place. He was an outside-right of devastating pace and fearsome finishing power. In his very first match for the club on 9 March 1955, while still a teenager, he scored a hat-trick in a 4–1 win over Falkirk at Ibrox. Six days later he drove in two stunning goals in a 2–2 draw against Arsenal at Highbury.

Alex was the ultimate flying winger, very fast, physically strong at 5' 10" and 12 stone, a good crosser of the ball and a menacing attacking force – altogether the perfect replacement for Willie Waddell. From Camelon Thistle in the Falkirk area, he was signed provisionally by Rangers in January 1954 and permanently in March 1955, when he went straight into the team and stayed there for the best part of eight years. He had a rather strange running style because, in spite of his speed, his left arm stayed by his side and scarcely moved.

With the advent of the young, brilliant and quite different Willie Henderson, Scott went to Everton in February 1963 for a fee of £39,000 and as he had done in Scotland with Rangers, won Championship and Cup honours with the Liverpool club. He came back north to Hibs in 1967 and was with Falkirk in the early seventies. As well as full senior internationals, he played for Scotland at Under-23 and B levels. He had the unusual if not unique honour of playing in a winning Scotland side against England at Hampden in 1962, Scotland's first win over England there in 25 years. And he did it while playing in Rangers' reserves, having lost his place in the League team to the young Willie Henderson. The selectors may well have gone for him because of his outstanding performance earlier that season at Windsor Park, Belfast where he scored three goals in Scotland's 6–1 win. Alex was one of Rangers' greatest assets in the European arena. In the 1959–60 European Cup he scored against Anderlecht and Red Star Bratislava as Rangers progressed to the semi-finals of that tournament and the following season scored what he himself rated the finest goal of his career in the Rheinstadion Dusseldorf as Rangers overwhelmed Borussia Munchengladback 3–0. He was in the Rangers team which lost the final of the 1961 European Cup Winners' Cup in Florence, when he scored the only Rangers goal. Indeed, he scored, in all, five goals en route to that final. He had scored in each of Rangers' semi-final matches with the then powerful Wolverhampton Wanderers, and jointly with Ralph Brand and Jimmy Millar, held the club's European goals record on 12 until Alistair McCoist passed it in the season 1996–97. From time to time Alex played centre-forward, never more effectively than in Rangers' 7–3 win over Ayr United on 29 April 1961, the last League match, which clinched a Championship and in which Scott scored three of the goals. Alex was the scorer of Rangers' 5000th League goal in that same fixture. His younger brother James played for Hibs and for Scotland. They went into business together in Falkirk.

Games:	331
Goals:	108
League Championship:	1955–56, 56–57, 58–59, 60–61
Scottish Cup:	1959–60
League Cup:	1960–61, 61–62
Honours:	16 Scotland caps (11 with Rangers)
Everton	
League Championship:	1962–63
FA Cup:	1965–66
Born:	Falkirk, 22 December 1936

JIMMY WALKER

1956-57

Big, strong, heavily built centre-forward from Clydeban, he played just two league games in 1956–57.

Games:	2
Goals:	0
Born:	Stenhousemuir

MAX MURRAY

1955-63

'Slapsie Maxie', as he was called, came from Queen's Park to Rangers with the reputation of being a prolific goal-scorer. Prior to arriving at Hampden, Murray's career had started at Falkirk High and Camelon Juniors, but with Queen's Park he won five amateur international caps with Scotland. Signed for Rangers on 12 May 1955, he scored on his debut, in his home town of Falkirk at the start of the following season when Rangers won 5–0 in a League Cup tie. An exuberant character, he had but one thought in mind – to hammer that ball at goal, with right foot, left foot or head. And as the records show, although he was essentially a reserve to Jimmy Millar, Max was entirely successful. He was thoroughly reliable, an all-action player who never let the team down. He was tall and slender with very little physical strength, but quick and with a good turn of speed. There was little that was sophisticated about his play and it is true to say that he was not highly popular with all Rangers fans. They thought him cumbersome – he had 'the action of a combine harvester with the brakes off', was one description. But with 121 goals in 154 games, substance was more important than style for Max.

He would slash at balls and blast them over the bar impetuously, when often a simple side-foot would have done. Yet he scored some important goals for the club. In the Scottish Cup semi-final of 1962, in place of Millar, he scored two of the Rangers goals in a 3–1 win over Motherwell. Max was transferred to West Bromwich Albion in November 1962 for £15,000. He returned to Glasgow to play with Third Lanark and find success in business. He was also a capable golfer, playing to a two handicap.

Games:	154
Goals:	121
League Championship:	1956–57, 58–59
Born:	Falkirk

SAMMY BAIRD

1955-61

A graduate of Rutherglen Glencairn, Sammy Baird, a powerful left-side player, became a senior professional with Clyde. He moved to Preston North End in June 1954 when Scot Symon, then Preston manager, paid £12,000 for him. When Symon returned to Ibrox as manager he quickly bought Baird once more, in June of 1955 for £10,000. At 5' 11" and 12 st 8 lb, Baird used his physique to good effect. It was quite unwise to foul him. His upright running style earned him the tag 'Straight backed S.B.'. Prior to the 1990 World Cup finals, Sammy was the only Rangers player to have scored in the World Cup finals. He could play either wing half or inside-forward, and loved above all to play against Celtic – he rejoiced in the atmosphere and combative nature of these matches.

Games:	179
Goals:	52
League Championship:	1955–56, 56–57
Scottish Cup:	1959–60
Honours:	7 Scotland caps
Born:	Denny, 13 May 1930

NORMAN ARNISON

1955-57

Norman, a South African centre-forward, brother of Billy, had a 100% scoring record – two games, two goals. He scored two in his first match, a 6–0 win over Queen of the South at Ibrox in the League Cup on 3 September 1955. Indeed he scored two more in his second game, a 6–0 win over Third Lanark two days later in a Glasgow Cup tie. His third match was in a League Cup semi-final against Aberdeen, which was lost 2–1. He never played again, and many Rangers fans felt that he had been harshly treated.

Games:	2
Goals:	2
Born:	Johannesburg

BOBBY CUNNING

1954-55

Scot Symon paid £2,500 to Hamilton Academicals on 2 September 1954 for this outside-left of startling pace, no doubt to add to the wing strength with the departure of Findlay and Rutherford. Bobby, alas, had serious vision problems – he was one of the first footballers to wear contact lenses – and his career was badly compromised.

Games:	5
Goals:	0
Born:	Dunfermline

JIMMY MILLAR

1955-67

Above all else a dashing centre-forward as courageous as any player Rangers have ever had, Jimmy Millar was brave, honest, a never-say-die player who gave the impression that he would in fact die for the cause if there were no alternative. But Jimmy was not just a charging warhorse. He had skills and talent for the game in abundance and led his forward line well. Although only 5' 6" tall, he was quite marvellous in the air and would knock balls down to Ralph Brand, who 'fed off' Jimmy for years, and with him formed a fearsome strike force. The 'M and B Tablets' they were dubbed in one of the greatest of Rangers teams, that of the early sixties which had Shearer, Caldow, Greig, McKinnon in defence, McMillan and Baxter in midfield, and Scott, Henderson and Wilson variously on the wings. Although Jimmy Millar was much more than just a goalscorer, it should be noted that his total of 30 goals in the Scottish Cup is a post-war Rangers record, one which is matched by Derek Johnstone alone, and not by one Alistair McCoist. On two occasions – 1960 and 1964 – he scored twice in Scottish Cup finals, a distinction shared by Derek Johnstone. The scorer of 13 goals against Celtic, Jimmy appeared to revel in Old Firm matches, particularly in the Ne'er Day games. He had the distinction of twice scoring the winning goal at Celtic Park on New Year's Day, in 1960 (a last-minute winner) and in 1964, both games ending 1–0 to Rangers. Many to this day will claim that Millar's finest hour with Rangers was the 1963 New Year's Day game at Ibrox, when Rangers overwhelmed Celtic by 4–0. The first of his 22 caps for Scotland came at Cardiff in 1960 against Wales. Scorer of goals in both 1962 and 1963 Scottish Cup finals, only both posts robbed Wilson, freakishly, of being the first player to score three goals in a Scottish Cup final. In the 1964 game against Dundee, his last-minute shot hit one post, rolled along and hit the other, and came out. Ironically it was then turned in by Ralph Brand, who achieved the distinction.

Millar was an outstanding half-back for Dunfermline when Rangers signed him for £5000 on 12 January 1955, and at times he played half-back at Ibrox. Fearless, gifted in ball control, Millar was a positive personality of much character who could be inspirational to team-mates. In May 1959, Millar was moved up to centre-forward in a match in Denmark when Max Murray was injured. The half-time score was 0–0. Rangers won 4–0 – Millar scored all four, and never looked back! Still he did win a Scottish Cup winners medal in 1966, as a wing-half towards the end of his Ibrox career. His international career was much compromised by injury. He went to Dundee United in the summer of 1967, was briefly manager of Raith Rovers, then took a pub in his native Edinburgh.

Games:	317
Goals:	162
League Championship:	1960–61, 62–63, 63–64
Scottish Cup:	1959–60, 61–62, 62–63, 63–64, 65–66
League Cup:	1960–61, 61–62, 64–65
Honours:	22 Scotland caps
Born:	Edinburgh, 20 November 1934

RALPH BRAND

1954-65

Ralph Laidlaw Brand was seen by the Rangers manager, Bill Struth, on television when he played in the England v Scotland schoolboy international at Wembley in 1952. In June of that year the boy Brand was provisionally signed for Rangers, and in April 1954 he became a fully fledged Ranger, six months short of his 18 birthday. Indeed, he had made his debut before that on 6 November 1954. Willie Waddell and Willie McCulloch were both injured, and the young Brand played at outside-right. The match was against Kilmarnock – Rangers won 6–0 and Ralph Brand scored twice. It was an omen of things to come. Brand became one of the truly great Rangers goal-scorers.

He spent most of 1955 and 1956 doing National Service and by December 1957 was back in a Rangers team rather demoralised by a 7–1 defeat from Celtic in the League Cup Final of that year. He made 22 League appearances that season, scoring 11 goals. By season 1960–61 his partnership with Jimmy Millar was established and was to be the sharp end of a very successful Rangers team over the next half-dozen years. They first impressed as a partnership in the opening League Cup fixture of 1959–60, in an away match against Hibs which Rangers won 6–1, four goals to Brand, one to Millar and one to Andy Matthew.

Brand travelled to Glasgow for training, from Edinburgh each day with Jimmy Millar and latterly John Greig, and it was said that much of the understanding between Brand and Millar was established by their conversations and planning en route. Brand scored in three successive Scottish Cup Finals (four if one considers a replay), the only player to achieve this in Scottish football history. The finals were 1962, 1963 plus replay and 1964. Only two players in the post-war era have scored more League goals than Brand – Derek Johnstone and Alistair McCoist. He was joint leading scorer in European matches, with Alex Scott and Jimmy Millar, with 12 goals, before the coming of McCoist.

Brand was a player of intense concentration and constant movement. He put so much into a match that he'd often be sitting in the dressing room an hour after the match, still anxious to talk about it. He was a deep thinker on the game, wanting to talk tactics at a time when such discussion was probably in short supply at Ibrox. He was beautifully balanced on either side, as sharp and fearless as a Law or a Greaves in the penalty area, on the ground or in the air. At 5' 7" Ralph was no giant. He never weighed more than 150 lb, but speed off the mark was the thing for him, and above all a burning desire to be a great player. Even in primary school in Murrayburn in Edinburgh, he wanted to be a footballer. In seven Rangers finals, he was never on the losing side and scored six goals. In eight international matches, he scored eight goals! He was perhaps unfortunate in that Denis Law was a contemporary.

Brand always wanted to do extra-skills training. He wore lightweight continental boots when others were rejecting them. Oddly, he was never over-popular with the Ibrox crowd, who dismissed him as a poacher. Some poacher!

No doubt for the money and perhaps a new tactical stimulus, and with an outstanding Rangers team breaking up, he moved to Manchester City in August 1965 for a £30,000 fee, and two years later to Sunderland. He became a qualified FA coach and moved back to Raith Rovers in 1969, before retiring as a player in 1970.

Games:	317
Goals:	206
League Championship:	1958–59, 60–61, 62–63, 63–64
Scottish Cup:	1961–62, 62–63, 63–64
League Cup:	1960–61, 61–62, 63–64, 64–65
Honours:	8 Scotland caps
Born:	Edinburgh, 8 December 1936

DON KITCHENBRAND

1955–58

Don Kitchenbrand was signed from the South African club Delfos on 26 September 1955, and the appearance of the South African immediately split the Ibrox supporters into two camps, for and against. Kitchenbrand was hugely strong and fast, was nicknamed 'The Rhino', and quite simply knocked defenders down with his bulk as much as anything else. He was neither smart enough nor skilful enough to be a 'dirty' player, but he would simply chase everything in sight, catching right on the line balls which everyone else would have written off. He could score goals – in season 1955–56, 24 League goals in 25 matches. And on 8 March of that season he hit five out of the eight Rangers scored against Queen of the South, in the very first Scottish League match to be played by floodlight. Don was transferred to Sunderland on 5 March 1958, and later returned to South Africa.

Games:	37
Goals:	30
League Championship:	1955–56
Honours:	I South Africa cap (against Scotland)
Born:	Johannesburg

BOBBY SHEARER

1955-65

A red-haired firebrand of a right-back, Bobby Shearer, or 'Captain Cutlass' as he was known, was a death-or-glory, take-no-prisoners defender for whom becoming captain of Rangers, as in time he did, was – the ultimate. Shearer was – is – the ultimate 'Blue-nose' and to this day will not tolerate a word of criticism of the club, no matter how well merited it might be. He was signed from Hamilton Academicals where his father was head groundsman, and for the best part of a decade was a good, if unpolished full-back who tackled with all the fierce intensity of a Jock Shaw. He formed a valuable full-back partnership with Eric Caldow in domestic football. His lack of pace would perhaps have left him exposed at higher levels of the game, in European and international competition, although he did play for Scotland four times. Few Rangers players have collected more trophies than Shearer. He once enjoyed a run of 165 consecutive games.

A clear illustration of his character came in a match at Tynecastle against Hearts, then the reigning champions, on 26 October 1960. After only eight minutes play, Billy Ritchie, the Rangers goalkeeper, went off with an injury later diagnosed as a chipped ankle bone. Shearer took his place, and for 82 minutes the new goalkeeper and ten men defied Hearts and won 3–1. Rangers won the Championship that season!

Games:	407
Goals:	4
League Championship:	1956–57, 58–59, 60–61, 62–63, 63–64
Scottish Cup:	1961–62, 62–63, 63–64
League Cup:	1960–61, 61–62, 63–64
Honours:	4 Scotland caps
Born:	Hamilton, 29 December 1931

45

BILLY RITCHIE

1955-67

Billy Ritchie from Newtongrange started his football career with West Calder High School and Addiewell Hearts, before signing for Rangers from Bathgate Thistle on 12 August 1954. He overlapped and eventually succeeded George Niven as the goalkeeper in one of the greatest of all Rangers teams, that of the early sixties.

Fate had taken a hand in his journey to Ibrox. He was at Bathgate Thistle, understudy to John Neill, who was provisionally signed by Rangers by manager Bill Struth. When Rangers asked Neill to play in a third team match, he was unavailable and at the last minute, Ritchie deputised, impressed Struth and promptly found himself signing provisional forms for the Ibrox club. Neill never did join Rangers. He played his first match on 5 May 1956, in a Charity Cup tie at home to Third Lanark, and secured a regular place in the second half of season 1957–58. National Service took him to Cyprus for all of the following season, and when he returned, George Niven's form was just too good. By 1961 he was in the team, and for the next five years was an outstanding goalkeeper in an outstanding Rangers team. Ritchie was undemonstrative and was considered the 'quiet man' of the team, but he was a solidly reliable goalkeeper who had a shut-out in every third game he played for Rangers. One of his greatest games for Rangers was in the European Cup Winners' Cup semi-final at Molyneux, against the then-formidable Wolves team. His save on the stroke of half-time from a Ron Flowers thunderbolt perhaps turned the game irrevocably in favour of Rangers.

He had one cap for Scotland when he came on as a substitute for Eddie Connachan of Dunfermline in Scotland's match against Uruguay at Hampden. Ritchie's first handling of the ball was to pick it out of his net! He was probably unlucky on the international scene in being a contemporary of Bill Brown, the Dundee and Tottenham goalkeeper who won 28 Scotland caps. Billy Ritchie's last game for Rangers was against Aberdeen in a League Cup semi-final at Hampden, drawn 2–2, on 19 October 1966. A year later, like George Niven before him, Billy Ritchie was transferred to Partick Thistle.

Games:	340
Shut-outs:	120
League Championship:	1962–63, 63–64
Scottish Cup:	1961-62, 62-63, 63–64, 65–66
League Cup:	1961–62, 63–64, 64–65
Honours:	1 Scotland cap
Born:	Newtongrange, 11 September 1936

ALAN ELLIOTT

1955-56

Alan was a centre-half from Irvine Meadow, very fit, particularly hardy. The need for a replacement for George Young was becoming imminent and Alan might have been considered, but at 5' 9" he was probably not quite commanding enough. One of his only two games in place of Young was against Celtic at Parkhead, which Rangers won 1–0! He was given a free transfer at the end of the season, and signed for Ayr United. His father played for Partick Thistle.

Games: 2
Goals: 0
Born: Glasgow

JOHN QUEEN

1955-58

An outstanding junior from the same team as Torry Gillick, Petershill Juniors, John was considered a potential successor to the great Rangers inside-right. Queen was a very skilful inside-forward with a near-mastery of the ball, but could not overcome the presence of Simpson, Baird and Murray and remained a reserve player.

Games: 2
Goals: 0
Born: Glasgow

SANDY THOMSON

1955-56

Centre-half who played in place of George Young in the opening League game of the season, but like Alan Elliot, failed to escape from the reserve team. That match, at home to Stirling Albion, was a 0–0 draw. Thomson was transferred to East Stirling on 26 December 1957.

Games: 1
Goals: 0
Born: Kilsyth

WILLIE LOGIE

1956-57

From Cambuslang Rangers, big and strong, Logie looked as good a left-half as Rangers had had in years, but in their first venture in the European Champions Cup, in a rough-house match in Nice, he was ordered off with the French centre-forward Bravo, and his career seemed to go downhill from there.

Games: 19
Goals: 0
Born: Montreal

HAROLD DAVIS

1956-64

Very strong, very hard, very popular, right-half Davis, with Shearer and Greig and even Jimmy Millar, gave the outstanding Rangers team of the early sixties its bite, just as Baxter, McMillan, Brand and the wingers gave it style, skill, class and polish. Harold was signed from East Fife on 31 October 1956 by Scot Symon, who had kept a close watch on him, and like Symon himself, Davis was an excellent ball-winner and a much better footballer than many people thought; he could play all three half-back positions. Although he looked slightly sluggish in action, he never seemed to be caught short of pace or out of position. He was particularly protective of Ian McMillan. Davis also had a sense of humour. In a 1959–60 European Cup tie at Ibrox against Anderlect, the Belgian tactics of checking and fouling and obstructing became exasperating, and when Harold decided he had had enough, he set off in chase of the famous Belgian forward Joseph Jurion. They went half-way up the field before Davis realised what he was doing. He stopped, laughing, and laughed all the way back to his position. Harold was a veteran of the Korean War, (in which he served in the King's Own Scottish Borderers) where he suffered suffered shrapnel wounds. Davis joined Partick Thistle after leaving Rangers in 1964, then went to Queen's Park as trainer before returning to Ibrox as a coach under David White. He later held a similar post under the same manager from 1972–75. He remained a perfect gentleman, and became a very successful hotelier in Gairloch, Wester Ross. Davis suffered very severe injuries on 1st May 1998 in a car crash on the A819 road in Argyll.

Games:	261
Goals:	13
League Championship:	1956–57, 58–59, 60–61, 62–63
Scottish Cup:	1961–62
League Cup:	1960–61, 61–62
Born:	Cupar

DAVIE WILSON

1956-67

Arguably Rangers' finest outside-left since Alan Morton, Wilson, only 5' 6" tall and very fair haired, was fast, direct, opportunistic, with a particular talent for penalty-area positioning when the crosses from the outside-rights, Scott and Henderson, were pouring in. He had an outstanding career with Rangers and Scotland, one of his most famous internationals being against England at Wembley in 1963 when he moved to left-back and played with great distinction after Eric Caldow had broken a leg. One of his many important international goals was Scotland's first in the 2–0 win over England at Hampden in 1962. It must have been sweet indeed for Wilson, who had played in the traumatic 9–3 defeat Scotland suffered at the hands of England at Wembley one year earlier. Davie Wilson was an almost automatic choice for Scotland in the era. They failed by the narrowest of margins to qualify for the World Cup finals in Chile, losing a play-off match to Czechoslovakia, eventually to finish runners-up to the champions Brazil. At one point, in that play-off game in Brussels, Scotland led 2–1, but eventually lost 4–2. In March of that year he scored six goals in Rangers' 7–1 win at Falkirk.

Wilson, a Glasgow boy, was signed from Baillieston Juniors in May of 1956. In August 1967, at the age of 28, he and Wilson Wood went to Dundee United in exchange for Orjan Persson, and he had five good seasons there. Many people felt that Rangers had released him too soon. He went to Dumbarton in 1972 where he became assistant manager, and later, successfully, manager.

Games:	373
Goals:	157
League Championship:	1960–61, 62–63
Scottish Cup:	1959–60, 61–62, 62–63, 63–64, 65–66
League Cup:	1960–61, 61–62
Honours:	22 Scotland caps
Born:	Glasgow, 10 January 1939

BILLY SMITH

1956–58

A centre-half or full-back who joined the club in June 1955, from Dundee North End, Billy was from Arbroath, where his family owned fishing boats. At 5' 9", and perhaps on the slow side, Billy never did break through with Rangers and played a total of only three first-team games, one of them a Glasgow Charity Cup tie in May 1957 being his debut. He was released a year later.

Games:	2
Goals:	0
Born:	Arbroath

BOBBY MORRISON

1956–58

Bobby was a tall, slim inside-left who had looked a really good player at Falkirk, where Rangers found him. His goals-for-games record in fact was impressive. His debut was a memorable match – a Scottish Cup tie at Celtic Park. Bobby scored in a game that finished 4–4 – Rangers came back from being 4–2 down with but a few minutes to play. Morrison also scored in his first League match, a home 3–3 draw with Queen's Park. His scoring total that season including Charity Cup matches was 9 in 10 games – he scored in the 2–1 Charity Cup Final against Queen's Park on 6 May 1957. He never commanded a place at Ibrox and was released a year later.

Games:	8
Goals:	7
Born:	Chapelhall

JOHN VALENTINE

1956–57

John was signed from Queen's Park on 2 May 1956, and Rangers thought they had a fine centre-half in the making. But John was unfortunate. He played in the League Cup Final on 19 October 1957, when Celtic won 7–1, and completely outclassed and even humiliated Rangers. Billy McPhail, the Celtic centre-forward against Valentine, scored three goals. Within a month, perhaps paranoid about that result, Rangers had signed the experienced Willie Telfer from St Mirren for £10,000. Some Rangers fans who saw the match, to this day will blame John for the fiasco. It hardly seems fair – he was very much a newcomer to the team. Valentine never again played for the first team and a year later was transferred to St Johnstone.

Games:	9
Goals:	0
Born:	Buckie

ALAN AUSTIN

1957–58

Austin was pitched into the early-season Celtic match at Ibrox, playing left-half in a game in which Rangers were by no means favourites. Some supporters saw this as a scapegoat selection. Rangers lost 2–3. The left-half position had been troubling Rangers at this time, and they used Davis, Millar and Baird at various times.

Games:	1
Goals:	0
Born:	Glasgow

WILLIE TELFER

1957-60

Telfer, already an experienced and international player and 32 years of age, was signed in November 1957 as a stop-gap following the defeat, humiliating for Rangers, of 7–1 by Celtic in the final of the League Cup a month earlier. If the £10,000 signing from St Mirren was a knee-jerk reaction by the Ibrox club, it was a resounding success and one of their most

profitable purchases. Powerfully built, Telfer was a bustling, vigorous, rational centre-half of experience who held Rangers together and allowed the club to assemble their outstanding team of the early-sixties. In spite of his physique, he was a gentleman and a player of honesty with a respect for the game. On one famous occasion in a Scotland-Wales match at Hampden which was Telfer's one international appearance, John Charles, the magnificent Welsh

centre-forward, got past Telfer and made for goal. Telfer, half a yard behind him, could easily have brought Charles down with a 'professional foul', but chose not to. Charles went on and scored. Telfer was much criticised, and was never again selected for Scotland. The match was drawn 3–3.

Games:	97
Goals:	0
League Championship:	1958–59
Honours:	1 Scotland cap
Born:	Larkhall, 26 October 1925

WILLIE MOLES

1957-58

Moles was a centre-half who to some extent replaced John Valentine following that League Cup Final defeat by Celtic, but held the place only until Willie Telfer had arrived and settled into the position after a few weeks. The sequence of Valentine-Moles-Telfer was the result of the quest by Rangers to find a worthwhile successor to George Young following the Woodburn suspension.

Games:	5
Goals:	0
Born:	Airdrie

GEORGE DUNCAN

1957-60

An outside-right, a little fellow who was a perfectly good player but who had bleak prospects with Alex Scott at the club.

Games:	15
Goals:	5
Born:	Glasgow

BILLY HOGG

1957-59

Centre-forward or inside-forward who was signed from Aberdeen on a free transfer. Billy scored on his debut, a 5–4 defeat at Airdrie in which Jonny Hubbard scored a hat-trick. His only other match was a 2–2 draw at Stirling Albion.

Games:	2
Goals:	1
Born:	Glasgow

TOM ROBERTSON

1957-58

An inside-forward from Edinburgh – a very skilful player in short, sharp bursts. His only game was a League Cup semi-final against Brechin City, won 4–0 by Rangers. He was freed on 1 May 1958.

Games:	1
Goals:	0
Born:	Kincardine

ANDY McEWAN

1958-59

A centre-forward from Queen's Park, Andy arrived in June 1958 and was freed in April 1959. He lined up at centre-forward in the opening League game of season 1958-59, a 2–2 home draw with Third Lanark. It was his only match.

Games:	1
Goals:	0
Born:	Glasgow

HARRY MELROSE

1957-58

An elegant, skilful little player from the Edinburgh area, Harry was freed on 1 May 1958 and went to Dunfermline Athletic where he had a perfectly good career, winning a Scottish Cup winner's medal in 1961 against Celtic. His one game for Rangers was that League Cup semi-final in which Robertson played. Harry had two of the four goals.

Games:	1
Goals:	2
Dunfermline Athletic	
Scottish Cup:	1960–61
Born:	Edinburgh

BILL PATERSON
1958-62

Bill Paterson, a former Scotland 'B' international player, was signed in July 1958 from Newcastle United for £3500. He became the bridging centre-half between Willie Telfer and Ronnie McKinnon, the latter playing through most of the sixties. Paterson was tall and stylish, good-looking and in the opinion of some of Rangers' fundamentalist fans, too gentlemanly and not physical enough to be the ideal Rangers centre-half. Without ever looking like a full international player, Bill played well, and stabilised the position for the club. He was a close friend of fellow half-back Harold Davis – they often went fishing together. Bill was given a free transfer on 21 September 1962.

Games:	116
Goals:	0
League Championship:	1960–61
Scottish Cup:	1959–60
League Cup:	1960–61
Born:	Kinlochleven

BOBBY ORR
1958-59

Bobby, a strong, direct, combative right-half from Kirkintilloch Rob Roy, signed for Rangers in May 1957 and played only two first-team games. In season 1958–59, he played a friendly against the British army, a 1–0 defeat at Ibrox, then in a League match against Third Lanark at Cathkin, on 27 December, which Rangers won 3–2. Nevertheless, Orr was a stalwart in the reserves, for whom he played 88 matches. Freed in April 1960, he joined the Lanarkshire Police and became an inspector in the Strathclyde Force. He died at the age of 52 in January 1992.

Games:	1
Goals:	0
Born:	Bellshill

ANDY MATTHEW
1958-60

Andy Matthew was signed from Fast Fife on 17 July 1958 for a fee of £4500, and he gave Rangers reasonable service. He was a fast, direct, orthodox outside-left with a natural left foot, and if not the bravest of wingers, he would nevertheless persist in getting to the byeline and getting his crosses in, thus doing exactly what his manager, Scot Symon, felt a winger should do. He was particularly successful in European matches. He scored in each of the 1959–60 European Cup matches against Anderlect and had totals of 14 goals in 45 matches, a good ratio for a winger. Rangers got their money back when he returned to Fife, and Raith Rovers, on 11 September 1960 for exactly £4500. Andy Matthew died in 1992, aged 60.

Games:	37
Goals:	12
League Championship:	1958–59
Born:	Kirkcaldy

BILLY STEVENSON
1958-62

A red-haired left-half from Edina Hearts and an excellent footballer in a good Rangers team, Billy seemed put out by the expensive arrival of Jim Baxter in June 1960, for his position, in a transfer that was to mean the completion of one of the greatest Rangers teams. In the pre-Baxter season of 1959–60 Stevenson had played 34 League games, indeed had missed only one game all season. In Baxter's first season, 1960–61, he played only eight games, and in the next season only five. Billy didn't care for this, and he swept off to Australia at the end of that season. He was back in the autumn, and was transferred to Liverpool for £20,000 on 19 October 1962 and had an excellent career at Anfield under Bill Shankly. Stevenson completed a Scotland-England Cup double in 1965, as his former Rangers compadre Alex Scott was to do with Everton a year later. Both players had also won Championships in each country.

Games:	103
Goals:	1
League Championship:	1958–59
Scottish Cup:	1959–60
Born:	Leith
Liverpool	
FA Cup:	1964–65
Football League Championship:	1963–64, 65–66

IAN McMILLAN

1958-64

Ian McMillan, dubbed the 'Wee Prime Minister' because of his control of affairs and in recognition of the then Prime Minister Harold McMillan, was an old-style inside-forward and a player of the highest class. He was arguably the most gifted inside-right Rangers have had since Torry Gillick. Adept at screening the ball from defenders, his technical skills gave him instant and total control of the ball. He was an exceptional strategist, and this with his ball control allowed him to dictate the pace and tempo of a game and in particular set up open, running chances with through-balls to the forceful strikers, Jimmy Millar and Ralph Brand. He was at Ibrox for only six years, but it was a period which brought as much concentrated success to the club as did any in its history.

When he joined Rangers on 2 October 1958 he was 27 years old and had a decade of senior football with Airdrieonians under his studs, and was already an international player, many Rangers fans felt it was a transfer long overdue. His first match was against Raith Rovers at Ibrox, producing the result of 4–4, with McMillan scoring the opening Rangers goal. Rangers had been having a spell of rather indifferent form, but from that match on, with the arrival of McMillan, they went 23 matches with only one defeat; Ian played a season's total of 26 matches, scoring eight goals, and Rangers won the Championship by two points from Hearts! If ever a player gave a team the kiss of life, it was McMillan for Rangers in 1958–59.

With the advent of Jim Baxter in the summer of 1960, one of the great Rangers midfield partnerships was in place. They would be called midfield players today, but neither McMillan nor Baxter was much for defending or tackling, and neither was much inclined to head the ball. But McMillan was sustained – to some extent protected – by his right-half Harold Davis, a hardy, hard-tackling, ball-winning Fifer, and Baxter by the defensive talents of Greig and McKinnon, and with the speed of Caldow behind him.

These two players, McMillan and Baxter, were the controllers, the architects, the engineers of Rangers in the first half of the sixties. Neither was addicted to running – they made the ball run for them. McMillan relied on his skills; he was not a physical player but he was a good, talented, old-fashioned dribbler who knew how to work with a winger. He formed exceptional right-wing partnerships with first Alex Scott, then with Willie Henderson, during his time at Ibrox. His work might well have been rewarded with more Scottish international honours than he enjoyed. Scoring seven goals in Rangers' European campaign, McMillan revelled in the challenge and the atmosphere of the matches against Continental players.

He played his last game for Rangers on 29 April 1964 against St Johnstone at Perth, a match which Rangers lost 1–0 to finish a season in which they won the Championship from Kilmarnock by six points, a 'Triple Crown' season. McMillan, a qualified quantity surveyor, had always been a part-time player at Ibrox. In December of that year he went back to Airdrie, retired from playing in the close season of 1967 after the best part of 20 years as a player, then became coach, manager and subsequently a director of his home-town club, no doubt his first and last love. But in between, there had been golden, light-blue days.

Games:	194
Goals:	55
League Championship:	1958–59, 60–61
Scottish Cup:	1959–60, 61–62, 62–63
League Cup:	1960–61, 61–62
Honours:	6 Scotland caps (1 with Rangers)
Born:	Airdrie, 18 March 1931

DAVID PROVAN

1958-70

David, a Falkirk boy standing 6' 2", came from Bonnyvale Star as a centre-half but was kept out of that slot by Paterson and McKinnon. Nicely balanced, he could play either full-back position, and his chance came when Eric Caldow suffered a broken leg in the Wembley international of 1963. He matured from being a solid club craftsman to international class in the mid-sixties, and in his long career at Ibrox was in full-back partnerships with Caldow, Bobby Shearer and Kai Johansen. He played in the European Cup Winners' Cup Final of 1967.

A severe tackle by Celtic's Bertie Auld on 11 September 1967 in only the second League match put him out for the rest of season. He had been ever present before then, but not until a close season tour of Scandinavia did he reappear in Rangers colours. And apart from a spell in 1969–70, he was never quite the same again.

Released by Willie Waddell in 1970, he played with Crystal Palace, Plymouth Argyle and St Mirren, retiring in the summer of 1975. He was assistant manager to Alex Ferguson at St Mirren, manager of Albion Rovers for a spell, and chief scout for Rangers under John Greig's management.

Games:	262
Goals:	11
League Championship:	1963–64
Scottish Cup:	1962–63, 63–64, 65–66
League Cup:	1963–64, 64–65
Honours:	5 Scotland caps
Born:	Falkirk, 11 March 1941

NORRIE MARTIN

1958-70

Norrie Martin came to Ibrox as third-choice goalkeeper to George Niven and Billy Ritchie, and succeeded in becoming surely the unluckiest footballer who ever played for Rangers. He played his first match, an important League Cup tie against Hearts at Tynecastle on 23 August 1958, and played quite brilliantly until he was carried off with what proved to be a fractured skull. It was to be more than two years before he played in the first team again. Almost seven years later to the day – 21 August 1965 against Aberdeen at Pittodrie when he was pressing to make the position his own – it happened again. He was carried off with a fractured skull. By 1966–67 he was number one with 38 matches, but fate was not finished with Norrie Martin. He was in goal on 28 January 1967 when Berwick Rangers beat Rangers 1–0 in the most sensational result in the history of Rangers, perhaps of the Scottish Cup competition. As Scot Symon said, 'This is the worst result in the club's history.'

That season Rangers were runners-up in League, League Cup and European Cup Winners' Cup. The following season Norrie lost his place to Eric Sorensen from Morton, then won it back again only to lose it to the German Gerry Neef. He played for the last time on 11 October 1969, against Hibs at Ibrox, when the visitors uncharitably won 3–1, and in April of 1970 he was given a free transfer by manager Willie Waddell.

Norrie Martin left with just a clutch of reserve-team honours and several runners-up medals, surely unprecedented for anyone who had spent 12 years with Rangers.

Games:	110
Shut-outs:	41
Born:	Ladybank

GEORGE McLEAN (2)

1962-67

Signed for a then-record fee between Scottish clubs of £26,500 from St Mirren in January 1963, George Tomlinson 'Dandy' McLean was one of the most enigmatic and controversial figures to play for Rangers since 1945. Originally a wing-half he forced himself on the attention of Rangers when he played very well against them for St Mirren in the 1962 Scottish Cup Final, which Rangers won 2–0. He could play equally well at inside-forward, and the Rangers thinking was that he might succeed Ian McMillan, although he was a quite different type of player. At 6' 1" and none too physical, he could appear almost cumbersome on the ball at times but his distribution was cultured and constructive, and when he was played as a striker by manager Scot Symon he scored netfuls of goals by the side of Jim Forrest.

George was indeed 'Dandy' – a sharp dresser, a driver of quality cars, a lad for the good life off the field. Scot Symon had some problems in trying to control him, but there was nothing malicious in it all. He was quick with the repartee, a match for Jim Baxter at any time.

He scored ten minutes from the end of the Scottish Cup semi-final of 1966 against Aberdeen to put Rangers in the final, missed the final, then played in the final replay in place of Jim Forrest, against Celtic. Rangers won 1–0, and in all matches that season of 1965–66 George scored no fewer than 41 goals. His last match for the club came the following January when he and Forrest were held to be the villains, the guilty men responsible for the infamous Rangers Scottish Cup defeat at Berwick. Rangers were certainly paranoid about it. In March, Forrest went to Preston North End for £38,000 and in April, George McLean went to Dundee in exchange for Andy Penman. He later played for Dunfermline Athletic, Ayr United and Hamilton Accies.

Games:	117
Goals:	82
League Championship:	1963–64
Scottish Cup:	1963–64, 65–66
Honours:	1 Scotland cap (0 with Rangers)
Born:	Paisley, 26 May 1943

GEORGE McLEAN (1)

1959-62

George was the first of two George McLeans, which can be confusing to Rangers archivists. He was a centre- or inside-forward who found the competition too stiff, and he was transferred to Norwich City on 22 March 1962. Nevertheless his three goals in six League appearances contributed to a Championship success in season 1960–61, two against Hearts in a 3–0 win on 8 March 1961 and the winning goal against Clyde at Ibrox three days later, in a 2–1 win.

Games:	8
Goals:	3
Born:	Paisley

BOBBY HUME

1959-62

A rather small, lightweight outside-left, Bobby was at the club in the reign of Davie Wilson, but in his few matches he never let Rangers down. He played in the first leg of the 1961 European Cup Winners' Cup Final at Ibrox, which Rangers lost 2–0 to Fiorentina. A forward line that read Wilson, McMillan, Scott, Brand and Hume was not a success. He played in both European semi-final matches against Wolves, and also the title-clinching 7–3 win over Airdrie on 29 April 1961. On 14 September 1962 Bobby Hume transferred to Middlesbrough for £10,000. He later went to play and live in South Africa. A year later, he returned to play for Aberdeen for a couple of seasons. Bobby, a product of the famous junior club Kirkintilloch Rob Roy, was rather short-sighted which probably somewhat affected his game. In 1965 he joined the Highland Park club in Johannesburg and settled there. With Highland Park, he played alongside his brother Ronnie, winning the South African League Championship, the club's fifth in seven years.

Tragically, he was murdered by two hijackers in that city in March 1997. They leaped in front of his car, demanded the keys, then shot him in the chest. He was 56. Bobby Hume was one of 24 people killed in car hijackings that day in Johannesburg.

Games:	23
Goals:	3
Born:	Glasgow

ALBERT FRANKS

1959-60

Albert Franks, an Englishman, was signed by Scot Symon from Newcastle United on 23 March 1960. He was never able to establish himself. He had been a policeman before becoming a footballer, and he went back to a police career. All three of Albert's League matches were lost.

Games:	3
Goals:	0
Born:	Boldon, County Durham

STAN ANDERSON

1959-60

A Hamilton boy, Stan had a short spell at Ibrox as a left-side midfield player before moving on to Queen of the South. He was a coach at Ibrox in the seventies for Willie Waddell, then for Jock Wallace, and was manager of Clyde for a time. In later life, Stan had a dreadful struggle against kidney disease. In 1995, both of his legs were amputated, and he died in December 1997 at the relatively young age of 58.

Games:	1
Goals:	0
Born:	Craigneuk

BOBBY GRANT

1959-60

A centre-forward, Bobby came directly from Edinburgh juvenile football in July 1959. Both Bobby and Stan Anderson played in the same, solitary game – a 4–1 defeat by Clyde at Shawfield on 27 April 1960. Inauspicious debuts indeed.

Games:	1
Goals:	0
Born:	Edinburgh

DOUG BAILLIE

1960-64

Douglas Baillie was a first-team centre-half at the age of 17 in an Airdrie team that included Tony Harris, Ian McMillan and goalkeeper Jock Wallace. He had been a schoolboy international player and was quite outstanding as a youth, winning the Scottish Youths sprint championship at Ibrox in the time of 10.1 seconds, and at the age of 16 joined Kirkmuirhall Juveniles as a centre-forward. Moving on to Douglas Water Thistle, he scored 49 goals in 25 games, before signing for Airdrieonians. Doug had already acheived the considerable honour of captaining his country as a schoolboy at Wembley in 1952 and further recognition came his way while he was still at Broomfield. He was chosen to play in the inaugural Under-23 international at Shawfield, for Scotland against England. He did not win another Under-23 cap for four years, when he captained Scotland against Wales at Tynecastle.

He was tall at 6' 2", huge and immensely powerful and could be instantly intimidating by virtue of his bulk. Scot Symon saw this giant as a colossus around whom future Rangers teams could be built, and in the summer of 1960 paid Airdrie £18,000 for him. Baillie was difficult to beat in the air and difficult to pass on the ground; there was so much of him. He was used occasionally as a centre-forward to upset and frighten defences, one such occasion being the Ibrox semi-final of the European Cup Winners' Cup in 1961 against Wolves, which Rangers won 2–0. Roger Hynd, in the final of the same competition six years later, played the same role with the same limited success. In September 1964 he was exchanged for Findlay McGillivray of Third Lanark, who never did play in the Rangers first-team. Baillie also played for Dunfermline and Falkirk before becoming chief football writer at the *Sunday Post*, succeeding the famous Jack Harkness.

Games:	40
Goals:	0
League Cup:	1961–62
Born:	Douglas, 27 January 1937

WILLIE PENMAN

1960-63

Willie, a Fifer, was a fine junior footballer and was in the St Andrews United team which won the final of the Scottish Junior Cup. He played inside-left, understudy to Ralph Brand, but was transferred to Newcastle United on 4 April 1963 for £11,500. He was substitute for Swindon Town when the Third Division team beat Arsenal 3–1 in the English League Cup Final of 1969. Willie had played in three League games in 1960–61, none of them won. His last League match was a 6–1 defeat at Aberdeen on 8 April 1961.

Games:	3
Goals:	0
Born:	Coaltown of Wemyss

JIM BAXTER

1960–65, 1969–70

Just as many good and sober judges would claim John Greig to be the greatest Rangers player of all, a claim needless to say that is beyond any proof, so they might well insist that Jim Baxter was the most extravagantly gifted of all Rangers players; many critics declared that he was the best left-sided player Rangers had seen since the fabled Alan Morton. Willie Waddell said boldly that he was 'the most skilful left-half ever produced by Rangers'. At all events, it would not be too prejudiced a claim to say that he was a keystone of one of the best of all Rangers teams, that of 1960–65.

He was superbly gifted – his ball skills were astonishing, especially with his left foot. His defensive qualities were not worth speaking of, however, and he was very fortunate to have a full-back of the pace and resolution of Eric Caldow behind him. It was said that 'Slim Jim' could not tackle, could not use his right foot, could not head the ball: Jimmy Greaves 'couldn't' tackle, Puskas of Hungary 'couldn't' use his right foot, Stanley Matthews 'couldn't' head the ball! Baxter was an individualist, his own man. Work rate did not loom high in his priorities – so much so that, had he been English, he might not have been considered for a place in Alf Ramsey's England team of the time. Baxter had to be the dominant personality, the orchestrator of the ensemble, the king of the castle. The bigger the stage, the better.

He was certainly a player for the big occasion. He loved the 'Old Firm' matches, loved 'taking the mickey' out of Celtic when he could. One of the most vivid examples of this was the replay of the 1963 Scottish Cup Final, when Rangers demoralised Celtic with a 3–0 win. Indeed, Baxter had a remarkable record in these matches. In the period 1960–65 he played eighteen times for Rangers against Celtic, ten League matches, five in the League Cup and three in the Scottish Cup, and was only twice on the losing side. What gave Baxter even more impish pleasure was in doing the same thing against England at Wembley in the matches of 1963, when he scored both goals in a 2–1 win, and again in 1967 in a 3–2 win. His career was marked by both brilliance and self-indulgence. Although Scottish fans, always neurotically obsessed with the ball-player above all else, worshipped these performances and maintain their memory in the lore of the game, they were no more than parades of the Baxter trait of an unlimited confidence which bordered on arrogance. Nevertheless, he was a player of the highest class. In October 1963, in England's centenary match against the Rest of the World, he was in the World squad of players and took part in the match in place of Masopust of Czechoslovakia.

Rangers paid a record Scottish fee of £17,500 when they signed him from Raith Rovers on 21 June 1960. A Fifer, he had been a part-time player with Raith, encouraged and directed to an extent by Willie McNaught, the team's Scottish international left-back. For a spell, Baxter had worked in coal mining. He was one of the last young men required to do National Service, which he did in the Black Watch. He established himself immediately in a Rangers team which manager Scot Symon had assembled and which was to dominate the Scottish game for five years. Baxter's languid left-sided attacking play combined perfectly with Ian McMillan's generalship on the right. But Baxter's was a wayward genius. He never seemed prepared to pay the price of discipline and dedication which great talent demands if it is to thrive and mature. Symon would say to him, 'You're the man who makes Rangers play. Go out and make them play.' He eventually captained the team, and it may be that such responsibilities were not for Jim. He did not much care for training; he never saw much merit in work for its own sake. He also drank quite heavily, as he himself has admitted.

Baxter's time at Ibrox was punctuated by several signing and wages squabbles and he was transferred to Sunderland in May 1965 for £72,500. He moved to Nottingham Forest in December of 1967 for £100,000 and no doubt his share of the fees was reason enough for these moves. By this time, Baxter's off-the-field activities had more media attention than his play. He returned to Rangers in May 1969, unsuccessfully, and retired in November of the following year to become a publican.

Games:	254
Goals:	24
League Championship:	1960–61, 62–63, 63–64
Scottish Cup:	1961–62, 62–63, 63–64
League Cup:	1960–61, 61–62, 63–64, 64–65
Honours:	34 Scotland caps (24 with Rangers)
Born:	Hill o' Beath, 29 September 1939

RON McKINNON

1960-73

Ronnie McKinnon was the best Rangers centre-half since Willie Woodburn with above all outstanding pace. He was a product of Benburb, the local Govan junior team, and of Dunipace Juniors, and he signed for Rangers in 1959 as a wing-half: However, he developed as a centre-half in the reserves. He was considered a stop-gap when coming into the team in 1961–62, with both Paterson and Baillie injured, but developed into an international class defender, and throughout most of the sixties shared the centre-half position in the Scotland team with Billy McNeill, the Celtic captain. At 5' 10 ½" he was not over-tall for a centre-half and in his early seasons he was criticised for being weak in the air. This was exploited by Spurs in a European Cup Winners' Cup match in 1962 when Rangers were beaten 5–2 at White Hart Lane.

But McKinnon worked hard at his game, and became a well-rounded footballer. He was composed, stylish, authoritative, and had a calming effect on the Rangers defence. He never seemed under much pressure in possession, and was entirely comfortable with the good players around him. The line of Greig-McKinnon-Baxter was one of the finest in the history of the club, and of Scotland, reaching a peak perhaps in the 3–2 win at Wembley in 1967. In the late sixties, in the face of Celtic's dominance, Greig and McKinnon were the heart of the Rangers defence, and carried the team on their shoulders. Ron broke a leg in the away European match against Sporting Lisbon in November 1971 and so missed a chance of playing in Rangers' European Cup Winners' Cup triumph in May 1972. He left Rangers at the end of season 1972–73, played for a year in South Africa, then moved on to Australia.

Games:	473
Goals:	3
League Championship:	1962–63, 63–64
Scottish Cup:	1961–62, 62–63, 63–64, 65–66
League Cup:	1963–64, 64–65, 70–71
Honours:	28 Scotland caps
Born:	Glasgow, 20 August 1940

WILLIE HENDERSON
1960-72

As popular with Ibrox fans as any player in modern times, Willie Henderson was at least the equal of any of the great wingers who have graced Rangers' long history. He was an outside-right of the most tremendous pace, muscled and closely coupled at 5' 4" like the sprinter he was. He could weave through a warren of defence, a maze of defenders, as he pleased, to the extreme delight of the fans. His speed, dribbling skills and ball control, his ability to change direction quickly on a dead run – dummying inside the full-back was a feature of his game – and the quality of his crossing to Millar and Brand, and even to Davie Wilson on the far side of the penalty area, made him one of Rangers' most highly profitable players. He possessed the knack of scoring critical goals for the club, goals that won important matches. Against Cologne in the Inter Cities Fairs Cup match in 1967–68, he produced an extra-time winner and did the same against Sporting Lisbon in the European Cup Winners' Cup with another extra-time goal. This was the season in which Rangers won that cup.

Willie was something of a boy prodigy. He was a schoolboy international with Airdrie Schools, one of the few who made the transition to full international status. He was capped by Scotland at the age of 18 years 269 days. Only Denis Law in the modern era played for Scotland at a younger age, about one month earlier than Henderson. Willie was in the Rangers team at eighteen and stayed there, hastening the departure of Alex Scott to Everton. He had his share of injuries, and in season 1964–65 a bunion operation caused him several months of inaction. He was a direct contemporary of Jimmy Johnstone, the brilliant Celtic outside-right, and in the first half of the sixties was probably the more effective player. In the second half of the decade, Johnstone, playing in an exceptional Celtic team, probably had the edge. Between them, they dominated the position in the Scotland team throughout the decade.

Henderson had some eyesight difficulties, and wore contact lenses. The story is told – it deserves to be true – of how, late in an Old Firm match, he rushed over to the bench and asked, 'How long to go, how long to go?' Jock Stein replied, 'Go and ask at the other dugout, you bloody fool – this is the Celtic bench!'

Henderson moved to Sheffield Wednesday in July 1972 and in 1974 to the Rangers of Hong Kong, where he captained the national team. He finished his career, aptly, with Airdrie in 1979.

Games:	426
Goals:	62
League Championship:	1962–63, 63–64
Scottish Cup:	1961–62, 62–63, 63–64, 65–66
League Cup:	1963–64, 70–71
Honours:	29 Scotland caps
Born:	Baillieston, 24 January 1944

69

JOHN GREIG

1961-78

John Greig is considered by many good and sober judges to have been the greatest of all Rangers players. It is a subjective claim, of course, but there is a powerful body of opinion, and of fact, to support the claim. Greig made 857 appearances in all for the club, second only to the total of Dougie Gray, the full-back who played in the twenties, thirties and forties. But for becoming manager of the club in May 1978, when he was still an active player, he would have passed Gray's total. He played for Scotland forty-four times, twenty-one matches in succession, and captained his country. Three times in his career he was part of a treble-winning Rangers team – League, Scottish Cup and League Cup – in 1963–64, 75–76 and 77–78. Twice he played in a European final, the Cup Winners' Cup on each occasion – in 1967 when Rangers lost to Bayern Munich 1–0 after extra time, and in 1972 when they beat Moscow Dynamo 3–2 in Barcelona. In his sixteen seasons with Rangers he averaged close to one honour per season. Many a footballer has played an entire career that long without winning one. For his services to football, John Greig was awarded an MBE.

In many ways he epitomised the spirit of the club. Even in the most hopeless of lost causes, Greig would fight to the finish; he was indomitable. He was not the most skilful of players – the quality of his passing was variable, and many defenders have been more accurate in their use of the ball. But he was above all a leader of men, a great club servant and captain for whom the club was life and who carried the team for many years when Jock Stein's Celtic was sweeping all before it, in the second half of the sixties. He did it by being 'one of the boys' off the field, and by example, exhortation and leadership on it. When it was necessary, Greig could take the team by the scruff of the neck and shake it into shape.

He was often selected for Rangers teams in an inside-forward position (he had a powerful shot, and scored in his first match, against Airdrie at Ibrox in the League Cup in September 1961), but his natural position was as a central defender or sweeper, where he was a hard but never evil competitor. Indeed, in the outstanding Rangers teams of the early sixties which won three Championships in four years, the core of the defence was Greig and Ron McKinnon, in front of goalkeeper Billy Ritchie. They were the foundation on which Jim Baxter and Ian McMillan could build their attacking patterns, while players such as Jimmy Millar and Ralph Brand put away the goals. Greig, McKinnon and Baxter was the outstanding half-back line of the day.

From 1966 to 1970, Rangers won nothing. In the League Championship they had a long barren spell from 1964 to 1975, as the greatest of all Celtic teams dominated the Scottish game with nine successive Championships. When Baxter, McMillan, Brand, Millar, Shearer and Caldow had gone, Greig and McKinnon soldiered on, and although many supporters viewed the late sixties as a time of failure and crisis, the fact is that Rangers were a very good second to Celtic at a time when both were streets ahead of all other Scottish teams. And Rangers were at least relatively successful in Europe – finalists in the Cup Winners' Cup in 1961 and 1967, quarter-finalists in the Fairs Cities Cup of 1968, semi-finalists in 1969 and, at last, with John Greig as an inspiring captain, winners of the European Cup Winners' Cup in 1972. The team of the late sixties/early seventies was probably better than many a Rangers team that did win the Championship.

As a player, Greig will never be forgotten by Rangers fans for his resolution, his leadership, his dedication. For his 1978 testimonial match no fewer than a staggering 65,000 packed into Ibrox. After five years as manager of the club, John was active as a travel consultant and a broadcaster on the game. In January 1990 he returned to Ibrox as manager of public relations for the club.

Games:	755
Goals:	120
League Championship:	1962–63, 63–64, 74–75, 75–76, 77–78
Scottish Cup:	1962–63, 63–64, 65–66, 72–73, 75–76, 77–78
League Cup:	1963–64, 64–65, 75–76, 77–78
European Cup Winners' Cup:	1971–72
Honours:	44 Scotland caps
Born:	Edinburgh, 11 September 1942

JIM CHRISTIE

1961-62

Signed on 22 May 1961 for £11,000 from Ayr United, for whom he had played in only ten first-team games, Jim was a direct, capable player whose appearances were restricted by Jimmy Millar. Nevertheless, his scoring record was a centre-forward's dream and included some important goals, not least two in Rangers' 3–2 win over Monaco at Ibrox on 5 September in the European Champions Cup of 1961–62.

Games: 8
Goals: 8
Born: Glasgow

BOBBY KING

1961-62

A full-back, and very much a reserve-team player, Bobby came directly from Shettleston Juniors as a youngster and was cover for Shearer or Caldow. One important match he did play was the first leg of the quarter-final tie of the Champions Cup against Standard Liège in Belgium. Rangers lost 4–1 and went out at that stage.

Games: 3
Goals: 0
Born: Edinburgh

ALEX REID

1964-68

An inside-right, Alex joined Rangers in April 1964, and was given a free transfer on 17 June 1968. He scored two goals on his debut, a 3–0 win over St Mirren.

Games: 3
Goals: 2
Born: Glasgow

CRAIG WATSON

1962-66

A reserve to David Wilson, Craig was a lively outside-left with a lot of pace. He played several matches in 1963–64, when Wilson was injured, including a European Champions Cup tie second leg, when Rangers were overwhelmed by Real Madrid in Spain 6–0. He went to Morton in exchange for Jorn Sorensen in August 1965. He won a League Cup medal when Rangers beat Morton 5–0 in the final on 26 October 1963.

Games: 20
Goals: 4
League Cup: 1963–64
Born: Glasgow

WILLIE HUNTER

1962-64

A left-side midfield player from Hamilton Schools, Willie finished playing when he left Ibrox, and settled in Canada. His one game had been at Kilmarnock on 13 May 1963; Kilmarnock won 1–0.

Games: 1
Goals: 0
Born: Cambuslang

DEREK TRAILL

1963-66

A fringe player from Edinburgh, outside-left Derek found the competition from Rangers wingers in the sixties too much for him.

Games: 5
Goals: 0
Born: Edinburgh

JIM FORREST

1962-67

A goal-scorer par excellence, indeed a goal-scorer extraordinary as his goals-to-games-played ratio testifies, Jim Forrest was the ideal centre-forward – balanced, good on either foot, with an electrifying burst of speed, fearless, forbidding in the air. In spite of being criticised (quite wrongly) for being nothing but a goal-scorer! Forrest could combine unselfishly with other players and hold an attacking line together very well. One of a handful of players since 1945 to score a hundred League goals in his career, his tally of 57 goals in all matches in 1964–65 remains a record to this day. Forrest displaced the highly popular Jimmy Millar and came in as the successful team of the early sixties was breaking up. His Ibrox career ended under the cloud of the infamous Scottish Cup defeat at Berwick in January 1967. He and George McLean (2) were deemed entirely to blame, which was a nonsense, and were dropped and transferred within a few weeks. The transfer of Forrest, a gentleman in every respect, was quickly seen to have been a major error on the part of a paranoid management.

He had come to Rangers as a schoolboy, then been sent briefly to Drumchapel Amateurs for development. After a year at Preston he returned to Aberdeen and won a Scottish Cup medal with the Dons of 1970. He went to Hong Kong Rangers in 1973. His cousin Alex Willoughby was a colleague at Drumchapel, Rangers, Aberdeen and Hong Kong, a remarkable instance of family loyalty (or affection, or coincidence, or whatever). When Forrest scored a record four goals in the League Cup Final of 1963 against Morton, Willoughby scored the other in Rangers' 5–0 win. Jim Forrest scored four goals more than once, and on 30 October 1965 scored five against Hamilton Accies at Douglas Park in a 7–1 Rangers win.

Games:	163
Goals:	145
League Championship:	1963–64
League Cup:	1963–64, 64–65
Aberdeen	
Scottish Cup:	1969–70
Honours:	5 Scotland caps (2 with Rangers)
Born:	Glasgow, 22 September 1944

73

ALEC WILLOUGHBY

1962-69

Inside-forward Alec joined Rangers at the same time as his cousin, Jim Forrest. They had both served a preliminary apprenticeship with Drumchapel Amateurs. Alec was a highly talented player who moved around in the stealthy fashion of the late John White in the famous Tottenham 'double' team of the sixties. Ironically, his real chance came after Rangers' in-famous defeat at Berwick in January 1967, for which cousin Jim was condemned, and Willoughby was converted from a stylish midfield player into a striker and successful goal-scorer.

His achievements saw a sequence after the Berwick match as follows: 4 February v Hearts, three goals; 8 February v Clyde, three goals; 11 February v Kilmarnock, one goal; 1 March v Real Zaragossa, one goal; 4 March v Motherwell, four goals – a total of twelve goals in five games. In the following eight matches, Willoughby scored four of the team's total of 13. He was an outgoing personality, friendly, popular with everyone, in particular the Rangers crowd – an early-day Alistair McCoist – and a keen student of the game. He was inexplicably dropped in favour of Roger Hynd for the second-leg match at Ibrox in the European Cup Winners' Cup against Slavia Sofia, and again for the final against Bayern Munich in Nuremberg, as well as for decisive League matches late in the season, these omissions surely leading indirectly to the loss of the Championship and the European trophy.

In hindsight, Willoughby's treatment was seen as a major error of judgement on the part of Scot Symon, and although Alec was an out-and-out Rangers fan, he asked for a transfer. However, with the advent of Davie White as the new manager he became more of a regular for the next two seasons. The arrival of Andy Penman limited his appearances and he was transferred on 31 May 1969 to Aberdeen for £25,000, later playing in Hong Kong. Alec is now very much involved in the club's public relations efforts, in particular liaising with former players.

Games:	95
Goals:	47
League Cup:	1963–64
Born:	Glasgow

ROGER HYND

1963-69

Roger, nephew of Bill and Bob Shankly (his mother was a Shankly), came out of Lanark Grammar School, big, strong, solid, an all-action, play-anywhere defender. He was whole-hearted, but alas never a player of the highest quality – by his own admission 'of limited abil-ity'. Roger was a good squad player for the club, covering a number of defensive posi-tions as required. His misfortune was that Scot Symon, on the basis of one, and only one, reserve game in which Hynd, playing centre-forward in an emergency, scored four goals in a 5–2 win, decided that he was ideally suited for the position. Four days later Hynd found himself playing centre-forward in a European Cup Winners' Cup semi-final against Slavia Sofia. At that level his shortcomings were savagely exposed, and he was simply miscast. Nevertheless, he was selected for the final of 1967 against Bayern Munich in Nuremberg, where he was consumed by a young central-defender, name of Franz Beckenbauer. With half-an-hour gone in this match, Hynd, from the six-yard line, missed the only decent chance Rangers had in the match and with the score then 0–0, one which might well have won them the match. Roger was completely committed to Rangers and in a fit of pique and disgust at the end of the match, he threw his medal into the Nuremberg crowd. Only then did he learn that winners' and losers' medals were identical. But his was gone for ever.

On 22 June 1969 he joined Crystal Palace for £25,000. There, his sense of humour was put to good use. When he was in the team, he was often barracked severely. When he was out of the team, he'd sit in the stand and chant 'bring back Hynd'. He'd soon have a clique chanting with him, to the discomfiture of the manager, Bert Head. Roger later played for Birmingham City, then managed Motherwell for a spell.

Games:	48
Goals:	5
Born:	Falkirk

WILSON WOOD

1963-67

A talented left-half who was never a first-team regular but had considerable ability, Wood suffered from being a contemporary of Jim Baxter, and many friends of Rangers felt that he should have been encouraged positively and groomed to be Baxter's successor in season 1965–66, when he managed only 11 games. He was one of the few players to have played in all three Scottish derby games, in Glasgow, Edinburgh and Dundee. He went to Dundee United with Davie Wilson in August 1967, in exchange for Orjan Persson. Wood has developed his own physiotherapy practice in Whitburn.

Games:	47
Goals:	4
Born:	Whitburn

JORN SORENSEN

1965-66

A Danish player from Morton, Jorn arrived at Ibrox in August 1965 in exchange for winger Craig Watson and a fee of around £12,000. He was a talented midfield player of high class, in the manner of Ian McMillan. He was approaching the veteran stage when signed by Rangers and the pace of the modern game was probably a problem for him, although his skills and European experience might have been better used helping young wingers like Willie Johnston. At the end of his one season, he went back to Denmark.

Games:	16
Goals:	3
Honours:	31 Denmark caps (none with Rangers)
Born:	Nibe, Denmark, 17 October 1936

WILLIE MATHIESON

1964-75

Dubbed Willie 'Wan Fit' (one foot) by Rangers fans, Mathieson, a left-back, was certainly partial to the use of his left foot and was much maligned for it. Since Mathieson had an 11-year stay at the club, this criticism was evidently over-dramatic and less than fair. Willie, from St Andrews United, was a perfectly good attacking full-back, and comparing him with predecessors like Eric Caldow and John Little was unacceptable. 'Jardine and Mathieson' was a successful and established full-back partnership for a goodly spell. Willie was in the European Cup Winners' Cup team of 1972 and played for the Scottish League, and successive Rangers managers Symon, Waddell, White and Wallace all thought him good enough to play in what were good Rangers teams during his time at Ibrox. He finished his playing days with Raith Rovers.

Games:	276
Goals:	3
European Cup Winners' Cup:	1971–72
Scottish Cup:	1972–73
Born:	St Andrews, 20 January 1943

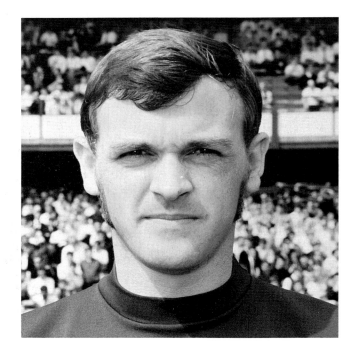

KAI JOHANSEN

1965-70

A Danish international full-back of outstanding talent, Kai Johansen was signed from Morton on 24 June 1965 for £20,000. This was at a time when Hal Stewart, the Morton impresario, was importing Scandinavian players galore. A right-back who could also play comfortably on the left, Kai took a little time to adjust to life at Ibrox, to some extent because of the restrictions Scot Symon sought to inflict on his play. Symon did not believe that defenders, and certainly not full-backs, should cross the halfway line. Johansen was a modern, attacking full-back, highly regarded throughout Europe with his crouching style, attacking the ball and coming forward at speed. This proved expensive in the League Cup Final of October 1965, when the powerful centre-forward John Hughes ran him ragged and scored with two penalty shots in Celtics 2–1 win. But Johansen was a quick study. In the Scottish Cup Final of 1966, and the replay, Kai dominated Hughes and entered Rangers folklore with a 25-yard drive to win the replay and the Cup.

Johansen was a prodigious talker – couldn't be stopped. He ran a pub in Glasgow, retired in 1970, then had a pub on Spain's Costa del Sol. Back in Denmark he became a player's agent, and he operated for a spell in South Africa.

Games: 238
Goals: 9
Scottish Cup: 1965–66
Honours: 20 Denmark caps (none with Rangers)
Born: Odense, Denmark, 23 February 1940

WILLIE JOHNSTON

1964-73, 1980-82

One of the most controversial footballers of modern times, Willie Johnston was an outside-left of blistering pace, dazzling dribbling skills and the highest international qualities, but he may be better remembered for an appalling disciplinary record and for being banned from the international game following a drugs test at the World Championship in Argentina in 1978. Johnston was ordered off at least 20 times in his career.

From the junior Lochore Welfare in Fife, 'Bud' Johnston signed for Rangers in 1964. He made his debut, aged 17, in a League match at home to St Johnstone on 29 August that year, and two months later played in the final, one of the more memorable Rangers–Celtic matches which Rangers won 2–1. So hugely skilled was Johnston that he progressed from Scottish youth international to full international status in six months, and was first capped at 18 in a World Cup qualifying match. He played well, but it was not the happiest of starts. Poland at Hampden scored two goals in the last five minutes to win 2–1. But Johnston was a regular international player from then on.

He played at inside-left early in his career, making a devastating wing partnership with Davie Wilson, whose maturity and experience brought the young man along nicely. Johnston was an entertainer. His speed, strength and commanding skills with the ball gave him a rapport with the fans. He could be argumentative, and was, clearly too often with referees. He was something of an expert at football quizzes, which he would organise on the team bus, and over the facts he would tussle with anyone. But Rangers tired of his lack of on-field discipline. His last suspension, a nine-week sentence following an ordering-off offence against Partick Thistle on 9 September 1972, led to his transfer to West Bromwich Albion for £135,000 on 1 December that year. Just six months earlier he had been a European Cup Winners' Cup medal winner, scoring two of Rangers' three goals in the final against Moscow Dynamo in Barcelona. Indeed, Johnston goals had been instrumental in taking Rangers to that final; his four goals included vital away scores at Rennes and Turin.

'Bud' and Colin Stein seemed to be the prima donnas of the Ibrox dressing room. Perhaps the new regime of Jock Wallace after 1972 was too harsh for them (Stein was sold to Coventry City on 5 October 1972 for £90,000 and the former Ayr United winger Quinton Young). A Wallace remark when Johnston and Stein had gone was telling – he said, 'We have sold two stars and found a team.'

Johnston played well at West Bromwich and was brought into the squad of Scotland players for the World Cup Finals in Argentina. Following the match against Peru (lost 3–1) he was routinely tested and found to have taken a banned substance. He was withdrawn from the tournament, sent home and banned from playing for Scotland ever again. The Scottish Football Association declared that it had been plain stupidity on Johnston's part. All the Scotland players had been asked, both collectively and individually, 'Have you taken any substance AT ALL, since you came here?' In every case, they said, the answer was no. Needless to say, Johnston had another version, published in a later book, in which he claimed that the Scotland team doctor Fitzsimmons had cleared the pills beforehand! He also claimed that the substance in question, 'Reactivan', was freely available to the public in the UK and had been taken by many members of the squad. Wherever the truth lay, Johnston's international career was over.

He went to Vancouver Whitecaps in March 1979, played with Birmingham City on loan, came back to Rangers for manager John Greig in August 1980, and played with some distinction during two more years with the club. His first match was on 16 August, at home to Partick Thistle. A month later, in a League Cup match against Aberdeen at Ibrox, Willie Johnston was – ordered off! He played finally with Hearts and Falkirk, retiring only in his 39th year, in 1985.

Games:	393
Goals:	125
Scottish Cup:	1965–66
League Cup:	1964–65, 70–71
European Cup Winners' Cup:	1971–72
Honours:	22 Scotland caps (9 with Rangers)
Born:	Glasgow, 19 December 1946

THEROLF BECK

1964-66

Therolf Beck from Iceland, known affectionately as 'Totty' Beck, which was as close as Glasgow cared to come to pronouncing his Christian name, was signed from St Mirren on 11 November 1964 for £20,000, perhaps because he had lately played very well against Rangers. Such performances often impressed them. But Totty, an inside-left, was not a success. There was a suspicion that the Rangers ambience and the city lights were too much for him, and he went back to Iceland.

Games: 14
Goals: 2
Born: Reykjavik, Iceland

DENIS SETTERINGTON

1965-70

A fringe player of the late-sixties from Edina Hearts, Denis was an inside-forward or midfield player who looked as though he might become very good, but who was hindered by injuries. He moved to Falkirk for £10,000.

Games: 14
Goals: 5
Born: Edinburgh

80 BILLY PAUL

1966-67

An outside-right from Pollok Juniors and limited opportunities, he played only part of one game. He was a substitute in a 5–1 win at Clyde on 8 February 1967. Following that, he played two friendlies, at Stoke and Leicester, but was never again in the first team.

Games: 1
Goals: 0
Born: Glasgow

BOBBY WATSON [1]

1964-70

Bobby Watson came out of Airdrie Schools football and as a right-half or inside-right was technically very sound, hardworking, whole-hearted and an effective tackler in midfield. He arrived in the post-Baxter and McMillan days, and found John Greig taking the right-half position, under Davie White's management. He played inside-right with distinction in the Scottish Cup Final matches against Celtic in 1966. Watson was badly injured in a bad tackle from Lothar Emmerich, the West German international, after forty minutes' play against Borussia Dortmund in a European Cup Winners' Cup match of season 1966–67.

He moved to Motherwell in 1970 with Brian Herron in exchange for goalkeeper Peter McCloy, became captain there and probably had his best seasons at Fir Park. He later became manager of Motherwell, and also of Airdrie. Always very articulate, Bobby Watson was a lay preacher, was successful in the steel business, and in the late-eighties was on the board of Partick Thistle as part of a group seeking to revive the club.

Games: 83
Goals: 7
Scottish Cup: 1965–66
Born: Airdrie, May 1946

COLIN JACKSON
1963-82

Colin Macdonald Jackson was a centre-half who gave Rangers 20 seasons of sterling service. He was tall and slender, of no great physique, yet he was an excellent stopper and a perceptive penalty-area player who could deny strikers space to move and manoeuvre. He was marvellously dependable, particularly in the air. He was also very patient, spending much time in reserve to Ronnie McKinnon and even Derek Johnstone. The greatest disappointment of his career must have been failing a fitness test on the eve of the European final of 1972 at Barcelona. He had played a significant role in getting Rangers to that final. Perhaps one of the highlights of his career was in the dying moments of the 1978–79 League Cup Final against Aberdeen – he headed the winning goal from a corner kick in the 19 minute!

Rangers had signed him from Sunnybank Athletic in Aberdeen, from under the noses of the Pittodrie scouting staff. Colin was born in London. He was one of a few Rangers players born outside the country and capped by Scotland. Others would include John Little, Richard Gough, Andy Goram and Stuart McCall.

Games:	505
Goals:	40
League Championship:	1974–75, 75–76, 77–78
Scottish Cup:	1975–76, 77–78, 78–79
League Cup:	1970–71, 75–76, 77–78, 78–79, 81–82
Honours:	8 Scotland caps
Born:	London, 8 October 1946

DAVE SMITH

1966-74

A superb, cultured left-half, Dave was already an international player when Rangers signed him from Aberdeen on 12 August 1966 for £50,000. He was an elegant player, a beautiful stylist whose cool positional sense and anticipation, as well as his precise passing of the ball, made him one of the outstanding players in the Scottish game of his time. He could also play very effectively as a sweeper, which he did in Rangers' victory over Moscow Dynamo in the European Cup Winners' Cup Final in 1972, when he won his only medal during his time at Ibrox. He succeeded Jim Baxter, but never quite had the acclaim he should have had. He certainly should have played more often for Scotland. He was a brother of Doug Smith, long-time (1958–76) centre-half of Dundee United and now a director of that club. Dave Smith moved to Arbroath on 4 November 1974 for £12,000, becoming player-coach. He was later player-manager of Berwick Rangers and Peterhead, and played in Los Angeles for the Aztecs and in South Africa.

Games:	303
Goals:	13
European Cup Winners' Cup:	1971–72
Honours:	2 Scotland caps (1 with Rangers)
Born:	Aberdeen, 14 November 1943

ALEC SMITH

1966–69

Alec Smith, no relation to Dave, was signed just three days before, from Dunfermline Athletic for £55,000. A droll tale hangs on this transfer. It seems that the Dunfermline chairman asked his manager, Willie Cunningham, how much they might get for Smith. 'Lucky to get £25,000' was the reply. However, Cunningham gave Scot Symon a big speech about what a good player Smith was, how many clubs were chasing him, and so on. Symon said he'd make a formal offer in writing. A few days later, Cunningham had a letter and an offer – of £55,000. Almost like the blind auction in Scottish property buying.

Smith was a good player, very able in the air, intelligent, strong, a right-half or inside-forward whose forte was strength on the ball and in breaking forward, but his major drawback was a lack of pace. In season 1966–67, he was leading scorer with 23 goals. He moved on to Aberdeen in June 1969. One of the mysteries of this mysterious game came in the dying moments of the 1966–67 League Cup Final against Celtic when the experienced Smith, only a few yards from goal with Celtic goalkeeper Ronnie Simpson beaten and the goal unguarded, unaccountably stumbled and Willie O'Neill was able to make a clearance. Celtic won 1–0.

Games:	68
Goals:	26
Dunfermline	
Scottish Cup:	1960–61
Born:	St Andrews

BILLY SEMPLE

1967–72

A dark, strongly built lad, Billy was an outside-left who was in and out of the team when wingers like Wilson, Johnston and Persson were on the books. He was a lively extrovert on the team bus, doing impressions of Billy Connolly, Chick Murray and others. He was given a free transfer in May 1972.

Games:	9
Goals:	2
Born:	Bellshill, 2 November 1946

WILLIAM JARDINE

1965-82

William Pullar Jardine, nicknamed 'Sandy' because of the colour of his hair, was one of the finest Rangers players in the entire post-war era. In that period, only John Greig made more appearances for the club. He was a cultured, elegant footballer, cool, strong, very fast, scrupulously fair. Originally a wing-half, he played there, at midfield, as a sweeper and full-back, and even as centre-forward for a spell under Davie White's management. He was developed by Willie Waddell as a full-back and could play comfortably on either side. Sandy came to Rangers from Edinburgh minor football – he lived quite near the Hearts ground – and he made his debut at 18 in the week after the 'Berwick Disaster' of January 1967. That was against Hearts, of all people, at Ibrox. Rangers won 5–1.

In his international debut, against Portugal at Hampden in 1971, he marked Eusebio out of the game, and after the European final in Nuremberg in 1967 he was much praised by his opposite number, Franz Beckenbauer. He was in the Rangers team which eventually did win the European Cup Winners' Cup, in Barcelona in 1972. At his best, Jardine was certainly a world-class player. He and Danny McGrain of Celtic formed a first-class partnership for Scotland as the full-back pairing on 19 occasions. He played in the World Cup Finals in Germany in 1974 and Argentina in 1978, and captained Rangers for a spell. He was one of the few players to be twice voted the sports writers' Player of the Year.

Sandy was released by John Greig after the Scottish Cup Final of 1982, at the age of 33, and he joined Hearts where he had a marvellous Indian summer to his career, bringing his lifetime appearance total in all matches to more than a thousand. As sweeper, he was a mainstay of the 1985–86 team which came so close to doing a Scottish 'double' but finished second in both League and Scottish Cups. He became assistant manager to Alex Macdonald, then joint manager before leaving Hearts in 1988. He now works in the Rangers commercial department.

Games:	674
Goals:	77
League Championship:	1974–75, 75–76, 77–78
Scottish Cup:	1972–73, 75–76, 77–78, 78–79, 80–81
League Cup:	1970–71, 75–76, 77–78, 78–79, 81–82
European Cup Winners' Cup:	1971–72
Honours:	38 Scotland caps
Born:	Edinburgh, 31 December 1948

ERIC SORENSEN

1967-70

The 'Man in Black' was bought from Morton on 26 July 1967 for £25,000. This was Eric Sorensen, Danish international goalkeeper brought over by Hal Stewart, the Morton boss and impresario who was conducting at the time a policy of importing leading Scandinavian players. For publicity reasons, Stewart kept Sorensen's identity unknown until he made his debut, but compounded the mystery by calling him simply the 'Man in Black', from the all-black strip which he wore. There was nothing extraordinary in the uniform – all continental goalkeepers wore black in the days before their present multi-coloured strips became fashionable.

Sorensen turned out to be a spectacular, top-class goalkeeper who played a full season in the first team. He made his debut on 12 August in a League Cup tie against Aberdeen at Pittodrie (1–1), and played his last match, also against Aberdeen, at Ibrox on 27 April 1968 (Aberdeen won 3–2 with a goal in the very last minute). It was Rangers' only League defeat; they amassed their highest points total since Scottish League reconstruction twelve years earlier, yet they still lost the Championship to Celtic by two points! He had lost critical goals in the League Cup eliminator against Celtic (1–3) and in the Scottish Cup against Hearts (0–1) when he was beaten by the near post by Donald Ford, and worst of all, in the final League match of the season, against Aberdeen at Ibrox (3–2), a result which cost Rangers all hope of the Championship (they finished second). The team went off to a storm of booing that day and Sorensen said later, 'Our long unbeaten run has been forgotten – now I know what it means to play for Rangers.' On 30 July 1968, he lost two early goals to high balls into the goal mouth in a friendly against Spurs at White Hart Lane (1–3). He was substituted at half-time and never played for the club again.

Perhaps a combination of ill-luck, misfortune or whatever meant that the blond, blue-eyed Sorensen never quite became the darling of the Ibrox fans. He remained at the club for two more years without ever playing another first-team match, then left on the same day, 28 April 1970, as his rival Norrie Martin, with whom he had contested the position. He went back to Morton, where he recovered his poise and played successfully for a few more seasons. He later took a pub in Greenock, and, a keen student of the game, became a goalkeeping coach working with, among others, Alan Rough.

Games:	47
Shut-outs:	16
Honours:	15 Denmark caps (none with Rangers)
Born:	Odense, Denmark, 22 January 1940

ORJAN PERSSON

1967-70

More mature Rangers fans will relish the memory of one particular Persson goal, the one that produced the first defeat of Celtic's post-Lisbon team. At Ibrox in September 1967, before a crowd of 90,000!, Persson, two minutes into the second half, set off on a mazy run of 30-yards or so, taking him past player after player in the Celtic defence. Then, from a near-impossible angle, he sliced his left-foot shot past Ronnie Simpson. Persson was something of a specialist in making the ball move through the air, swerving, curling and slicing it, particularly dangerously from free kicks, even corner kicks.

He was a Swedish international signed from Dundee United in exchange for Davie Wilson and Wilson Wood, a hugely talented if inconsistent player who could score, it seemed, from any angle, any position. Another of his goals was a scissors kick from 25-yards which gave Rangers a 1–1 draw with Hearts in a Scottish Cup tie. Orjan played for Sweden in the World Championship Finals of 1970 in Mexico, while still a Rangers player. Later that year he went to Orgryte in Sweden for a small fee.

Games:	113
Goals:	31
Honours:	48 Sweden caps (6 with Rangers)
Born:	Sweden, 27 August 1942

ANDY PENMAN

1967-73

When Andy Penman arrived at Ibrox in April 1967 from Dundee, in exchange for George McLean and £30,000, Rangers had acquired a mature international player who could boast of an extraordinary career. Penman had been something of a boy prodigy. From Dunfermline Schools he had gone to Everton, making his debut there in a Lancashire Senior Cup match against Liverpool at the age of 15 Back in Dundee, he made his debut for them when not quite sixteen and still an amateur. He was capped for Scotland at schoolboy, youth, amateur (prob-ably the youngest-ever amateur player for Scotland), Under-23 and senior levels. He won a League Championship with Dundee in 1961–62, and played in a Scottish Cup Final (in 1964, against Rangers) before coming to Ibrox where, surprisingly, and like Orjan Persson, he won nothing at all. Penman had the distracting experience of playing for no fewer than four managers – Scot Symon, David White, Willie Waddell and Jock Wallace – and in terms of rewards he was an unlucky player. He played in three losing finals, one with Dundee. A mysterious illness, eventually diagnosed in February 1968 as diabetes, kept him out of the team for two months, and was seen as contributing to the defeat in the Scottish Cup by Hearts, and the loss of momentum in the team in their title chase with Celtic. Once again Rangers finished second.

Andy Penman was a midfield player of class and startling vision, a fine passer of the ball who could clip balls precisely through, round and over defences to give his forwards clear, untrammelled runs at goal. In the Scottish Cup Final of 1971 against Celtic, he carved openings time and again only for Willie Johnston and Colin Stein to spurn them. He used dead-ball situations to telling effect, and in a better Rangers team (Rangers in his time, the late-sixties, were always chasing and struggling against Celtic) he could have been one of the historically memorable Rangers players. In 1973 he moved to Arbroath, in 1976 to Inverness Caley, and in 1979 he retired. Andy died at the early age of 51 on 19 July 1994.

Games:	150
Goals:	49
Honours:	4 Scotland caps (3 with Rangers)
Dundee	
League Championship:	1961–62
Born:	Rosyth, 20 February 1943

ALEX FERGUSON

1967-69

One of the most consistently controversial figures in football over the past 25-years, Alex Ferguson is the local boy who made more than good. Brought up in Govan, the Rangers heartland, he was 'Rangers-daft' in boyhood. At Queen's Park in the late-fifties, he played for Scotland youth as a rip-roaring centre-forward. In 1960 he joined St Johnstone, and in 1964 he was bought by Dunfermline, a transfer justified by his tally of 66 goals in 88 League games in a team that missed winning the Championship of 1964–65 by a single point. He was signed by Rangers for £65,000 in July 1967.

In his first season at Ibrox, Alex was leading scorer with 19 goals from 29 League matches. Ferguson was lean and hard, a hustling, bustling, elbows-out striker, uncompromising and rumbustious. Defenders became nervous when Alex was about, and he and Colin Stein formed a powerful attacking force for Rangers. He left the club following a row with Davie White, the man-ager, over the 1969 Scottish Cup Final. That was the match in which Billy McNeill, the Celtic centre-half, unmarked, headed in a Bobby Lennox corner kick after just two minutes' play. Celtic went on to overwhelm Rangers 4–0. White insisted that Ferguson should have been marking McNeill. He moved to Falkirk in November 1969 for £20,000, and was in their promotion team the following season. At Falkirk he played beside Andy Roxburgh – both men were to become Scotland team managers. After four years with Falkirk and one with Ayr United, Alex was forced to retire because of injuries.

He then learned the management game with East Stirlingshire, and in taking St Mirren into the Premier Division before going on to Aberdeen with the avowed ambition of 'smashing' the Old Firm hegemony. He did it by going on the attack in the citadels of Ibrox and Parkhead. The result was vigorous matches and for Aberdeen three Championships, four Scottish Cup and one League Cup victories and one European title in Ferguson's time at the club – an exceptional achievement. In 1983 he turned down an invitation to manage Rangers when John Greig left, and he became Scotland team manager on a temporary basis for the World Cup Finals competition in Mexico following the death of Jock Stein. He was appointed manager of Manchester United in November 1986. After a few lean years, he had outstanding success at Old Trafford – four Championships in five seasons, three FA Cup wins, a European Cup Winners' Cup win included.

89

Games:	66
Goals:	35
Honours:	4 Scotland caps (0 with Rangers)
Born:	Glasgow, 31 December 1941

COLIN STEIN

1968-73, 1975-77

Colin was signed from Hibernian in October 1968 for £100,000, the first six-figure transfer between Scottish clubs. A product of Linlithgow Schools football, he was almost an 'old-fashioned' centre-forward, strong, bustling, with rather a short fuse; his temperament saw him sent off several times in his career. His impact on the club was immediate. He scored a hat-trick in his opening games, at Arbroath and at home to Hibernian, and that meant instant popularity with the Ibrox crowd. He scored four goals in a World Cup qualifying match against Cyprus in May 1969. He was not the cleverest player in football but, blond and busy, Colin would simply hammer the most meagre of chances at goal, from any range. He scored in Rangers' European Cup Winners' Cup success in Barcelona in 1972.

In October of that year he was transferred to Coventry City for £90,000 plus Quinton Young, former Ayr United winger, and after some initial success there he came back to Rangers in February 1975 when it appeared that Coventry could no longer maintain the transfer instalments. His 'second coming' was restricted by the presence of the two Dereks, Johnstone and Parlane, but he did score a critical goal, his first since returning to the club, at Easter Road in March 1975. It was an equaliser that gave Rangers a draw and their first Championship win in 11 years. On loan to Kilmarnock in season 1977–78, Colin Stein was given a free transfer at the end of that season.

Games:	206
Goals:	97
League Cup:	1970–71, 75–76
European Cup Winners' Cup:	1971–72
Honours:	21 Scotland caps (17 with Rangers)
Born:	Philipstoun, West Lothian, 10 May 1947

ALEX MACDONALD

1968-81

One of Rangers' most valuable signings, Alex Macdonald's long career at Ibrox began with his transfer from St Johnstone, for £50,000, on 19 November 1968. Alex took a little time to settle at Ibrox and was not immediately accepted by the fans. But playing as a left-side midfield player, or inside-forward, he became the powerhouse of a Rangers team that was immensely successful through the seventies. Fiery, red-haired, small, combative, a ball-winner and a great competitor, Alex eventually became overwhelmingly popular with the fans, who dubbed him 'Doddie'. He was adept at stealing into the blind side of opposing defences and snatching important goals, never more so than the solitary winning goal he headed against Celtic in the 1975–76 League Cup Final. Alex was in Rangers' winning team in the European Cup Winners' Cup Final of 1972. He moved to Hearts in August 1980, became player-manager in 1981, then took over as manager where his ability and energy brought him the award of Manager of the Year in 1986. In that season, Hearts were runners-up in both League and Scottish Cups. Alex moved on to manage Airdrie with success, taking them to Scottish Cup Finals against Rangers in 1992 and Celtic in 1995. He was one of the few Rangers players to register 500 games in the post-war period.

Games:	503
Goals:	94
League Championship:	1974–75, 75–76, 77–78
Scottish Cup:	1972–73, 75–76, 77–78, 78–79
League Cup:	1970–71, 75–76, 77–78, 78–79
European Cup Winners' Cup:	1971–72
Honours:	1 Scotland cap
Born:	Glasgow, 17 March 1948

GERRY NEEF

1968-73

93

The goalkeeper, the first German to play for Rangers, had had trials with Aberdeen before coming to Ibrox in the spring of 1968. Gerhard's first match was at home to Morton on 19 April 1969 (3–0) and he kept his place for most of season 1969–70 until the coming of Peter McCloy from Motherwell in March 1970. He was on the bench as a substitute in Barcelona in 1972 for Rangers' successful European Cup Winners' Cup Final against Moscow Dynamo.

He took a good deal of ribbing in the Ibrox dressing room because of his nationality, but he gave as good as he got, and was a popular lad. At 5' 10" and of slender build, he was never very big for a goalkeeper, but he had exceptional agility.

Games:	48
Shutouts:	17
Born:	Hausham, West Germany,
	30 December 1946

ALFIE CONN

1968-74

Alfred James Conn was the son of a famous father, Alfie Conn, the international inside-right of the famous Conn-Bauld-Wardhaugh attacking trio in an excellent Hearts team of the forties and early-fifties. Thus the young man reached senior level from a family background and environment which left him steeped in the game, and he was bursting with natural talent and confidence. Almost inevitably, he was an international player at schoolboy, youth, Under-23 and senior levels. Alfie was a right-side player with, like his father, a tremendous shot in his right foot. He played his first match for the club in Dundalk in November 1968, in what was then the 'Fairs Cities Cup'. Affected by injuries intermittently throughout his career, he was in Rangers' European Cup Winners' Cup team, a winning team, in Barcelona 1972. One of his more memorable goals was Rangers' second in their 3–2 Scottish Cup win in 1973, when his run on goal exposed the lack of pace of Billy McNeill, the Celtic centre-half.

Conn moved to Tottenham Hotspur in July 1974 for £140,000 and was capped while at White Hart Lane. Alfie committed the ultimate sin in March 1977 by signing for Celtic in a £65,000 transfer and to this day has never been forgiven by Rangers supporters. In 1977 he made history by appearing in a winning Celtic team in a Scottish Cup Final against Rangers. Thus he had played for both Old Firm clubs against the other in winning Scottish Cup Final sides. He was with Pittsburgh in 1979, Hearts in 1980–81, then with Blackpool and Motherwell.

94

Games:	149
Goals:	39
Scottish Cup:	1972–73
League Cup:	1970–71
European Cup Winners' Cup:	1971–72
Honours:	2 Scotland caps
	(none with Rangers)
Celtic	
Scottish Cup:	1976–77
Born:	Kirkcaldy, 5 April 1952

BRIAN HERON

1969-70

Outside-left was Brian's original position, but he was converted to left-back during Davie White's last season at Ibrox, for his only lengthy spell in the team. Brian went to Motherwell with Bobby Watson in exchange for Peter McCloy.

Games:	9
Goals:	0
Born:	Glasgow

BILLY McPHEE

1968-70

Inside-forward, fringe player who never found a regular place.

Games:	3
Goals:	0
Born:	Methil

WILLIE WHITE

1969-70

Another young full-back of great but unfulfilled promise. His one game was against Airdrie in 1970, at right-back partnering Davie Provan to a 1–1 draw.

Games: 1
Goals: 0
Born: Irvine

KENNY WATSON (1)

1969-71

A powerful left-side player who had played for Scotland youth before joining Rangers, Kenny had a fierce shot and showed much early promise. A weight problem was one of the factors that prevented his obvious promise from maturing.

Games: 4
Goals: 0
Born: Edinburgh

IAIN MACDONALD

1969-73

An outside-left in the mould of Willie Johnston and Willie Henderson, Iain showed great talent as a youngster, breaking into the team under Willie Waddell in 1969–70. A cartilage operation in March 1970 ended that season for him, and after a spell with Dundee United injuries forced him to give up the game.

Games: 14
Goals: 2
Born: Edinburgh, 26 August 1952

PETER McCLOY

1970-86

At 6' 4" beyond much doubt the tallest goalkeeper in British football in his time, Peter McCloy was dubbed the 'Girvan Lighthouse' after his coastal birthplace in Ayrshire. The son of a St Mirren goalkeeper, he began his senior career with Motherwell in 1964. In exchange for Bobby Watson and Brian Heron, he moved to Rangers in the spring of 1970, towards the end of what had been a rather barren season for the Ibrox club. Indeed in McCloy's first match, Rangers were beaten 2–1 at Dunfermline. But for the next four seasons, he made the position his own. He was capped by Scotland and won his share of honours with the club, notably a place in the European Cup Winners' Cup Final of 1972, when Rangers beat Moscow Dynamo in Barcelona. He played a record number of games for a Rangers goalkeeper, 647 in all, thus passing the mark of 545 which the famous Jerry Dawson had set between 1929 and 1945.

In international terms, Peter was contemporary with Alistair Hunter of Kilmarnock and Celtic, David Harvey of Leeds United, Bobby Clark of Aberdeen and later, Alan Rough of Partick Thistle – formidable opposition. And when Stewart Kennedy joined Rangers in 1973, he and McCloy fought over the position for some four years. McCloy was the better survivor and was mainly in possession from 1978 to 1981. Then Jim Stewart, yet another international player, arrived in March of 1981 and McCloy had a battle on his hands yet again. Yet again he prevailed, at least until the coming of Graeme Souness and Chris Woods in 1986. Then Peter became a coach at Ibrox and subsequently became a freelance coach, working with Hearts and other clubs.

His height, of course, was a prodigious advantage with high crosses and lobs, although he would sometimes slap at balls rather than punch or catch. His huge downfield clearances became an attacking gambit for Rangers, in particular when Derek Johnstone, a target for the kicks, was playing in attack. It has often been claimed that Peter was capped for Scotland at golf. Not so – another myth has to be exploded, even if Peter was a first-class player. The Scottish Golf Union has no record of a Peter McCloy having played, at boy, youth or senior level.

Games:	535
Shut-outs:	214
League Championship:	1975–76
Scottish Cup:	1972–73, 75–76, 77–78, 78–79
League Cup:	1970–71, 78–79, 83–84, 84–85
European Cup Winners' Cup:	1971–72
Honours:	4 Scotland caps
Born:	Girvan, 16 November 1946

GRAHAM FYFE

1969-76

Graham played in almost all the forward positions for Rangers, and was a very skilful, very talented player even if he held a place in the team only intermittently. He was a very clever ball-player and an old-fashioned dribbler of the ball, and fitfully would play quite spectacular games, scoring spectacular goals. One of these games, including a cracking goal, came in a 'Juan Gamper' tournament in Barcelona which had the local press comparing him to his opposite number in the Barcelona team, one Johan Cruyff.

For long spells in the Jock Wallace reign he was the regular substitute, rather like David Fairclough at Liverpool, a role he performed successfully, often coming on to score decisive goals. Unpredictable and inconsistent, Graham went to Hibs in 1976 with Alistair Scott in exchange for Iain Munro. His career there was no different.

However, in later years he created great controversy with his statements on why he had left Ibrox. On the age-old topic of Rangers' policy with regard to employing Roman Catholic players, the media in the mid-eighties highlighted cases where Rangers players had married Catholic girls, and tried to persuade them to admit that this had affected their careers. They approached three players in particular. Robert Russell told them point-blank that it had not affected his career (he went on to play several more seasons at the club). Derek Johnstone quite simply refused to discuss it, declining to be interviewed or quoted, but within three months of having married he had been made club captain. Graham Fyfe, on the other hand, said that he was absolutely certain that the real reason he could not get a regular place at Ibrox was because he had married a Catholic girl. Despite the furore it caused at the time, and regular rumblings since then, Rangers' signing of Maurice Johnstone in 1989 surely put an end to such nonsense.

Games: 91
Goals: 31
Born: Motherwell, 18 August 1951

ANGUS McCALLUM
1970-71

A Scottish youth centre-half known as 'Gus', who did not develop to Rangers' requirements. Gus played his only competitive game at Brockville, where a weakened Rangers team went down 3–1 on New Year's Day 1971.

Games: 1
Goals: 0
Born: Glasgow, 19 March 1953

TOM ALEXANDER
1970-73

Tall, slim, another promising young full-back earning only minimal exposure. His two appearances came at the end of season 1970–71 – a 3–1 away win at Cowdenbeath, and in the last home League match of the season, a 2–0 defeat by St Johnstone.

Games: 2
Goals: 0
Born: Ayr, 20 October 1951

BOBBY WATSON (2)
1970-73

Goalkeeper Bobby Watson had a meteoric start to his Ibrox career. Signed from Ardrossan Winton Rovers in July 1970, having had an outstanding career in junior football, he made his first-team debut that same month, coming on as a substitute for Gerry Neef in a pre-season friendly in Hamburg. He retained his place in further matches against Kaiserslautern and Tottenham Hotspur and played in the opening League Cup match, against Dunfermline Athletic at Ibrox on 8 August 1970. After a 1–3 Glasgow Cup Final defeat at the hands of Celtic two days later, Watson was dropped and never again played in the first-team. He was released at the end of season 1972–73.

Games: 1
Shut-outs: 0
Born: Glasgow, 22 March 1950

JIM DENNY
1970-79

Membership of a unique club came to Jim Denny with his very first game for Rangers. It was the Scottish Cup Final of 1971, and Jim thus emulated a predecessor, Willie Reid, who had done exactly the same more than 60 years earlier. (This was perhaps the only similarity in their careers.) Denny played right-back in the replay, which Celtic won 2–1, and although a novice aged 21, played perfectly well and was not responsible for the defeat. He was in the team because Rangers had something of an injury crisis.

Jim was versatile. He played in every position for Rangers, including goalkeeper, mainly in the reserves. He was of medium height, medium build, medium ability. His club-mates cynically called him 'Pele' because of his lack of ball control, and he was something of a utility, or even fringe, player. But he did play in Europe more than once, for example in Cologne in 1979, listed as outside-left. He moved to Hearts on a £30,000 transfer on 4 September 1979.

Games: 66
Goals: 0
Born: Paisley, 13 March 1950

DEREK PARLANE

1970-80

Son of the former Rangers inside-forward Jimmy Parlane, Derek James Parlane was a midfield player converted into a centre-forward by Jock Wallace. Tall, strong and energetic, Derek made a success of the move. In four seasons out of five he was leading goal-scorer, despite being a contemporary of Derek Johnstone for much of the time. He was particularly strong in the air, and an invaluable attacking force for both Rangers and Scotland. Willie Waddell and Willie Thornton together had gone down to the village of Rhu on the Clyde estuary to sign him as a teenager, against very strong competition from many clubs, when he was a Queen's Park player.

He impressed himself on a wider audience in the European Cup Winners' Cup semi-final of 1972, against Bayern Munich, when he replaced the injured John Greig at right-half. Parlane played 'the game of his life', volleying home a Willie Johnston corner kick for Rangers' second goal. Derek scored Rangers' 6000th League goal against Hearts at Tynecastle on 19 January 1974, scoring all four goals in a 4–2 victory. He was transferred to Leeds United in March 1980 for £160,000 and after playing successfully there, he moved on to Manchester City in July 1983. He later played for Swansea Town, and after retiring in 1985 he became a director of non-league club Macclesfield Town, while in business in Cheshire.

100

Games:	300
Goals:	111
League Championship:	1974–75, 75–76, 77–78
Scottish Cup:	1972–73, 78–79
League Cup:	1975–76, 77–78, 78–79
Honours:	12 Scotland caps
Born:	Helensburgh, 5 May 1953

ALEX MILLER

1967-83

Alex came from Clydebank Juniors in 1967. A centre-forward, he scored goals galore in the reserve team, but developed as a full-back and indeed played many positions in a long career with the club. He may very well have suffered from this versatility. When the present principles of substitution were established, Alex became the ideal 'sub'. Tall and slim, Miller was not over-skilled but he was sure and steadfast and always produced a thoroughly reliable game. He was an expert penalty-scorer, the best Rangers had had since Johnny Hubbard. Alex was popular, rather quiet, an altogether nice man and dedicated to the cause. He played the entire Scottish Cup Final of 1971 despite having suffered a broken jaw in the first half. In the mid-seventies he played well enough to keep Sandy Jardine out of the team for a spell. He was released by John Greig, and quickly built a successful management career in turn with Morton, St Mirren and finally Hibernian.

After a decade at Easter Road, Miller resigned in the Autumn of 1996, and moved south to become an assistant to Gordon Strachan, manager of Coventry City. At the same time he maintained his relationship with the SFA as assistant to the national team manager, Craig Brown.

In January 1998, he returned to Scottish club football as manager of Aberdeen where his hard work and organisational skills saved the Dons from relegation. At the same time, ironically, Hibs, the club which dispensed with his services, was relegated.

Games:	306
Goals:	30
League Championship:	1974–75, 75–76, 77–78
Scottish Cup:	1975–76, 78–79
League Cup:	1970–71, 77–78, 78–79, 81–82
Born:	Glasgow, 7 April 1949

DEREK JOHNSTONE

1970-83, 1985-86

Derek Johnstone has been arguably the most versatile player the club has ever had in the post-war era. In an outstanding career he played at centre-half, in midfield and at centre-forward for the club. He also played for Scotland in all three sections of the team and believes he is the only man to have done that. He scored the only goal, the winning goal in the 1970–71 League Cup Final in his first Old Firm match. He was 16 years and 355 days old, the youngest footballer surely ever to have scored the winning goal in a national cup final. Jock Wallace, then the coach at Ibrox, can take some of the credit: he insisted that the young Johnstone be selected. It was Rangers' first trophy in four years. Johnstone went on to score 132 League goals, a post-war Rangers record in the days before Alistair McCoist, and for these facts alone his place in the lore of the club is secure.

He was something of a boy wonder. A product of Dundee Schools football, he played for Scotland at schoolboy, youth, amateur, Under-23 and senior international level. His first love was Dundee United, and he trained with them for a spell but found their methods monotonous. He signed schoolboy forms for Rangers in December 1968 and a full professional contract in July 1970. Derek was a big lad, six-feet tall and powerfully built even then. He played his first match on 19 September 1970 against Cowdenbeath at Ibrox. Rangers won 5–0 and young Johnstone had two of the goals. The 'immortal' goal, in the League Cup Final, came only one month later. From then on Derek was seldom out of the team.

His club record was outstanding. He won Scottish Cup medals in three different positions; he scored goals in Scottish Cup Finals from both centre-half and centre-forward positions. Centre-half was his favoured position. He was and certainly deserved to be compared to the fabled John Charles of Wales in his physical power, his exceptional heading abilities, his nimbleness and quickness over the ground for such a big man, and as a goal-scorer. Johnstone by any standard was an exceptional player. As a centre-forward he scored dozens of goals with his head, mainly from the precise crosses of Tommy McLean on the right wing, and since he did little roaming to the wings, he forced many goals at close range in the goal area.

He was a member of the Scotland international squad for the World Championships of 1978 in Argentina but was not selected to play in any of the matches, an omission that was condemned by the Rangers faithful, and others, as a fatal error of judgement and a tactical disaster on the part of the team manager, Alistair McLeod. Certainly Johnstone had scored in two of the three preceding international matches. It was believed that his omission was because he had asked to play centre-half and not centre forward.

Derek's later years at Ibrox seemed dogged with problems. John Greig, on becoming manager, made him club captain, but Johnstone for some reason was not completely happy and three years later asked to be relieved of it. Many Rangers fans felt that Johnstone's considerable abilities had not been used to the full. The signing by Greig of Colin MacAdam from Partick Thistle in 1980, who was preferred to Johnstone as a centre-forward although he had much less talent, was a straw in the wind of change. The manager's decision to leave out 'D.J.', David Cooper and John MacDonald was seen as a serious tactical error when the 1981 Scottish Cup Final with Dundee United proved a dull goalless draw. These three players transformed the replay; Rangers played their finest football in years and won 4–1 with Johnstone outstanding at centre-forward.

He eventually left in 1983, transferring to Chelsea for £30,000. He played on loan for Dundee United for one month in October 1983 before Jock Wallace, now Rangers' manager, re-signed him in January 1985 for £25,000. His second stint at Ibrox was not a success; he had increasing weight problems, and he was freed by Graeme Souness in 1986. After a brief spell as manager of Partick Thistle, he joined Radio Clyde. An extrovert with a sharp sense of humour and fun, broadcasting has become an ideal second career for 'D.J.'.

Games:	546
Goals:	210
League Championship:	1974–75, 75–76, 77–78
Scottish Cup:	1972–73, 75–76, 77–78, 78–79, 80–81
League Cup:	1970–71, 75–76, 77–78, 78–79, 81–82
European Cup Winners' Cup:	1972
Honours:	14 Scotland caps
Born:	Dundee, 4 November 1953

QUINTON YOUNG

1972-76

Quinton 'Cutty' Young came to Rangers from Coventry City in October 1972, in part exchange for Colin Stein, and had previously been with Ayr United. In fact his origins were in Drongan, a small mining village in Ayrshire. Young was another example of Rangers' long memory concerning players who had played particularly well against them. He had scored a thumping goal on their visit to Somerset Park back in 1969! Cutty settled in quickly as a winger very much in the style that Jock Wallace admired – strong, hard, busy, direct, well able to take care of himself against the most aggressive defenders. If he was no Henderson, no Johnston, still Young was successful at Ibrox, his style much in keeping with the direct philosophy of Wallace. In the end there were differences between these two sparky characters, and Young was given a free transfer in 1976.

Games:	116
Goals:	38
League Championship:	1974–75
Scottish Cup:	1972–73
League Cup:	1975–76
Born:	Drongan, 19 September 1947

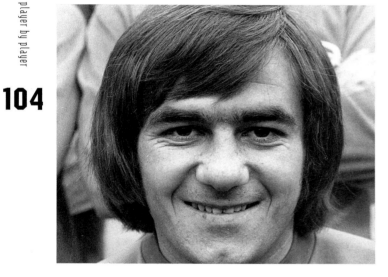

GEORGE DONALDSON

1972-74

In 1970, at the age of 15, 'Boy' Donaldson was taken on tour to Germany by Willie Waddell, to let him see a brave new world and give him a taste of what the future might offer him. Alas, it held a two-year wait before he reached the 'big' team. George was a strong, stockily built wing-half who did not graduate. He was given a free transfer in April 1974.

Games:	10
Goals:	0
Born:	Edinburgh, 24 November 1954

TOM FORSYTH

1972-82

Dubbed 'Jaws', a nickname which not surprisingly he detested, Tom was one of the most popular players to appear with the club. The nickname came from his style of play, which was uncompromising, and the quality of his tackling, which was fearsome. He was bought from Motherwell in October 1972 for £40,000. Originally a mid-field player, he was developed as a centre-half by Jock Wallace, and his qualities of power and accurate and confident passing of the ball brought balance to the Rangers defence and added a strong support element to its attack. With Colin Jackson, he formed a solid core at the centre of a very successful team through the seventies. Tom was a very important player for the club.

He is also famous in Rangers' annals for his first goal. It came in the Scottish Cup Final of 1973, fittingly against Celtic. Forsyth's goal was scored from approximately six inches. A Derek Johnstone header had struck one post and rolled along the goal-line; Forsyth, charging in, could not quite reach the ball. It rebounded from the other post and Forsyth, on the goal-line and off balance, stuck out a foot, managed to make contact, and over the line it went. Forsyth was probably a lucky talisman in that match – it was his 27th consecutive undefeated domestic match.

Forsyth captained Scotland in but his third international appearance, against Switzerland in 1976, and was a prominent member of the squad in the 1978 World Cup Finals competition. He retired because of injury in March 1982, and became manager of Dunfermline Athletic in the autumn. Having formed a close affinity and friendship with Tommy McLean at Ibrox, Forsyth became his coach and assistant manager at Motherwell in 1985 and proved himself enthusiastic and influential with young players.

Games:	326
Goals:	6
League Championship:	1974–75, 75–76, 77–78
Scottish Cup:	1972–73, 75–76, 77–78, 80–81
League Cup:	1975–76, 77–78
Honours:	22 Scotland caps (21 with Rangers)
Born:	Glasgow, 23 January 1949

JOE MASON

1972–74

Joe Mason was a mature player signed from Morton only a few days after Rangers had been beaten at home by Stenhousemuir (of all people) in a second-round League Cup match. The Rangers team at the time was erratic, all the pieces not yet having fallen into place to make the forceful and successful team of the middle and late-seventies. Mason brought intelligence and some style and pattern to the team's play He was an astute midfield player with a sharp football brain, who became a capable coach to the reserve team during the management of John Greig. He left the club when Greig did, in November 1983.

Games: 19
Goals: 2
Born: 17 August 1940

PHIL BONNYMAN

1972–73

Phil was a left-side midfield player, signed from Hamilton Avondale, who managed only one game with the club – the 1–2 defeat at Ibrox by Stenhousemuir on 4 October 1972 in a League Cup second-round match. He played inside-right that day – rather a bitter souvenir of his season with the club. He was freed and later played with Hamilton Academicals and Carlisle United and became a player-coach with Dunfermline Athletic.

Games: 1
Goals: 0
Born: Glasgow, 6 February 1954

ALEX O'HARA

1973–77

Alex made his debut for the club at the age of sixteen in a League Cup tie at Falkirk, scoring two goals. He had a very substantial talent for the game, either in midfield or as an inside-forward, and at 5' 10" he certainly looked the part. It may have been that a lack of the discipline and dedication which Rangers demand sent him into the lower divisions with Partick Thistle and Morton.

Games: 45
Goals: 10
Born: Glasgow, 1 October 1956

DOUG HOUSTON

1973–74

Signed at the end of season 1972–73 by Jock Wallace, from Dundee for a fee of £50,000, Doug Houston played full-back or midfield on the left side of the field. He was an experienced player in his late-twenties, intelligent, thoughtful, sophisticated and by no means over-physical in action. Injuries inhibited his time at Ibrox, and he never became a regular. He went to Dundee United within a year.

Games: 17
Goals: 0
Born: Glasgow, 13 April 1943

ERIC MORRIS

1973–79

Eric was an exceptional player as a junior, playing outside-left with Irvine Meadow in the Junior Cup Final when they beat Cambuslang Rangers. He was 23 when he reached Ibrox, and never did break into the team on any regular basis. He signed for Ayr United in September 1979.

Games: 11
Goals: 1
Born: Stranraer, 30 September 1951

JOHNNY HAMILTON

1973–78

Freed by Hibernian, 'Dingy' Hamilton was snapped up in May 1973. He was a deep-lying inside-forward with a Benburb junior background, and he was very much the play-maker. Pace was probably not his forte, but his passing skills were finely honed and he would keep his outside-right well supplied. He played a prominent role in the League Championship of the treble-winning team of 1975–76 and won a Scottish Cup medal that year. He was freed in the summer of 1978 with Colin Stein despite having won a League Cup medal that season, a fate he had also suffered with Hibernian in 1972–73.

Games: 77
Goals: 8
League Championship: 1975–76
Scottish Cup: 1975–76
League Cup: 1977–78
Born: Glasgow, 10 July 1949

TOMMY McLEAN

1971-82

One of the most intelligent and perceptive footballers to play for Rangers, indeed one of the best players produced in Scotland in the past 30 years, Tommy McLean followed a sequence of outstanding outside-rights – Willie Waddell, Alex Scott, Willie Henderson – and in many respects might be considered the greatest of them all. His height of 5' 4" belied his ability, which was immense. He was not, like Henderson or Johnston, a dribbler. He was not, like Waddell or Scott, a powerful runner. But he was meticulous in his crossing, primly precise in his passing, the accuracy of his entire game, with either foot, making him a goal-maker supreme and a mainstay of Rangers throughout the decade of the seventies, when his positional sense and distribution were unequalled in Scotland. His long passing, and in particular his crosses, brought goals galore from the men in the centre, specifically Derek Johnstone, Derek Parlane, even Alex Macdonald.

He was signed by Willie Waddell in Copenhagen in 1971, when on international duty, for a fee of £65,000 from the Kilmarnock club. Waddell had earlier signed him as a youngster when he was manager of Kilmarnock. When Tommy came to Ibrox he was already an international player, mature and in his mid-20s; he had already tasted European competition.

McLean retired after the Scottish Cup Final of 1982, becoming coach and assistant manager to John Greig at Ibrox. When Greig left in October 1983, McLean took command of the team, and did very well until Jock Wallace arrived. He became part-time manager of Morton, then in the summer of 1984 he became manager of Motherwell. His brothers have been prominent in Scottish football management. Older brother Jim has been progressively manager, managing director and chairman of Dundee United, and Willie is a former Motherwell manager. Tommy moved from Motherwell to Hearts, then in the autumn of 1996 moved to Raith Rovers, where he stayed for one week! Dundee United had made a faltering start to the season, and when the call came from brother Jim, Tommy went to Tannadice and transformed the performance of the United team.

Games:	452
Goals:	57
League Championship:	1974–75, 75–76, 77–78
Scottish Cup:	1972–73, 75–76, 77–78, 78–79
League Cup:	1975–76, 77–78, 78–79
European Cup Winners' Cup:	1971–72
Honours:	9 Scotland caps (1 with Rangers)
Born:	Larkhall, Lanarkshire, 2 June 1947

IAN McDOUGALL

1973-77

A wing-half signed from Pollok Juniors, Ian played quite often without establishing himself in the team. One of his pleasant memories may be a goal scored against Celtic at Parkhead in September 1974, when Rangers won 2-1. He was transferred to Dundee in August 1978 for £15,000.

Games:	37
Goals:	3
League Championship:	1974–75
Born:	Baillieston, 14 August 1954

DONALD HUNTER

1973-75

Reserve goalkeeper in the time of McCloy, Kennedy and company, there were few chances for Donald to shine. He was loaned to St Mirren for a spell and went to Dumbarton in 1975.

Games:	4
Shut-outs:	2
Born:	Dumbarton, 1 April 1955

108 ALLY SCOTT

1973-76

Scott made an immediate impact with Rangers. Signed from Queen's Park in the summer of 1973, he went straight into the team in the first match of the new season, a League Cup tie against Falkirk – and scored two goals! Repeating that, sustaining that kind of performance, was more than anyone could expect. Alistair Scott was a big fellow, six-feet tall, a bustling, all-action, rumbustious striker, a disturber of defences. Articulate and something of an intellectual, his mannerisms and hairstyle (and lack of it) earned him the tag of 'Bamber Gascoigne' in the dressing room. He and Graham Fyfe went to Hibs in exchange for Iain Munro on 7 April 1976. Alistair was subsequently in the insurance business in Glasgow.

Games:	54
Goals:	20
Born:	Glasgow, 26 August 1950

DAVID ARMOUR

1974-79

A midfield player signed in 1974 from Shamrock Juveniles, David moved to Ayr United in September 1979, each of his four games in light blue having been as a substitute.

Games:	4
Goals:	0
Born:	11 April 1953

RICHARD SHARP

1974-75

Brother of Graham, of Everton and Scotland fame, Richard played only one game for Rangers, a League Cup tie against Hibs at Easter Road which was lost 3–1. He was a centre-forward, tall and strong, who left Rangers for a police career.

Games:	1
Goals:	0
Born:	Glasgow, 26 January 1956

MARTIN HENDERSON

1974-78

A tall, rangy centre-forward, Martin was particularly prominent, and a regular scorer, in the treble team of 1975–76. It was the one season of sustained form he enjoyed in the four he spent with the club. Many games that season were won 'single-handedly' by decisive Henderson goals. He went to Hibs on loan for three months, then in April 1978 was transferred to Philadelphia Furies for £30,000.

Games:	47
Goals:	14
League Championship:	1975–76
Scottish Cup:	1975–76
Born:	Kirkcaldy, 3 May 1956

GORDON BOYD

1975-76

A midfield player, highly talented, Gordon showed quite staggering promise as a schoolboy, so much so that he was being compared to Pele at that age. He showed the same skills on joining Rangers, but a lack of self-discipline and dedication, and an obvious abhorrence of training, brought his career to an end. So highly did Rangers think of him that he was given another chance, around 1980, but the same thing happened. A Barrhead boy, he simply drifted from the football scene. His only game had been against Hearts at Ibrox on 8 November 1975 – Rangers lost 2–1.

Games:	1
Goals:	0
Born:	Glasgow, 27 March 1958

STEWART KENNEDY

1973-80

The main contender to the crown of Peter McCloy in the Rangers goal of the seventies was Stewart Kennedy, a Stirling lad who came from Stenhousemuir on 2 April 1973 for a fee of £10,000. Kennedy reached Ibrox by an unusual route. He joined Dunfermline Athletic from his local Camelon Juniors in 1967, was reinstated to junior football with Linlithgow Rose in 1969, then decided to try the senior game again with Stenhousemuir in April 1971. His first match for Rangers was against Falkirk at Brockville on 29 August 1973, in a 5–1 win. The following season, 1974–75, when he was an ever-present, saw Rangers win their first League Championship since 1963–64, and from then until 1978 Kennedy and McCloy exchanged the position, swapping seasons, and effectively sharing the honours.

At 6' 1" and 11 stone 5 lb, Kennedy was well equipped for the job. He was a fine athlete, sure in handling with quick reflexes, and made a major contribution to Rangers' Championship win in 1974–75. That season he played five times for Scotland, and seemed settled in the national team until its defence was overrun at Wembley in a disastrous, comprehensive 5–1 defeat by England. Kennedy was never capped again. Many friends of Rangers felt that his unjustified treatment by the Scottish selectors was such that he was never quite the same goalkeeper again. He moved to Forfar Athletic on a free transfer at the end of April 1980 and continued his career there, still playing at the age of 40 Rangers thought so highly of him that they sent a team to play in his testimonial match at Station Park, Forfar, on 26 February 1985.

Games:	131
Shut-outs:	45
League Championship:	1974–75, 77–78
League Cup:	1975–76, 77–78
Honours:	5 Scotland caps
Born:	Stirling, 31 August 1949

BOBBY McKEAN

1974-78

A product of the junior Blantyre Victoria, Bobby was signed from St Mirren in September 1974 for £60,000. Originally an outside-right, he could play on either side of the team and became a competent midfield player. He was fairly skilful and could go off on mazy dribbles. But he was a purposeful player, a good tackler, strong all round and could score goals. He formed a particularly effective right-wing partnership with Tommy McLean in the Championship of 1974–75. In fact, he was a clear success in his first two seasons at Ibrox, but then inconsistency cost him a regular place, although he remained a useful squad member. He may have been distracted by problems off the field. On 16 March 1978 Bobby McKean was found dead in his car beside his home in Barrhead.

Games:	119
Goals:	17
League Championship:	1974–75, 75–76
Scottish Cup:	1975–76
Honours:	1 Scotland cap
Born:	East Kilbride, 15 March 1952

ALLY DAWSON

1975-87

Alistair Dawson joined Rangers as a 16-year-old boy in 1975 and was promptly taken on a world tour by manager Jock Wallace. He made his debut in Canada. Alistair was a skilful, cultured full-back who could play on either side. He became the club captain, although he perhaps never quite became the wholly exceptional player everyone expected him to be, possibly because of a serious injury he sustained on a club tour of Canada in 1980 when he fractured his skull. He recovered, of course, and went on to become a poised, neatly balanced central-defender, winning his League Cup medal of 1986–87 in that position. He was highly thought of by Jock Stein, the Scotland team manager. Dawson joined Blackburn Rovers for £25,000 in 1987.

Games:	316
Goals:	8
Scottish Cup:	1978–79, 80–81
League Cup:	1978–79, 83–84, 84–85, 86–87
Honours:	5 Scotland caps
Born:	Johnstone, 25 February 1958

KENNY WATSON (2)
1975-81

Signed from Montrose for £30,000 on 3 August 1975 by Jock Wallace, Kenny was originally a left-side midfield player, but he also played in central defence and as a sweeper. He was rather one-footed, but nevertheless established himself for a spell under John Greig, playing 'out of his skin' in a superb Rangers European Champions Cup win in Eindhoven over PSV, and he had a decisive hand in one of the Rangers goals! That was in March 1979, and was PSV's first defeat at home in any European competition. Kenny moved to Partick Thistle in 1981.

Games:	**94**
Goals:	**6**
Scottish Cup:	**1977-78, 78-79**
Born:	**15 December 1951**

CHRIS ROBERTSON
1977-80

Brother of John, of Hearts, Newcastle United and Hearts again, Chris is also a striker and was an able goal-scorer in the reserves, but not in the first-team. On release he went to Hearts, then to Meadowbank Thistle.

Games:	**21**
Goals:	**3**
Born:	**Edinburgh, 25 December 1957**

JIM STEELE
1976-77

As his name suggests, Jim was a Stalin of a player, a defender with very red hair who came up from Southampton on loan for a month, which was littered with bookings. Impossible to play against, Jim came, saw and made many impressions. His loan period was not extended.

Games:	**5**
Goals:	**0**
Southampton	
FA Cup:	**1975-76**
Born:	**Edinburgh, 11 March 1950**

IAIN MUNRO
1976-78

Alexander Iain Fordyce Munro had a remarkable playing career. It began in that forcing ground for young Glasgow footballers, Drumchapel Amateurs, and took him in turn to St Mirren, Hibernian, Rangers, St Mirren again, Stoke City, Sunderland, Dundee United and back to Hibernian.

Skilled, stylish, cultured, Iain was a left-side midfield player who reached Ibrox from Hibs in April 1976 in exchange for Graham Fyfe and Ally Scott. He was converted into a left-back and in terms of his overall career, this was greatly beneficial to the player – although for no apparent reason, he played a rather limited number of games in his short time with Rangers. His abilities might have been used much more and to better effect. He moved to St Mirren (where he had already been from 1968 to 1973) for £25,000 and in this spell at Love Street was capped seven times for Scotland in 1979 and 1980. In October 1980 he went to Stoke City for £150,000, six times what St Mirren had paid for him, then for the same fee to Sunderland in July 1981. In 1984 he was at Dundee United, in 1985 back at Hibs. His polished skills, with the single defence-splitting pass a speciality, and a high work-rate sustained this long and varied career, which took him into coaching at Dunfermline Athletic. He later became assistant manager to, and then in 1989 joint manager with, Jim Leishman at the Fife club, before ascending to sole managership, under controversial circumstances in July 1990. He subsequently managed Hamilton Accies, and in season 1996–97, Raith Rovers.

Games:	**11**
Goals:	**1**
Honours:	**7 Scotland caps (none with Rangers)**
Born:	**Uddingston, 24 August 1951.**

ROBERT RUSSELL

1977-87

Robert Russell came from Shettleston Juniors in 1977 and made his debut that year in a pre-season game against Nairn County in which he scored a fine goal. This goal was a portent of goals to come, this game the overture to 10 marvellous years at Ibrox. Quite simply, Robert Russell was one of the best players Rangers have had since 1970. He had great talent, a stunning first touch on the ball which he used with vision, and he could dribble like an old-timer. He played inside-right or right midfield, and was comparable in style perhaps to the late John White of Blanchflower's famous double team of the early-sixties at Tottenham.

If he is remembered for nothing else, it will be for one of the most startling, most audacious, most perfect goals ever scored in European competition. In a second-round European Champions Cup match in October 1978, PSV Eindhoven had come away from Ibrox with a 0–0 draw. In the second-leg match in Holland, PSV scored in just 34 seconds! But Rangers, playing with verve and rare discipline, twice equalised, and with three minutes to play and the score 2–2, were under siege by PSV seeking the goal that would take them through. If Rangers held that score, they would go through on the away-goals rule. Yet another PSV attack was headed clear by Derek Johnstone, and the ball picked up by Gordon Smith on the edge of the penalty area. He slanted a pass with his left foot out to Tommy McLean, wide and free on the right wing in his own half. There were two defenders between him and the goalkeeper. McLean shattered these two defenders by clipping a beautiful ball beyond them, and Russell, coming through the centre at speed, had possession. In an instant he was in control and went on calmly to the edge of the penalty area. The goalkeeper, van Engelen, came out and did everything he should have done, did everything right; he came out the correct distance, closed off the angle. Russell could have chipped him or dribbled round him. Instead, he bent his shot round the goalkeeper and into the net. In accuracy, speed and brilliant execution, from Johnstone's head to Russell's shot, it was a stupefying goal. And it brought PSV their first defeat at home in any European match.

After his Rangers decade, Robert went to Motherwell, where he showed the same style and form. Often selected for Scotland, injury each time denied him his cap.

Games:	370
Goals:	46
League Championship:	1977–78
Scottish Cup:	1977–78, 78–79, 80–81
League Cup:	1978–79, 81–82, 83–84, 84–85
Born:	Glasgow, 11 February 1957

BILLY MACKAY

1975-85

Diminutive, red-haired outside-right who made his debut at Pittodrie, August 1977. He had a powerful shot and a tremendous turn of speed, but the presence of Tommy McLean, then David Cooper, denied him a regular place. Sadly, injury led him to retire in 1985, the club giving him a testimonial match against New Zealand. He did come back later to play a few games with Hearts.

Games:	37
Goals:	4
Born:	Glenrothes, 27 October 1960

DEREK STRICKLAND

1977-80

Signed for Rangers in July 1977, he was a skilful inside-forward much in the Derek Ferguson mould. He made his first-team debut as a substitute in the John Greig testimonial match of April 1978 (5–0 v a Scotland XI). Derek was transferred to Leicester City in part-exchange for Gregor Stevens on 6 September 1979.

114

Games:	2
Goals:	0

BILLY URQUHART

1978-80

Billy, a Highland lad, was another of John Greig's early signings, on the strength of a pre-season game Rangers had played against his team, Inverness Caledonian, in July 1978 (Rangers won 6–3). Urquhart was a strongly built, enthusiastic type of player who, if he would never win the skill award of any year, could score goals. He played in the European Champions' Cup quarter-final tie against Cologne in 1978–79 after having won a League Cup medal earlier that season. He went to Wigan Athletic for £20,000 in November 1980.

Games:	26
Goals:	7
League Cup:	1978–79
Born:	22 November 1956

GORDON SMITH

1977-80, 1982-83

Bearer of a noble football name, this Gordon Smith would vie with Stuart Munro as Jock Wallace's biggest bargain signing. Gordon came from Kilmarnock in August 1977 for £65,000 and contributed to a very large extent in the transformation from a barren 1976–77 into a treble-winning 1977–78 for the club, when Rangers played their best football of the seventies. The forward line of McLean, Russell, Johnstone, Smith and Cooper at times ran amok. Johnstone had 37 goals, Smith 26. He had never been known as a goal-scorer with Kilmarnock, but his partnership with Derek Johnstone tore defences apart.
He had arrived at Ibrox as an outside-left, but Wallace made him a deep, left-side midfield player, breaking forward at speed, or alternatively an out-and-out striker. Smith relished it all. He was dark, good-looking, had good pace with a loping stride and a hard right-foot shot. He had pedigree, too – his great-grandfather 'Mattha' Smith had won Scottish Cup medals with Kilmarnock in 1920 and, as captain, in 1929.

Gordon Smith played an important part in Rangers' European Championships and domestic Cup campaigns in 1978–79. He went to Brighton and Hove Albion for a quite astonishing fee of £400,000 in 1980 and, unhappily, will be best remembered for his spell there for a close-range miss in the dying moments of the FA Cup Final of 1983 against Manchester United, seen of course by millions on television. When Smith was clear through on goal he provoked the scream from the commentator 'Smith must score!' It became the title of a Brighton fanzine. Cruelly for Smith was the fact that, overlooked, he had scored the opening goal of the match.

Gordon was recalled to Rangers in controversial circumstances, on loan, only a matter of days before the League Cup Final of 1982 against Celtic, and put straight into the team. Rangers lost 2–1. It was a gamble by John Greig which did not come off. Gordon later played in Austria and Switzerland, then had his own insurance and financial consultancy business in Glasgow, advising Scottish footballers on investments.

Games:	157
Goals:	51
League Championship:	1977–78
Scottish Cup:	1977–78, 78–79
League Cup:	1977–78, 78–79
Born:	29 December 1954

GEORGE YOUNG [2]

1978-80

A solid, competent, dependable goalkeeper, George was signed from Stirling Albion for £20,000. The presence of Peter McCloy and Stewart Kennedy meant that he was deprived of any chance of competing for a first-team place.

Games:	**2**
Shut-outs:	**0**
Born:	**8 November 1949**

GREGOR STEVENS

1979-84

Gregor Stevens had what can be described as an interesting career – it was certainly different from that of your average Rangers footballer. As a young player with Motherwell he attracted the attention of many clubs, Celtic and St Etienne among them, but he went to Leicester City for £165,000. He joined Rangers in September 1979 for £150,000 and Derek Strickland, and seemed sure to have a wonderful career chance at Ibrox as a central-defender.

Gregor was slim and fiery, went for everything and everybody, and argued with everyone. Off the field he was the perfect family man, living quietly in Torrance. During his five years with Rangers he was sent off five times and booked 19 times. He was sent off three times in season 1980–81, and his days at the club were surely numbered when, controversially, he was suspended by the SFA for six months in March 1982 following his ordering-off during a friendly! with Kilmarnock. He was given a free transfer in May 1984, and later played with Brechin City and Dumbarton. He was ordered off in his debut match with Dumbarton, and, early in the 1989–90 season, with Brechin. Gregor is said to have been sent off 12 times in his career.

Games:	**92**
Goals:	**4**
Scottish Cup:	**1980–81**
League Cup:	**1981–82**
Born:	**Glasgow, 13 January 1955**

DAVID COOPER

1977-89

Clearly one of the most gifted players in the Scottish game, Davie Cooper was also one of the most enigmatic, inconsistent and irritating, a player whose brilliant mazy dribbles could take him waltzing past bewildered defenders, but at other times lead him into blind alleys and dead-ends from which he would have to extract himself. An outside-left, his left foot has been compared to that of Jim Baxter. They operated in different areas of the field, of course, and many observers have felt that he was more effective on the right when coming inside the full-back to favour his left foot in that way.

Cooper was a menacing crosser of a ball, and possessed a thundering shot from dead-ball situations – for example one scored against Jim Leighton from a free kick in the Rangers–Aberdeen League Cup Final of 1987; a decisive goal for Scotland against Australia in a World Cup qualifying match in 1985; and a critical penalty kick against Wales at Cardiff in the same competition in the same year. Perhaps his most dazzling goal, preserved to this day on video tape, came in the Dryburgh Cup Final against Celtic on 4 August 1979, when he flicked the ball in the air over successive defenders, then volleyed the goal without ever allowing the ball to touch the ground. Many people felt that if Scotland manager Alex Ferguson had made better use of him in the 1986 World Cup Finals in Mexico, the team may have qualified for the later stages for the first time. One of his exceptional games was in the 1981 Scottish Cup Final replay when, almost on his own, he tore the Dundee United defence apart.

David was signed from Clydebank in June 1977 for £100,000. Quiet and reserved, in his early years he shunned publicity, and as a printer in Hamilton he turned down numerous transfer offers from English clubs before joining Rangers. When he did, there was much talk of him being indifferent to going to Ibrox and being perfectly happy at Clydebank. The truth is more likely to be that the transfer had been arranged and agreed long before it happened, since Cooper is by way of being a modest 'Blue-nose'. He moved to Motherwell in August 1989 for a fee of £50,000 and enjoyed a new lease of life with the Lanarkshire club. He won another Scottish Cup medal in 1991 when Motherwell beat Dundee United in the final, and was recalled to the Scotland team for the deciding World Cup qualifying game against Norway. He planned to end his career back at Clydebank, his first love, at the end of season 1995–96, then concentrate on coaching, but on 22 March at Clyde's Broadwood Stadium, he collapsed. He had been making a coaching video with his old adversary Charlie Nicholas of Celtic, Arsenal and Aberdeen. They had just agreed to have a drink when they had finished work when Cooper suffered a massive brain haemorrhage. He died the next day in a Glasgow hospital, a matter of days after his 39th birthday.

The death of Davie Cooper stunned the nation. Rangers fans in particular were devastated and the massive blue gates at the Copland Road end of the stadium became an instant shrine. Thousands came to smother the gates with flowers, scarves, shirts and messages. Celtic fans too paid tribute with their club scarves at Ibrox, and Motherwell fans paid similar massed tributes at Fir Park. His funeral service was attended by the entire Rangers and Motherwell playing staffs and every club in the land was represented.

Games:	540
Goals:	75
League Championship:	1977–78, 86–87, 88–89
Scottish Cup:	1977–78, 78–79, 80–81
League Cup:	1977–78, 78–79, 81–82, 83–84, 84–85, 86–87, 87–88
Motherwell	
Scottish Cup:	1990–91
Honours:	24 Scotland caps (20 with Rangers)
Born:	Hamilton, 25 February 1956

ALEX FORSYTH

1978-81

One of John Greig's first signings, Alex came to Ibrox from Manchester United in the first place on a one-season loan arrangement, at the end of which he was signed on a permanent basis. Rangers thus had a mature, vastly experienced and thoroughly able full-back who was mainly held in reserve. He had been on Arsenal's ground staff at the age of 15, but homesickness drove him back to Scotland after eight or nine months and he joined Partick Thistle. There he gained his first Scotland cap, and played in the League Cup winning team of 1971–72, becoming therefore, in the eyes of Thistle fans, immortal. Tommy Docherty, who had first selected him for Scotland, took him to Manchester United in December 1972 for £85,000, and in half-a-dozen years at Old Trafford Alex became a well-balanced, hard-tackling, stocky defender who could play on either side and get forward into attack, if he perhaps lacked pace in recovery against the faster wingers. He also had a quite thunderous shot. He was given a free transfer in the summer of 1982 and had a season with Motherwell and a season with Hamilton Accies before retiring.

Games:	41
Goals:	5
Partick Thistle	
League Cup:	1971–72
Honours:	10 Scotland caps (none with Rangers)
Born:	Swinton, Lanarkshire, 5 February 1952

GORDON DALZIEL

1976-84

Gordon was a forward – fast, pacy, and with a nose for goals. He was first noted by Rangers fans for a goal he scored after five minutes in a cracking 3–3 draw with Celtic at Parkhead in November 1981. He linked well with John MacDonald in attack, but like MacDonald did not reach full potential with Rangers and became rather a fringe player. He was transferred to Manchester City in 1984, later playing with Partick Thistle and Raith Rovers.

With the Kirkcaldy club, he won the First Division Championship in 1994–95, and in the sensational League Cup Final the same season, Gordon scored a last-minute equaliser to allow Rovers to beat Celtic on penalties 6–5, after the 2–2 draw. Dalziel became a manager with Ayr United.

Games:	48
Goals:	11
League Cup:	1981–82
Raith Rovers	
League Cup:	1994–95
Born:	Motherwell, 16 March 1962

ROBERT CLARK

1980-82

Robert, from Blantyre Victoria, was a tall, slim defender who distributed the ball well and looked like a good player. His sole first-team outing was as a sub at Tynecastle in 1981. He later played for Motherwell and Kilmarnock.

Games:	1
Goals:	0
Born:	Hamilton, 4 November 1962

IAN REDFORD

1980-86

Rangers set a new record transfer fee between Scottish clubs when they paid Dundee £210,000 for Ian Redford in February 1980. He was a tall, stylish, powerful-running player, good in the air and with a strong shot. An articulate man, Redford was the son of a farmer in Perthshire. He achieved a certain notoriety with Rangers fans for his last-minute penalty failure against Dundee United in the Scottish Cup Final of 1981. Ian's shot was hard and straight, and goalkeeper McAlpine got his legs to it. But it should be said that it was Redford's dramatic last-minute equaliser against St Johnstone at Perth in the fourth round that kept Rangers hopes alive. Redford also produced a winner two minutes from the end of the League Cup Final of 1981–82. He was transferred to Tannadice in August 1985 and played for United in their golden season of 1986–87, when they reached the UEFA Cup Final, with wins against Barcelona and Borussia Münchengladbach. They lost the two-leg final narrowly to IFK Gothenburg. Ian moved on to Ipswich Town and in the twilight of his career won a League Cup winners medal with Raith Rovers.

Games:	247
Goals:	42
Scottish Cup:	1980–81
League Cup:	1981–82, 84–85
Raith Rovers	
League Cup:	1994–95
Born:	Perth, 5 April 1960

JIM BETT

1980-83

One of the strangest routes ever taken to Ibrox was trodden by Jim Bett, the Aberdeen and Scotland midfield player. A Hamilton boy, he went from schools football there to Airdrieonians by way of being, briefly, an 'associate schoolboy' with Dundee. In May 1978 he was transferred to, of all places, Valur FC of Reykjavik, Iceland, for £1500, and during a short spell there married an Icelandic girl. Bett moved on and up, to SK Lokeren in Belgium where John Greig 'discovered' him and paid £180,000 to bring him to Ibrox in June 1980. Although he had complete success with Rangers, and won Cup medals with them, domestic reasons took him back to Lokeren in the summer of 1983. Two years later Aberdeen persuaded him back to Scotland at a cost of £300,000. With the north-eastern club he won further medals and established himself firmly as a member of the Scotland team.

Jim Bett was an outstanding Rangers player, a first-class footballer much admired, incidentally, by Graeme Souness. A midfield player, he was two-footed, intelligent, skilful, with a killing first touch on the ball. In a sense he may have been a little before his time at Ibrox, when the team played a more vigorous game than those which came later in the eighties. Like Ray Wilkins, he was not inclined to release the ball until he was sure of its target. In that respect Jim was the strong, safe, conservative type in distribution, preferring the simple pass, the simple option. On arrival at Ibrox he made an immediate impact on the team with the quality and control of his play. He was somehow never wholly accepted by the fans, who recognised him as highly capable but thought him inconsistent.

Games:	152
Goals:	30
Scottish Cup:	1980–81
League Cup:	1981–82
Aberdeen	
Scottish Cup:	1985–86, 1989–90
League Cup:	1989–90
Honours:	26 Scotland caps (2 with Rangers)
Born:	Hamilton, 25 November 1962

119

JOHN MACDONALD

1978–86

Yet another of John Greig's earliest signings, John MacDonald was one of the most promising young players in Scotland during the seventies. As a striker he was on the small side (5' 9"), dark, bustling, always in place when the crosses came in, a goal-scorer. He got most of them from around the six-yard range, a scrambler of goals as much as anything, picking up chances, pecking at crumbs. He did it all very well, and was probably most effective playing alongside a big, target centre-forward. In his early years at Ibrox he was a prominent scorer, but his form fell off, in spite of the chances given to him by a succession of managers. He went to Barnsley.

Games:	230
Goals:	77
Scottish Cup:	1980–81
League Cup:	1981–82, 83–84
Born:	Glasgow, 15 April 1961

COLIN MACADAM

1980–85

Colin MacAdam was the first player to feature in a 'tribunal transfer' in Scottish football history. Rangers' notion of his worth in the summer of 1980, when they sought to buy him from Partick Thistle, was £80,000. Thistle were sure he was a £500,000 player. The tribunal priced him at £165,000. Colin forced himself into the record books again by playing for Rangers against Celtic at Parkhead in August 1980 – a game in which Jim Bett scored – in direct opposition to his brother Tom, centre-half for Celtic. He did it more than once, notably three months later in November, when centre-forward Colin scored twice against his brother in a 3–0 Rangers win at Ibrox.

In his first season with the club, Colin scored 22 goals. MacAdam was a big (6' 1") powerful lad, versatile and strong in the air, if ball skills and close control were not his strongest suits. Before Partick Thistle he had played at Dumbarton and Motherwell, and it was Bertie Auld at Partick Thistle who converted him from centre-half to centre-forward with a good deal of success. After his bright start at Ibrox, Colin rather languished in the reserves until Jock Wallace revived his career somewhat by moving him back to central-defence. As a PE teacher, Colin had always been a part-time player prior to his arrival at Ibrox. He was released by Rangers on 30 March 1985.

Games:	99
Goals:	32
League Cup:	1983–84
Born:	Glasgow, 28 August 1951

JIM McINTYRE

1981-82

Jim McIntyre must be rated one of the great disappointments of the early-eighties, indeed of this whole period under review. He first came to national notice in the annual Under-15 international against England, when he was quite outstanding. He played briefly with the junior Irvine Meadow and came to Ibrox as a teenager. At 5′ 7″ and sturdily built, he was a super-active wing-half, covering the entire field, and seemed to have the potential of becoming another, say, Billy Bremner. But Jim had a moment of madness by turning out without permission for another, minor, club while a registered Rangers player. He was released. No other senior club came along with an offer, and he went back to Irvine Meadow.

Games: 1
Goals: 0
Born: Kilwinning, 26 October 1962

KENNY BLACK

1981-84

A left-side full-back or midfield player, Kenny was originally with Rangers on a schoolboy form. He reached the League team in 1981 and in his first two appearances was booked, against Hibs at Easter Road, then sent off against Dundee United at Tannadice, thereby making an immediate name of sorts for himself. He was an attacking full-back, hard-tackling although small, very compact, and altogether a rather fearsome, combative player. In December 1983 he and Kenny Lyall were transferred to Motherwell in exchange for goalkeeper Nick Walker. Black later moved to Hearts and, in 1989, to Portsmouth. Returning to Scotland he became a very successful captain of Airdrie and he played in the 1995 Scottish Cup Final.

Games: 34
Goals: 2
Born: Stenhousemuir, 29 November 1963

JOHN McCLELLAND

1981-85

John McClelland was the Irish international central-defender who had played with Portadown in Ireland, Cardiff City in Wales, and came from Mansfield Town in England to Rangers, just possibly a unique four-country career record. John Greig paid the English club £100,000 for him in May 1981, and he became a cornerstone in the Rangers backline, forming a sound partnership with Craig Paterson in the core of the defence in 1982 and 1983, by which time he had become Rangers' captain. McClelland was tall at 6′ 2″ and heavily built, but in spite of that, very fast on his feet. Greig took him on a pre-season tour to Sweden in 1981, where he played at left-back, and an ankle injury received there dogged his early days with the club. Before joining Rangers he had played left-back and even midfield for Northern Ireland, and during his days at Ibrox he was one of the best defensive footballers in the UK, conservative in positional play and never a taker of any risks whatsoever. Rangers fans were genuinely sorry to see him go in November 1984, following a dispute over money with manager Wallace. He was smartly transferred to Watford for a record £265,000. By 1990 he was back with St Johnstone with whom he had a taste of management. He later became a coach at Bradford City.

Games: 153
Goals: 8
League Cup: 1983–84, 84–85
Honours: 52 Northern Ireland caps (25 with Rangers)
Born: Belfast, 7 December 1955

JIM STEWART

1981-84

Circumstances, and perhaps particularly the change of management from John Greig to Jock Wallace in November 1983, meant that James Garven Stewart, the Scottish international goalkeeper, had rather a short career with Rangers. He was signed by Greig on 15 March 1981 for £115,000 from Middlesbrough. Three days later he played against Dundee United when they had one of their very infrequent wins at Ibrox – 4–1 – a rather less than joyous start for any goalkeeper. By the end of the season, however, that score was reversed and Stewart had a Scottish Cup winners' medal in his glove, as Rangers beat Dundee United in the final. Against that same United he won a League Cup Final the following season.

Stewart, a Kilwinning boy, became the regular Kilmarnock goalkeeper, by way of Troon Juniors, when he was but 18. He was capped at youth, Under-21 and Under-23 as well as at senior level, and went to Middlesbrough in May 1978 for £110,000. He stood 6' 2", built for the job, and was a fine goalkeeper. Some people believed that the word 'fine' was particularly applicable to him and that he was too polite in action to be a real Rangers goalkeeper. He had had to play second best in his later time at Middlesbrough to Jim Platt, the North of Ireland goalkeeper, and of course Peter McCloy was still around at Ibrox.

He was blamed for the loss of critical 'away' goals to Dukla Prague at Ibrox in September 1981, and to Cologne at Ibrox in 1982. The German goal in fact should never have been allowed – it came from a free kick by Allofs, who actually played the ball twice. Stewart's form for Rangers declined. He went to Dumbarton on loan for a spell in 1983–84 and, following a free transfer from Rangers in the summer, moved on to St Mirren as understudy to Campbell Money. He played in the infamous League match, the last of the season in May 1986, when St Mirren lost to Celtic 5–0 at Love Street, a controversial result which allowed Celtic to win the Championship.

Games:	92
Shutouts:	34
Scottish Cup:	1980–81
League Cup:	1981–82
Born:	Kilwinning, 9 March 1954

BILLY DAVIES

1980-86

Signed as a schoolboy – another graduate of Crookston Castle Secondary School – Billy made his debut in Hamilton, Ontario, as a substitute in the final of a close-season tournament, the 'Red Leaf Cup', against Ascoli of Italy. Rangers lost 2–0. He was a left-side midfield player, medium height, active, stocky, a perfectly good little player who proved not quite good enough and who was never fully established in the team. He was released when Graeme Souness arrived at Ibrox, went to Sweden briefly, then came back to play with St Mirren. During his time with Rangers, he won Scottish youth honours.

Games:	23
Goals:	2
Born:	Glasgow, 31 May 1964

KENNY LYALL

1981-84

Kenny Lyall, an Edinburgh boy, was a left-side midfield player of very few appearances who was transferred to Motherwell with Kenny Black in exchange for Nicky Walker in December 1983.

Games:	12
Goals:	0
Born:	Edinburgh, 23 March 1963

DOUGLAS ROBERTSON

1981-84

A bustling inside-forward who forced his way into the first-team for a few matches in 1981 but could not sustain his place, Dougie had something of a weight problem which hindered him. He went to Morton in 1984 for a small fee.

Games:	8
Goals:	0
Born:	Torphichen, 15 March 1963

CRAIG PATERSON

1982-87

A club record fee of £225,000 was paid for Craig Paterson in July 1982 when John Greig bought him from Hibs, but the transfer in a sense turned out to be one of the most disappointing of his managerial career. Craig, son of John Paterson, centre-half in the Hibs team of the late-fifties and early-sixties, had shown immense promise and ability at Easter Road, but injuries dogged his time at Ibrox. Rangers were so anxious to have him signed for a pre-season tournament in Lille that they did not insist on a medical examination before the transfer. Paterson marked his debut in the tournament by scoring the winning goal in the semi-final against St Etienne in a penalty shoot-out. Rangers lost the final to SK Lokeren.

Craig quickly established himself in the Rangers team, forming a very successful central defence partnership with John McClelland. He became captain after McClelland left the club, leading the team to success in the League Cup of 1984–85. His greatest strength was in the air, and he was a ball-player rather than a plain stopper. Injuries and intermittent lapses in form prevented him from being the player he should have been, from fulfilling all his talents. Such was his ability that he should have been, for example, a Scottish international. Drifting around the fringes of the team, he was sold to Motherwell by Graeme Souness early in his Ibrox regime. Craig won a Scottish Cup medal with the Fir Park club, against Dundee United, in 1991.

Games:	130
Goals:	12
League Cup:	1983–84, 84–85
Motherwell	
Scottish Cup:	1990–91
Born:	South Queensferry, 2 October 1959

ROBERT PRYTZ

1982–85

A Swedish international signed from Malmo for £100,000, Robert was a seasoned player who had played in the European Champions Cup Final which Malmo lost to Nottingham Forest in Munich in 1979. He was a central or left-sided midfield player. Prytz was strong and stocky, used the ball well and had a terrific finishing shot. He was popular with the players, but perhaps not so with the crowd – they thought he gave less than 100 per cent effort. Perhaps the direct Rangers style was none too compatible with his continental thinking on the game and how it should be played. He scored the winning goal at Pittodrie in a League match in September 1982 to give Rangers their first win there in six years. Robert went to IFK Goteborg for £130,000, and went on to play for Bayern Uerdingen in Germany.

Games:	118
Goals:	20
League Cup:	1984–85
Honours:	56 Sweden caps (10 with Rangers)
Born:	Malmo, 12 January 1960

DAVID McPHERSON

1981-87, 1992-95

As a graduate of the famous football 'academy', the Crookston Castle secondary school, David McPherson was a genial giant who twice signed for Rangers and twice signed for Hearts. He joined Rangers as a schoolboy fresh from Gartcosh United, and growing to 6' 3" tall, was a natural as a centra-defender. He also played at full-back and occasionally in midfield, making a first-team debut in a League Cup tie against Brechin City at Ibrox in September 1981, when Rangers made rather heavy weather of winning 1–0.

Many Rangers supporters felt that his progress through the youth ranks was identifying him as a Rangers captain of the future. His debut in European football saw him score four goals in a Rangers 8–0 win over Valetta. David won League Cup medals in 1984 and 1985 against Celtic (3–2) and Dundee United (1–0). When the Souness era began, McPherson won the first of his three Championships in 1986–87. He missed only two league games, but that consistency was obliterated by a calamitous mistake in a Scottish Cup tie at Ibrox. He failed to control a long through ball and the Hamilton Accies' Adrian Sproat went on to score the solitary goal which put Rangers out of the Cup and brought the lowly Accies a memorable victory.

In that close season, David was transferred to Hearts for £400,000 – the general inference was that Graeme Souness was taking his revenge for that Cup blunder, although years later Walter Smith insisted that financial considerations had applied. McPherson became Hearts' captain and a solid and successful central-defender in partnership with Alan McLaren. It brought him a place in the Scotland team and the first of 27 caps in a career which covered the World Cup Finals in Italy in 1990 and the European Championship Finals in Sweden in 1992.

His partnership with Gough in central defence in these Scotland matches may have persuaded Walter Smith to bring him back to Ibrox for £1.35 million in the summer of 1992. There was the suggestion that Smith had done Hearts a financial favour.

In the 1992–93 season, David played in all of the memorable European matches and recorded a season's total of 56. Alas, another McPherson blunder cost Rangers a Scottish Cup success, this time in the final. Against Dundee United in 1994, a hesitant back pass by David and a subsequent tangle with goalkeeper Alistair Maxwell, allowed Craig Brewster to score the only goal, to give United a long-awaited cup victory and destroy Rangers' dream of successive trebles.

The arrival of Basile Boli and Rangers' determination to sign Alan McLaren meant that McPherson was off to Edinburgh again. He had been entirely consistent in his last season and typically gave an outstanding performance in his final appearance at Motherwell on 22 October 1994.

He joined an elite band in the Scottish Cup final of 1998, when he helped Hearts to defeat his old club, having won a Scottish Cup medal with Rangers in 1993.

Games:	322
Goals:	32
League Championship:	1986–87, 92–93, 93–94
Scottish Cup:	1992–93
League Cup:	1983–84, 84–85, 92–93, 93–94
Heart of Midlothian	
Scottish cup:	1997–98
Honours:	27 Scotland caps (4 with Rangers)
Born:	Paisley, 28 January 1964.

125

ANDY BRUCE

1981-86

Andy was a Scottish youth international goalkeeper who made a limited number of appearances because of the presence of Peter McCloy and Jim Stewart. He was a perfectly capable goalkeeper, released by Graeme Souness. He went to Hearts, where he was yet again an understudy.

Games:	2
Shutouts:	0
Born:	Edinburgh, 9 August 1964

ANDY KENNEDY

1982-84

Signed from youth football, Andy Kennedy was a striker, very, very fast, in the mould of an Ian Rush, but of course not remotely as good. He was brought into the team by John Greig, and with contemporaries such as Billy Davies and Kenny Black, it seemed that the Rangers youth policy was succeeding. After a lively start, Andy could not maintain his momentum and when Jock Wallace arrived, he lost his place, never to regain it. Released by Wallace, he went to Birmingham City, then to Blackburn Rovers, where he was perfectly successful.

Games:	20
Goals:	4
Born:	Stirling, 8 October 1964

DAVE MITCHELL

1983-85

Defenders always knew when Dave Mitchell was around – Dave made sure of that. A six-foot centre-forward hustler from Australia, Mitchell paid his own expenses to Scotland for trials with Rangers and was signed by Greig. He made himself a regular first-team player, and was rather surprisingly transferred by Wallace. He went back to Australia, played against Scotland in the World Cup Finals in 1986, and played in Germany's Bundesliga with Eintracht Frankfurt.

Games:	45
Goals:	14
Honours:	Australia caps
Born:	Glasgow, 13 June 1962

SANDY CLARK

1983-85

If the traditional concept of the 'old-fashioned' centre-forward is one of a strong man, full of running, taking and giving knocks, often injured but spurning the injuries, challenging for everything, active with the elbows, and so on, Sandy Clark was the vintage example. He was, of course, much more than that. Sandy was forceful in the air, courageous in the penalty area, but he could work well and closely with inside-forwards and keep a forward line moving nicely. He played originally with his home-town team, Airdrieonians, then went to West Ham United, from whom Rangers bought him on 17 March 1983 for £160,000. Sandy had been a long-time Rangers supporter, and it had always been an ambition to play for the club. The return to Ibrox of Jock Wallace seemed to restrict Sandy – Wallace appeared to prefer such other forwards as McCoist, Iain Ferguson and David Mitchell. Clark was transferred to Hearts for £40,000 in October 1984, where he played successfully until 1989 when he joined Partick Thistle as player-manager before going back to Hearts to coach in 1990. He became manager at Tynecastle for a spell, then succeeded Iain Munro at Hamilton Accies in season 1996–97.

Games:	62
Goals:	22
League Cup:	1983–84
Born:	Airdrie, 28 October 1956

DAVE MACKINNON

1982-86

In one of John Greig's surprise transfer deals, MacKinnon was signed from Partick Thistle for £30,000 in May 1982. Dave was a red-haired, wholehearted full-back who had pace and was addicted to storming forward to use a powerful shot. He was not a highly cultured player and Rangers fans failed to comprehend this signing – MacKinnon had previously been with Arsenal, Dundee and Partick Thistle, so what, they asked, could he do for Rangers? He was given a free transfer by Graeme Souness and moved on to Airdrie.

Games: 141
Goals: 2
Born: Glasgow, 23 May 1956

JIMMY NICHOLL

1983-84, 1986-89

A seasoned player of high quality, as a career with Manchester United, Sunderland and West Bromwich Albion and more than 70 caps for Northern Ireland confirms, Jimmy joined Rangers originally on loan from Toronto Metro Croatia. A cheerful, outgoing Ulsterman, he was much respected by Rangers fans. Second time around at Ibrox, Graeme Souness brought him from West Bromwich Albion, exchanging Bobby Williamson in the deal in August 1986, and he became a defensive cornerstone in the first Souness team, before the advent of Gary Stevens. Nicholl was technically very sound, experienced and mature and was a useful, valuable and classy player for Rangers. Whilst at Ibrox he coached the second-team, and Souness wanted him to stay and develop as a coach. Nicholl felt that he could play on in Premier Division football for a little longer, and he went to Dunfermline Athletic in 1989. Later, as manager of Raith Rovers, he led the Fife team into the Premier Division in 1994–95, crowning it with the League Cup Final win over Celtic in the same season. Nicholl was then tempted to the management of Millwall, but after a year there, the club was declared bankrupt, and he returned to Raith Rovers to work with manager Munro in coaching.

Games: 106
Goals: 0
League Championship: 1986–87
League Cup: 1983–84, 86–87, 87–88
Manchester United
FA Cup: 1976–77
Honours: 73 Northern Ireland caps (4 with Rangers)
Born: Toronto, Canada, 28 December 1956

BOBBY WILLIAMSON

1983-87

A strong, knock 'em down type of centre-forward who could score spectacular goals, Bobby was signed by Jock Wallace from Clydebank for £100,000 in December 1983. In 1984 he suffered a severe leg break, an injury which kept him out of football for the best part of a year. He was transferred to West Bromwich Albion in August 1986, in exchange for Jimmy Nicholl. Bobby returned to Scotland to play for Kilmarnock in the nineties, and became manager there when Alex Totten left in season 1996–97, leading them to their first Scottish Cup success since 1929.

Games:	52
Goals:	20
Born:	Glasgow, 13 August 1961

ERIC FERGUSON

1983-86

Many friends of Rangers felt that Eric, a tall, loose-limbed centre-forward, was worth a more extended run in the team than he had. He scored many goals in the reserves. Released in 1986, he went to Dunfermline Athletic.

Games:	14
Goals:	1
Born:	Fife, 12 February 1965

NICKY WALKER

1984-89

Jock Wallace, lately the Motherwell manager, swapped Kenny Black, Kenny Lyall and cash, in a deal reckoned to be worth £100,000, to bring his erstwhile goalkeeper Nicky Walker to join him at Ibrox a month or so after he was appointed Rangers manager for a second time. Walker, a native of Elgin and scion of the Walker shortbread family, had his first match at Easter Road on 27 December 1983, when Rangers beat Hibs 2–0. Like Kennedy and Stewart before him, he found himself disputing with Peter McCloy for the position, but season 1985–86 was a particularly successful one for him. He missed only a couple of matches in a season which was completely barren for a team of appalling inconsistency, so much so that after Rangers lost a rather prestigious home friendly with Tottenham Hotspur (a club that has caused them trouble down the years) by 2–0, Jock Wallace departed from the club and Graeme Souness arrived from Sampdoria as his successor in April 1986.

The expensive signing of Chris Woods in the summer of that year, at the same time as Peter McCloy was signing a new two-year contract, meant that Walker went into reserve, although many fans were prepared to say that he should have been the preferred goalkeeper when Woods seemed to be suffering various crises of confidence. Nicky Walker was a competent goalkeeper, and something of a heroic one in the League Cup Final of 1987–88 against Aberdeen, when he replaced the suspended Chris Woods although he was not really fit. Under freedom of contract Walker signed for Hearts in 1989, inexplicably since he became a reserve yet again, this time to Henry Smith. His travels took him to Partick Thistle, then Aberdeen.

Games:	95
Shutouts:	37
League Cup:	1987–88
Born:	Aberdeen, 29 September 1962

SCOTT FRASER

1983-85

A full-back introduced by Jock Wallace in January 1984 in a home match against Aberdeen, Scott never became a regular choice and was freed in May 1985.

Games:	10
Goals:	0
Born:	Edinburgh, 28 April 1963

STUART MUNRO

1984-91

Stuart Munro was a model professional, a survivor of the Souness 'revolution' of the late-eighties, an unsung, often underrated, left-back who saw off challenges from such as Jan Bartram, the Dane, and Jimmy Phillips from Bolton Wanderers. Signed by Jock Wallace in February 1984 from Alloa, for what seems now the ridiculously low figure of £25,000, Stuart was fast, mobile, perfectly balanced, and always very fit – all told, a highly competent, well-rounded footballer who registered more than 200 games with the club. He was transferred to Blackburn Rovers for £350,000 in the summer of 1991.

Games:	233
Goals:	3
League Championship:	1986–87, 88–89, 89–90
League Cup:	1986–87, 87–88, 90–91
Born:	Falkirk, 15 September 1962

ROBERT FLECK

1983-88

Glasgow born and bred, Robert Fleck was a product of the 'system', both of Rangers and of Scotland. Like Derek Ferguson, Hugh Burns and Ian Durrant, Robert took the route through youth teams and Under-21 selections and emerged as a fast, pacy, brave striker with stunning acceleration. Although only 5' 6" tall, he was a powerful runner and finisher. He was the ideal foil to Alistair McCoist (according to McCoist), and they formed a potent strike force, particularly in 1986–87. Financial differences, it was believed, led to Fleck making a transfer request, which was certainly not welcomed by Rangers, but in December 1987 he went to Norwich City for £560,000. His going left Rangers woefully short of striking force that season, and may have cost them their chance of advancement in the European Cup. Fleck's talents blossomed in the English First Division, where he scored regularly for the Canaries prior to a £2 million move to Chelsea where he spent three seasons before returning to Carrow Road.

Games:	104
Goals:	34
League Championship:	1986–87
League Cup:	1986–87, 87–88
Honours:	3 Scotland caps (none with Rangers)
Born:	Glasgow, 1 August 1965

129

DEREK FERGUSON

1982-90

A midfield player who has represented Scotland at youth, Under-21 and senior international level, Derek Ferguson was seen by many friends of Rangers to have the potential to become quite outstanding. Injuries, misdemeanours and other problems off the field hindered his progress. He was brought to the club in the reign of John Greig as one of a group of considerable young players – Hugh Burns, Andy Bruce, Ian Durrant, Robert Fleck and Dave McPherson. He was able to contribute little to the Rangers team in season 1989–90, and in midwinter, when the possibility of his transfer arose, it was clear that the Rangers management had lost patience with the player. The Graeme Souness observation was ominous – he said, 'We've been paying him good money for no return in the past couple of years.' Ferguson was loaned to Dundee early in 1990. He was transferred to Hearts in July 1990 for £750,000. He later played with Sunderland, then Falkirk, with little consistency.

Games:	145
Goals:	9
League Championship:	1986–87, 88–89
League Cup:	1986–87, 87–88
Honours:	2 Scotland caps
Born:	Glasgow, 31 July 1967

IAIN FERGUSON

1984-86

Iain arrived at Ibrox in May 1984 from Dundee for a 'tribunal' fee of £200,000. He had out-standing ability and was a scorer of thrilling goals, but a certain lack of discipline and com-mitment meant that he never became another Kenny Dalglish, whereas at one time that had looked entirely possible.

He scored the only goal in the League Cup Final of 1984–85 (v Dundee United) and with an ironic twist, scored against Dundee United in the Scottish Cup Final – for victorious Motherwell in 1991. In the interim he played for the Tannadice club and was prominent in their 1986–87 UEFA Cup run – scoring in Barcelona and Monchengladbach. Europe had always been his forte; Iain had once scored two for Rangers against the mighty Inter-Milan.

Games:	46
Goals:	11
League Cup:	1984–85
Motherwell	
Scottish Cup:	1990–91
Born:	Newarthill, 4 August 1962

CAMMY FRASER

1984-87

Like Iain Ferguson, Cameron Fraser was a 'tribunal' transfer from Dundee, only two months later, for a fee set at £165,000. He was a midfield player, strong, stylish, competent but also hard, and he had his problems with referees. He was one of the few players who have appeared in all three major Scottish derby matches – Glasgow, Edinburgh and Dundee. Cammy was a fairly important member of the first Graeme Souness side at Ibrox in the League and League Cup, but was forced to retire at the end of the 1986–87 season because of injury. He did make something of a comeback, and played some games with Raith Rovers.

Games:	75
Goals:	9
League Championship:	1986–87
League Cup:	1984–85, 86–87
Born:	Dundee, 22 July 1957

HUGH BURNS

1983-87

Hugh Burns, a lively, attacking right-back, broke through into the team during the second Jock Wallace regime. He had been capped at youth and Under-21 levels and was popular with the Rangers crowd because of his exciting forward runs. Under Graeme Souness he lost his place in the team, and following a difference of opinion he was transferred to Hearts. Hugh subsequently joined Dunfermline Athletic, then Fulham.

Games:	63
Goals:	4
League Cup:	1983–84
Born:	Lanark, 13 December 1965

ALISTAIR McCOIST

1983-

The extrovert kid from East Kilbride was one of the greatest goal-scorers that Rangers ever had, certainly the finest for 50 years. He is now worshipped by the Rangers legions. 'Twas not ever thus. Alistair signed for Rangers only at the third time of asking. As a schoolboy, he said no to a John Greig approach, and signed for St Johnstone in 1978, aged 16. He made his debut for them on 7 April 1979 and had three more games in succession at the end of that season. In season 1980–81 he snapped up 23 goals for the Saints, and a flock of clubs were in pursuit of him, Rangers included – and thereby hangs a tale. The story goes that McCoist and a St Johnstone director were at Ibrox, discussing his transfer, in August 1981. There was a telephone call for the St Johnstone director, who left the discussions to take the call. It was from Sunderland, offering £100,000 more than Rangers. So McCoist, still only 18 years old, went to Sunderland for £400,000. Thus Rangers had been spurned twice.

His period at Sunderland, in a team that was always struggling, was not a success and in June 1983 Alistair met John Greig and his assistant manager, Tommy McLean, in a Carlisle hotel and signed, at last, for Rangers. The fee was £185,000. Alistair was not welcomed rapturously by the Rangers fans. They were well aware of his his history and rather questioned his commitment to a club he had twice rejected. His first two seasons at Ibrox were difficult and at one point manager Wallace suggested he should leave, saying he could arrange a transfer back to Sunderland. But McCoist was determined and persisted with Rangers, forcing himself into the Scotland International team, with a first cap in April 1986, against Holland. Since then he has become overwhelmingly popular with the fans, because of his play and personality alike. Alistair is lively, extrovert and articulate, and brilliant at handling the media.

Technically, as a striker, McCoist has some shortcomings, mainly his lack of a killing first touch, and instant ball control. At 5' 10" and 12 stone, he was never going to be a fiercely physical forward. But he was surprisingly good in the air, brave and well-balanced and above all he could score goals, knocking them in with mishits, deflections, scrambles, through crowded goal mouths, snapping up the most meagre of chances from the most unlikely situation. In season 1989–90, he became the scorer of the highest number of Premier Division goals, his 133 passing the 127 of Frank McGarvie. His 133 was a Rangers post-war record, passing the 132 of Derek Johnstone.

For 'Super Ally', 1991–92 became a golden year. With 41 goals, he reached a career total of 200 Scottish League goals. He scored Rangers' 100th goal of the season (they totalled 101) and was dubbed, 'Player of the Year' by both the Scottish football writers, and the Scottish professional players themselves. He won the European 'Golden Boot' award and promptly did the near-impossible by repeating the following season, becoming the only player to date to win that award in successive seasons, with 34 goals in 34 League matches.

His career was badly compromised in 1993 when he broke a leg playing for Scotland in Portugal but in 1995–96 he was back with 20 goals. Early in the season, he had passed Bob McPhail's club record, dating from the thirties, and ended the season with a new club mark of 236 League goals. Injuries meant that for the second time, he missed a Scottish Cup final.

Omitted from the team for long periods in 1997–98, due to the phenomenal goalscoring performances of Marco Negri, McCoist came back to prove his worth with 16 goals in 26 games for the season. These included a crucial strike in the Scottish Cup semi-final against Celtic, a goal which saw him equal the Old Firm tally of Jimmy McGrory with 27, his surpassed only by the 36 of Robert Hamilton of Rangers. Season 1997–98 saw him net his 250th League goal for Rangers; his 350th competitive goal for the club, and the setting-up of a Scottish club goalscoring record of 54 surpassing the 50 League Cup goals of Jim Forrest.

With his contract expiring at the end of the season, and the arrival of a new manager at Ibrox, it was possible that McCoist would seek pastures new for season 1998–99. If this should be the case, then fittingly, he scored in his last game for Rangers – in the Scottish Cup final of 1998.

Games:	581
Goals:	355
League Championship:	1986–87, 88–89, 89–90, 90–91, 91–92, 92–93, 95–96, 96–97
Scottish Cup:	1991–92
League Cup:	1983–84, 84–85, 86–87, 87–88, 88–89, 90–91, 92–93, 93–94, 96–97
Honours:	58 Scotland caps
Born:	Bellshill, 24 September 1962

IAN DURRANT

1984-98

An outstanding midfield player, Iain is a local boy from Govan who joined Rangers as a schoolboy and has come through the club's coaching and training system. He has played for Scotland at youth, Under-18, Under-21 and full international levels. Durrant was a player of high quality, an exciting, quick player with the confidence to run at defenders. He could play, and did, as a forward, but was seen as a player who would be a regular in midfield for Scotland in the future. He suffered an appalling tackle by Neil Simpson of Aberdeen in October 1988; his right knee was virtually shattered and demanded much surgery. The injury meant that Durrant was out of football for virtually three full seasons, a tragic loss to the player, and his club and country. Yet he did return to play at the highest level, most notably with an outstanding display in the 1992 Scottish Cup semi-final, against Celtic at Hampden. In heavy conditions, with Rangers reduced to 10 men after only six minutes, Durrant played the full 90 minutes, covered every inch of the field and was quite exceptional in one of the finest wins, 1–0, in Rangers' history.

In the following season, the season of the treble and the unbeaten 10 game run in the European Champions League which came so close to bringing the European Cup to Ibrox, Durrant played a major role, 30 of the 44 League games, League Cup and Scottish Cup winning teams, and nine of the 10 European matches. He had three goals in these games; the winning goal in Copenhagen against Lyngbye, the opener against FC Brugge at Ibrox, and the equaliser in Marseille against the eventual European Cup winners.

The following season, he was again a regular, scoring a fine opening goal in the League Cup Final against Hibernian. Ian Durrant had finely drawn skills, good control, an excellent passer of the ball, particularly confident at running at defences in possession, running on the blind side of defences when not in possession. He was a precise finisher. In September 1986 he scored the winning goal against Celtic at Ibrox when he ran through the Celtic defence, played a one-two with David Cooper, then clipped the ball past Pat Bonner.

No doubt that fearful injury had taken the edge off Ian. By 1995–96 he was more of a squad than a regular first-team player. He played only 15 of the 36 League games that year, but did win a Scottish Cup medal. Perhaps he had lost heart, lost the will to do the work and fight for his position, lost the desire. His career seemed to be drifting to a close. When he was brought into the team for the Championship deciding match at Celtic Park in March 1997, it was but his second start that season. Rangers were in something of a crisis by their standards – they had lost the two previous matches, a cup tie against Celtic, and in the League to Dundee United. Durrant played very well and had a major part in Rangers' solitary, and winning goal. As with his friend and colleague Alistair McCoist, the end of season 1997–98 saw Durrant out of contract and perhaps, with the arrival of new manager Dick Advocaat, moving to another club. If so, his final game for the club, in the

Scottish Cup final against Hearts in 1998, showed that he had lost none of his skills when coming on as a substitute after 65 minutes when Rangers were one down. He played a major role in almost saving the game in the closing 25 minutes, certainly having a foot in the one goal scored in that time. Wise after the event or not, many Rangers fans felt that Durrant's creativity should have been used from the start of that final, and that if it had, there would have been a different outcome to the game. He enjoyed a testimonial match on 28 April 1998, against Sheffield Wednesday which finished 2–2.

Games:	347
Goals:	45
League Championship:	1986–87, 92–93, 94–95
Scottish Cup:	1991–92, 92–93, 93–94
League Cup:	1986–87, 87–88, 92–93, 93–94
Honours:	11 Scotland caps
Born:	Glasgow, 29 October 1966

KEVIN McMINN

1984–87

Kevin 'Ted' McMinn would have to be considered an odd, almost comic figure in the Scottish game. A tall, haphazard winger, he would take off on runs without the opposition – or his team-mates for that matter – having the slightest notion of what he had in mind. Nicknamed the 'Tin Man', no doubt because of an apparent lack of physical coordination, Ted could nevertheless score spectacular, sometimes preposterous, goals. He had pace, power and stamina, and his wing play, combined with that of David Cooper, however different, was of major importance in Rangers' League Cup win of 1986–87.

Ted had been bought by Jock Wallace from Queen of the South in October 1984 for £100,000, and he may not have cared much for the Graeme Souness discipline. On the other hand, Souness may not have cared for the McMinn unorthodoxy. He was transferred to Seville for a reunion with his former manager, Wallace, and when he left Seville, McMinn came back to the UK and joined Derby County.

Games:	75
Goals:	5
League Championship:	1986–87
League Cup:	1986–87
Born:	Castle Douglas, 28 September 1962

DAVID MACFARLANE

1984–89

A fringe player who played several positions in defence, and who was in the League Cup winning team of 1986–87, David, 6' 2" tall and a youth international, never found a regular place in the team. He was transferred to Kilmarnock in 1989 for £100,000, an exceptional piece of business by Graeme Souness.

Games:	9
Goals:	0
League Cup:	1986–87
Born:	Irvine, 16 January 1967

STUART BEATTIE

1985–87

A youth international centre-half from Ayrshire, Stuart showed much promise as a young player, but his chance in that position surely went with the arrival of Terry Butcher. He was signed from Ardeer Rec. BC, and went to Doncaster Rovers.

Games:	5
Goals:	0
Born:	Stevenston, 10 July 1967

COLIN MILLER

1985–87

Scots-born Colin, a left-side full-back or wing-half, signed in July 1985 from Toronto Blizzard. He played for Canada in the 1986 World Cup qualifying tournament. He was very fast, but rather slightly built, and was released by Graeme Souness, subsequently playing for Doncaster Rovers, Hamilton Steelers (Canada), Hamilton Academicals and Dunfermline Athletic.

Games:	4
Goals:	0
Honours:	Canada International (2 caps with Rangers)
Born:	Lanark, 4 October 1964

DOUGLAS BELL

1985-87

Signed from Aberdeen for £125,000 in May 1985, Dougie Bell had been a very important member of the Aberdeen European Cup Winners' Cup team of 1983, although he did not play in the final. As a ball-winning midfield player with good skills, he was an important squad player at Ibrox in 1986–87, but he may not have been consistent enough for manager Souness. He went on to play variously at St Mirren, Hibs, Shrewsbury Town and Hull City.

Games:	44
Goals:	1
Aberdeen	
European Super Cup:	1983–84
League Championship:	1983–84, 84–85
Scottish Cup:	1981–82, 83–84
Born:	Paisley, 5 September 1959

COLIN WEST

1986-87

Graeme Souness's first major signing, Colin was bought from Watford on 15 May 1986 for £200,000. Big and strong, awkward and none too mobile albeit powerful in the air, a combination of injury and the emergence of the McCoist-Fleck striking partnership limited Colin's achievement at Ibrox, and he went back south after one year.

Games:	15
Goals:	3
Born:	Wallsend, 13 November 1962

SCOTT NISBET

1985-93

Scott Nisbet was forced to retire from the game at the age of 25, because of injury. He became one of the legion of players who are sacrificed by the intensity of the modern game, the pressure of competitions, and their relentless sequence of fixtures.

He joined from the Edinburgh Salvesen Boys' Club on 31 May 1985, and made his first-team debut later in the year in Malta. A centre-forward in those days, 'Nissy' hit five goals in the matches against Hamrun Spartans, and Valetta. He made his League debut on 7 December in a 1–0 victory over Motherwell and remained in the team for three more matches. At the end of the season he was a substitute for Cammy Fraser in Rangers' Glasgow Cup Final victory over Celtic, 3–2 – Graeme Souness's first trophy win as manager of the club.

Scott was capped by Scotland at schools, youth and Under-21 levels and would surely have consolidated his place as a useful team, or certainly squad, member had it not been for the arrival of Souness and his policy of glamorous, expensive imports. Nevertheless, Nisbet developed into a reliable defensive player, a big fellow who could play either full-back or central defence.

This was clearly proven in the decisive League match on the last day of season 1990–91, when Aberdeen were beaten 2–0 at Ibrox and the championship was won by two points. Nisbet started in central defence and had to move to right-back when Tom Cowan suffered a broken leg, and John Brown also was injured.

His career's golden moment, without any doubt, came in the Champions League match at home to Club Brugges on 17 March 1993. His cross-cum-shot, from a good 25 yards wide on the right, took a deflection then a wicked bounce in the penalty area over the stranded Belgian goalkeeper. The 'Nissy' goal gave Rangers a famous victory. Three days later Nisbet succumbed to a groin strain which was to end his career. It developed into a pelvic injury. The world's best medical advice left him with no hope of continuing. His final appearance was on 20 March 1993.

Games:	118
Goals:	9
League Championship:	1990–91, 91–92
Born:	Edinburgh, 30 January 1968

CHRIS WOODS

1986-91

One of the earliest of a stream of expensive purchases by Graeme Souness in what became known as the 'Souness era', Chris Woods joined Rangers in June 1986 from Norwich City for £600,000, and in his very first season at Ibrox demonstrated that he was a goalkeeper of the highest class. Already an England international and World Cup player, he had understudied Peter Shilton, whom he was expected to succeed as the regular England goalkeeper, at Nottingham Forest. Indeed, he had won an English League Cup medal with Forest, and had also played for Queen's Park Rangers and Norwich City. In the Championship season of 1986–87, his first with Rangers, he made many dramatic and vital saves and set a British record of successive games without conceding a goal, this run brought to an end by the painful home defeat from Hamilton Accies by one solitary goal in the first-round Scottish Cup tie at Ibrox in January 1987. Tall, blond, with blue eyes, and splendidly athletic, Chris looked as an English goalkeeper should look.

In 1988–89 he was stricken by an uncommon and persistent virus which seriously affected his vision and balance, so much so that he missed most of that season. Then in season 1989–90, in the opening game against St Mirren, he damaged his right shoulder, which cost him more appearances. His manager, not unnaturally since he had paid a small fortune for him, was convinced that Chris was the best goalkeeper in British football.

Given freedom from injury, Woods was seen as being a defensive bastion for Rangers for many years. But when Souness left the club in April 1991, Woods followed close behind, being transferred to Sheffield Wednesday that summer. It was a move that puzzled many Rangers fans, the explanation lying apparently in a UEFA ruling limiting "non-national" players to four. Ironically, the successor to Woods was to be Andy Goram, signed from Hibs for £1 million – technically a Scot, but English-born!

Games:	230
Shut-outs:	119
League Championship:	1986–87, 88–89, 89–90, 90–91
League Cup:	1986–87, 88–89, 90–91
Nottingham Forest	
Football League Cup:	1977–78
Norwich City	
Football League Cup:	1984–85
Honours:	43 England caps (20 with Rangers)
Born:	Boston, Lincs, 14 November 1959

TERRY BUTCHER

1986-90

One of the most famous and respected figures in world football, Terry Butcher captained the team and showed inspirational leadership qualities throughout the Souness era, and was probably the most calculated signing Graeme has made. He came from Ipswich Town in August 1986 for £725,000. The Butcher signing, and the price, coming so closely behind that of Chris Woods, was a clear declaration to the Rangers public and to Scottish football that there was fresh thinking in the Rangers boardroom and on the part of management, and that the club was preparing to challenge the best teams in Europe and to meet them on level terms. As deputy captain of England – he had led his country more than once in the absence of Bryan Robson – Butcher was a seasoned international and World Cup player, a giant of 6' 4" who dominated the team and the entire field. Over the four years since he joined the club Butcher was the core of the team, all the other players relating to him in action, all revolving round him. With a pleasant off-field personality at ease with the media, he was a great ambassador for the club.

As a centre-half, or more accurately a left-side central-defender, he formed an almost invincible central unit in defence with Richard Gough. As one would expect, he was unchallengeable in the air in defence, while in his advances into opposition space for corner kicks and free kicks, his height and sheer size made him enormously difficult to contain.

A broken-leg injury in 1987–88 cost him half of the season, and very probably Rangers' Championship chance. The consequences of his loss to England in the European Championships of 1988 can only be guessed at, and he was a cornerstone in their planning for the 1990 World Cup Finals. In his dedication to the team and hunger for victory, Butcher could be compared to the great John Greig. He played every one of the 90 minutes, and beyond, and cared passionately for success – so much so that it has been noted that he was sometimes crotchety in his protests to referees. He captained England in the 1990 World Cup semi-final tie against West Germany.

Butcher's career at Ibrox effectively came to an end following a game at Tannadice against Dundee United on 22 September 1990, when he scored a spectacular own goal by heading a long United clearance over his own goalkeeper, the advancing Chris Woods. When he later missed a tackle which led to a second and winning goal for United, it was clear that there would be little forgiveness from his manager, Graeme Souness.

Terry Butcher moved to Coventry City in November 1990, as player-manager, then managed Sunderland for a spell. He later became a hotelier in Bridge of Allan, combining this with media activity. Many Rangers fans to this day believe that the club has still not found a comparable successor in the heart of the defence.

Games:	**176**
Goals:	**11**
League Championship:	**1986–87, 88–89, 89–90**
League Cup:	**1986–87, 88–89**
Ipswich Town	
UEFA Cup:	**1980–81**
Honours:	**77 England caps (32 with Rangers)**
Born:	**Singapore, 28 December 1958**

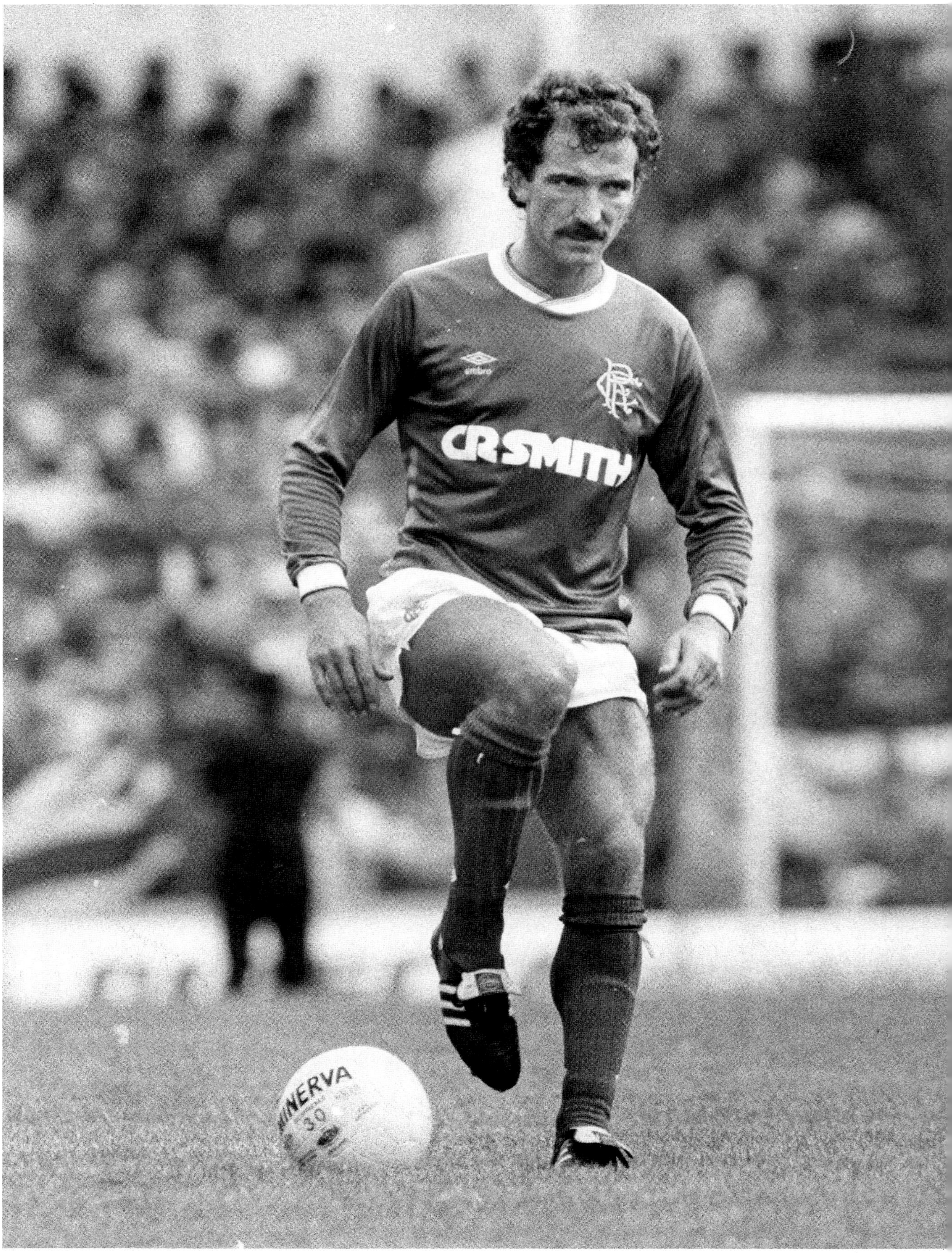
CRSMITH

GRAEME SOUNESS

1986-91

In the past ten years, possibly in the past twenty years, Scotland has produced only two players who beyond any reasonable doubt can be described as truly world-class footballers. They are Kenneth Mathieson Dalglish and Graeme James Souness, contemporaries at Liverpool. Both men have had dazzling careers in the game, and in the eighties both men made dazzling starts to managerial careers with Liverpool and Rangers respectively, by winning Championship and Cup doubles in their very first season.

Graeme Souness was a Tottenham Hotspur apprentice player in April 1969, aged sixteen, and a full professional at seventeen. He was a schoolboy and youth international as a midfield player. Homesickness and strong competition for selection at Spurs thwarted him, and he moved to Middlesbrough in January 1973 for £30,000. His next move was to Liverpool for £352,000, then a record between English clubs, in January 1978, and at Anfield he had a golden career – three European Championship victories, five English Championships, four English League Cups. During this glittering career were three World Cup competitions, and captaincy of his country.

Souness was a brilliant player – a controller of the middle of the field, a player who could set the pace, rhythm and tactics of his team. He was not noted particularly for pace, or heading ability, but seldom needed either. He was the master of the pass, and especially the long pass, and had a fulminating shot from outside the penalty area when backing up his forward players. Highly talented, he was also a hard player, giving best to no one on the field or, it seems, in his later life, off the field. In World Cup matches in Iceland, and at Hampden against Wales, he was fortunate to stay on the field. In his very first match for Rangers, as player-manager, against Hibs at Easter Road, he was not so fortunate – he was ordered off for blatantly kicking George McCluskey, the Hibs forward. And in his treatment of such players as David McPherson, Graham Roberts and Davie Cooper off the field, as manager, he seemed quite ruthless.

As a ball-winner and play-maker combined, perhaps his most important single game was the European Champions' Cup Final of 1984, when Liverpool beat AS Roma on penalties after a draw in extra-time. Souness so stamped himself on that match that Sampdoria promptly bought him, and he spent two successful and educational years in Italian football.

Although remaining registered as a player at the end of the eighties, Graeme's playing career was effectively over in 1990. He was then in his late thirties.

Games:	73
Goals:	5
League Championship:	1986–87
Middlesbrough	
2nd Division Championship:	1973–74
Liverpool	
European Champions' Cup:	1977–78, 80–81, 83–84
League Championship:	1978–79, 79–80, 81–82, 82–83, 83–84
League Cup:	1980–81, 81–82, 82–83, 83–84
Honours:	54 Scotland caps (2 with Rangers)
Born:	Edinburgh, 6 May 1953

GRAHAM ROBERTS

1986-88

Graham Roberts came to Rangers from Tottenham Hotspur in December 1986 for £450,000 with the reputation of being a very hard man, a kicker, a fouler. Paradoxically, he was sent off only once in competitive fixtures during his time with the club, in circumstances which Rangers people, naturally, considered amounted to dreadful refereeing decisions. Roberts was certainly a passionate player, the ultimate competitor who would tackle through anything, simply remove people from his path, to get to the ball. He came to Ibrox as a seasoned player – he had helped Spurs to a UEFA Cup win over Anderlecht in 1984 – and fell easily into a successful partnership with Terry Butcher in the centre of defence.

He was a very important player in the Rangers Championship campaign of 1986–87, and captained the League Cup winning team of the next season. Indeed, he was captain of Rangers throughout Terry Butcher's absence with his broken-leg injury, and was an inspirational player in never knowing when he was beaten. He could also be a ball-winning midfield player, and even a goal-scorer in forcing things home powerfully, perhaps ruthlessly (at 5' 11" and 13 stone) at close range in opposing penalty areas.

His end came dramatically following a 1–0 defeat by Aberdeen, when Roberts felt unfairly accused of having caused the loss of the goal, and of the match. Hard words were exchanged between him and manager Souness, and Roberts played no more for Rangers. He was transferred to Chelsea in time for the 1988–89 season for £475,000.

Games:	69
Goals:	3
League Championship:	1986–87
League Cup:	1987–88
Tottenham Hotspur	
FA Cup:	1980–81, 81–82
UEFA Cup:	1983–84
Honours:	6 England caps (none with Rangers)
Born:	Southampton, 3 July 1959

AVI COHEN

1987-89

An Israeli international and a contemporary of Graeme Souness at Liverpool, Avi was a central-defender or full-back, and a player of style and quality; a solid defender. He came from Maccabi Tel Aviv for £100,000 in the summer of 1987, and his talents gave the Rangers defence a bit of polish, and classy cover. No doubt Souness used him until he could recruit younger players. Cohen's availability was restricted by international calls from Israel for World Cup and Olympic matches, and many Rangers people felt that he could have made a major contribution to the European Champions Cup campaign of 1987–88. The lack of his poise in Bucharest through injury, for example, was a fatal blow. He went back to Israel in 1989, and later played in France.

Games: 12
Goals: 0
League Cup: 1987–88
Honours: 4 Israel caps (while with Rangers)
Born: Cairo, 14 November 1956

NEIL WOODS

1986-88

Neil was a young striker, bought from Doncaster Rovers for £100,000. He was transferred to Ipswich Town in 1988.

Games: 3
Goals: 0
Born: York, 30 July 1966

DAVID KIRKWOOD

1986-89

Davie came from East Fife as a midfield player in 1987 for £30,000. Initially he showed outstanding promise, but .... he was transferred to Hearts and in 1992 played for Airdrie against Rangers in the Scottish Cup Final.

Games: 10
Goals: 0
Born: St Andrews, 27 August 1967

JIMMY PHILLIPS

1986-89

A full-back or central-defender bought from Bolton Wanderers for £75,000, Jimmy was a very useful player indeed who challenged for Stuart Munro's left-back position. He was transferred to Oxford United in 1989 for £150,000.

Games: 33
Goals: 0
Born: Bolton, 8 February 1966

CHARLES RICHARD GOUGH

When Richard Gough left Rangers at the end of season 1996–97 to play out his career with Kansas City Wizards, he went in the certain knowledge that he has a proud place in the history of the club as one of its greatest captains.

Gough was the complete, dedicated professional footballer, a leader by example in a decade of continuous success at the club; his career culminated in leading the team to its now historic 'nine-in-a-row' Championships.

Richard was born in Stockholm of a Swedish mother and Scottish father, but grew up in South Africa where his father, a former player with Charlton Athletic and a lifelong Rangers supporter, was in business. His father arranged a Rangers trial for him and the young man – he was 18 – played against a Queen's Park team at Lesser Hampden. He did not impress, it would seem. Dundee United gave him a trial, and he did impress them, going on to become an international player and in 1982–83 a League Championship winner, at Tannadice.

With the coming of Graeme Souness to Ibrox, Rangers tried to sign him in 1986, offering £500,000, but Jim McLean, then Dundee United manager, refused to release him to any Scottish club, and Gough went to Tottenham Hotspur. At White Hart Lane, he was a success, captaining them to an FA Cup Final, so much so that Souness at last signed him, in December 1987, for £1.1 million. Since then only injury kept him out of the team. At right-back in the early days, then in forming a formidable central defence with Terry Butcher, Gough was an outstanding Rangers player.

A sound tackler with sharp timing and excellent, careful distribution, Gough is fast in recovery, confident in going forward. Despite a slender physique, he has honed his fitness to an impressive level, adhering to the Souness dictum that a footballer's most precious asset is his body. Gough was quite brilliant in the air, in defence or offense, particularly dangerous in ranging forward for corner kicks or free kicks. One of his most critical goals was for Scotland. In the very last minute of a World Cup qualifying match in Cyprus in 1989, from a corner kick, he headed the goal which gave Scotland a desperately narrow qualifying victory. Alas after more than 50 appearances for Scotland, his international career came to an end after a difference of opinion between him and the Scotland manager, Andy Roxburgh, following a 5–0 defeat in Portugal.

Had they reconciled their differences, Gough might have reached a career total of 90 caps. Unable to play, because of injury, in the title-clinching match at Tannadice on 7 May 1997 Gough was on hand to receive the trophy on behalf of the club, in the middle of the field. He, Alistair McCoist and Ian Ferguson were the only three who had played through nine-in-a-row and indeed Gough has the individual honour of being the only one of the three to actually win all nine Championship medals. He was clearly very, very moved – this was thought to be his last act as a Rangers player after a decade of unrelenting success. Signing for Kansas City Whiz, Gough's intention was to spend perhaps two years there before retiring, but an emergency call from Walter Smith, stricken by serious injuries to central defenders Lorenzo Amoruso and Alan McLaren, both long-term absentees, brought Gough back to Ibrox in October 1997. He took the captaincy from Brian Laudrup and led the team through the rest of the season with his accustomed skill and tenacity. In the summer of 1998, he returned to the United States, this time to play for San Jose Earthquakes. It is believed that he had been asked to remain to assist Dick Advocaat, lending him knowledge and experience of the Scottish scene, but Gough preferred to continue as a player for the time being.

Games:	397
Goals:	32
League Championship:	1988–89, 89–90, 90–91, 91–92, 92–93, 93–94, 94–95, 95–96, 96–97
Scottish Cup:	1991–92, 92–93, 95–96
League Cup:	1987–88, 88–89, 90–91, 92–93, 93–94, 96–97
Dundee United	
League Championship:	1982–83
Honours:	61 Scotland caps (28 with Rangers)
Born:	Stockholm, 5 April 1962

RAY WILKINS

1987–89

A thoroughbred even as a teenager with Chelsea, Ray came to Ibrox with 84 England caps behind him and a career at the highest level of the game embracing Manchester United, AC Milan and Paris St Germain. Rangers paid the French club £250,000 for him, and it proved to be an excellent investment. As a footballer Wilkins was intelligent, dedicated, technically highly skilled and above all cool in temperament, perhaps his single outstanding characteristic. He played the role of anchorman in midfield, making himself a focal point which gathered balls from defence and moved them on to the advance players. Wilkins was a superb passer of the ball, particularly with the long pass from deep positions. He was occasionallky criticised for not being more direct; indeed, Ron Atkinson, manager of Manchester United, dubbed him 'The Crab' because of his liking for the square pass.

If not a ball-winner as such, Ray was a good, firm tackler and an immensely creative player who would above all always seek to find the simple pass, the free receiver. He may well have vied with Graeme Souness as the finest midfield player Rangers have had since Baxter. Many people thought that highly of him, and when for family reasons he left Rangers in December 1989 to return to London with Queen's Park Rangers, he was given a farewell unsurpassed in Ibrox history, the entire ground, as they say, 'rose' to give Ray Wilkins a standing ovation. A return to Ibrox as a player with Hibernian in 1996, saw Wilkins once more enjoy a tremendous welcome from the Rangers faithful.

146

Games:	96
Goals:	3
League Championship:	1988–89, 89–90
League Cup:	1988–89
Manchester United	
FA Cup:	1982–83
Honours:	84 England caps (none with Rangers)
Born:	Hillingdon, 14 September 1956

JOHN McGREGOR

1987–92

Signed in the summer of 1987, John had been given a free transfer by Liverpool. He was first seen with Queen's Park in the early eighties, when many clubs, Rangers and Celtic included, showed interest in him. He decided on Liverpool, where he served a long apprenticeship. A serious leg injury while on loan to St Mirren, which recurred later while he was at Ibrox following a hard tackle by Stuart McKimmie at Aberdeen, cut short John's playing career. He was forced to retire, and joined the Rangers coaching staff.

Games:	34
Goals:	0
League Cup:	1987–88
Born:	Airdrie, 5 January 1963

IAN McCALL

1987–90

A left-side midfield player, Ian joined from Dunfermline Athletic in September 1987 for £200,000, having previously been with Motherwell and Queen's Park. He was occasionally used in attack, but was never a regular first-team man. He fell foul of the management by failing to appear for a training session in December 1989. In January 1990 he was transferred to Bradford City for £200,000 – Rangers got their money back on this one.

Games:	24
Goals:	2
Born:	Dumfries, 30 September 1964

GARY McSWEGAN

1986-93

A Glasgow boy, Gary was a product of Rangers Boys' Club and signed in 1986. His first-team debut was in a Glasgow Cup tie on 28 April 1987. The match, against Clyde at Firhill, was won on penalty shots after a 1–1 draw and one John Spencer, with whom McSwegan was to form a scoring, striking partnership in Rangers reserve teams, made his debut in the same match. Both of these young players won Glasgow Cup medals nine days later in a final 1–0 win over Celtic. McSwegan was a strong-running forward with the speed and determination to go at, and past, defenders. He scored goals galore in the reserves. In fact his reserve-team statistics are remarkable – 243 goals in 298 games.

He was the victim of a dreadful tackle by Celtic goalkeeper Ian Andrews in a reserve match at Ibrox in August 1989. Andrews was ordered off, McSwegan was carried off with a badly broken leg and did not play for almost a year. He recovered to make sporadic appearances in the first team, being unfairly treated, in the opinion of many, when the leading strikers Alistair McCoist, Maurice Johnston and Mark Hateley were absent, and the management preferred to use, out of position, such midfield players as Ian Durrant and Trevor Steven.

Gary was on hand to score at least two memorable and critical goals; on 25 November 1992 at Ibrox, he headed the first goal in the 2–2 draw with Marseille in the European Champions' League and on the first of May 1993 he sealed a League Championship success with an opportunistic strike in a 1–0 win at Airdrie.

His contract expired that summer, and he decided to move on, joining Notts County. He later returned to Scotland to play successfully with Dundee United with whom he returned to Ibrox to haunt Rangers with a winning goal in a League Cup quarter-final tie in 1997–98.

Games:	24
Goals:	5
Born:	Glasgow, 24 September 1970

MARK WALTERS

1989-91

The first black player to play for Rangers in fifty years, Mark Walters came from Aston Villa for £500,000 in January 1988 and brought a mercurial talent with him. His ball skills were such that he could turn defenders inside out, and he was something of a master of the 'Ali Shuffle', fluttering his right foot over the ball. He boasted a tremendous shot, and the skill to chip or float the ball around or over goalkeepers. He was also menacing with free kicks from the fringes of the penalty area. Mark was, however, inconsistent, sometimes indolent, and tended to vanish if the going got rough, especially in away matches. He was a controversial figure, to a large extent because of his colour, but also because it was not unknown for him to retaliate. He was ordered off twice in his early Rangers years, both times against Hearts at Tynecastle. Graeme Souness tended to use him wide and somewhat withdrawn on either wing, although he had plenty of pace to go through the centre.

Walters was one of several players who left Rangers in the wake of the departure of Graeme Souness and the arrival of Walter Smith. He first joined Souness at Liverpool, then moved on to Southampton.

Games:	143
Goals:	52
League Championship:	1988–89, 89–90, 90–91
League Cup:	1988–89, 90–91
Honours:	1 England Cap
Born:	Birmingham, 2 June 1964

MARK FALCO

1987-88

Mark was a striker, a big fellow bought from Watford for £270,000 in the summer of 1987 and a player who certainly did not let Rangers down. He was strong and forceful, very good in the air, more mobile and more polished than, say, Colin West. An illustration of his coolness and quickness came from the first goal against Dynamo Kiev at Ibrox in 1987 in the European Champions' Cup. A dreadful goalkeeping mistake made it possible, but Falco accepted the gift smartly and made quite sure of the conversion. He moved to Queen's Park Rangers after only a few months at Ibrox – one suspects reluctantly. It was a strange transfer, particularly since Robert Fleck moved to Norwich a month later, leaving Rangers with only one recognised striker eligible for European competition (the quarter-finals in fact). This may well have cost Rangers the tie, against Steau Bucharest, since Alistair McCoist had a cartilage operation only a matter of days beforehand.

Games:	19
Goals:	10
Tottenham Hotspur	
UEFA Cup:	1983–84
Born:	London, 22 October 1960

JAN BARTRAM

1987-88

Jan Bartram, a fast and skilful Danish international player, had an Ibrox career lasting six months. He came from AGF Aarhus in January 1988 for £180,000 and was transferred to Brondby in June for £315,000. Bartram certainly paid for his Danish pastries at Ibrox.

His career was highlighted by a spectacular goal against Celtic at Ibrox – in which both the match and the Championship were lost for Celtic – and by an even more spectacular difference with manager Graeme Souness. In an interview with a Danish magazine while on international duty, he was comprehensively critical of Rangers training methods and Souness's tactical thinking, and more.

This was not the sort of thing to delight the Rangers manager and Bartram was quickly on the move. He kept busy, playing for Bronby, Bayer 05 Uerdingen (Germany), AGF Aarhus (again) and Ascoli in the Italian league.

Games:	14
Goals:	3
Honours:	32 Denmark caps (2 with Rangers)
Born:	Denmark

JOHN BROWN

1987-96

A capable, all-round utility player, John came from Dundee in January 1988 for £350,000. His senior career had started at Douglas Park, Hamilton, home to the Academicals, whom he head joined from Balntrye Welfare. During five seasons as an Accies player, Brown played in more than 100 League games and received some national acclaim on the opening day of the 1980–81 season when he scored a hat-trick from left-back against Berwick Rangers.

A strong tackler and reasonable user of the ball, he was a forceful, never-say-die redhead. He played full-back, central defence or even on the left of midfield, and had a rocketing shot which could bring goals from better than twenty-five yards when backing up his forwards. He was a goal-scorer against Rangers in his time, with the only and winning goal in a Scottish Cup tie at Ibrox in 1984, and a hat-trick in a League match in November 1985. These must have hurt – John is a lifelong 'Blue-nose'.

That was evident in his loyalty, and consistency over nine years. Often it has seemed that he was to be no more than a squad player. Various big-money signings were introduced to the club making Brown, apparently, dispensable – Basile Boli in 1994–95, Gordon Petric in 1995–96, even Davie McPherson, returning in 1992–93. But for a variety of reasons – loss of form, injuries to key players – Brown was always on hand.

In season 1992–93, the season of Champions League and Treble successes, Brown was a critical player, in 39 of 44 League games, in every Scottish and League Cup tie and in all 10 European games. Indeed he missed only five games all season. And his courage in playing when not fully fit was most marked in the League decider against Aberdeen at Ibrox in 1991. Rangers were decimated by injuries. Brown played, injected with painkillers, and collapsed after an hour.

In 1995–96, following the signing of Gordan Petric, many felt that Brown's time was over, what with Rangers' central trio of Petric, Richard Gough and Alan McLaren established. But yet again, when Gough was injured in a Scottish Cup tie at Keith in January, Brown came in and was irreplaceable, shoring up the defence when it was sorely needed. And in the second half of that season, when Rangers were pressed 'to the wire' by Celtic in the championship, Brown's performances were quite outstanding. Injured for much of 1996–97, he turned to coaching young players at Ibrox. His last performance in a Rangers shirt came in Ian Durrant's testimonial in April 1998.

Games:	278
Goals:	18
League Championship:	1988–89, 89–90, 90–91, 91–92, 92–93, 93–94
Scottish Cup:	1991–92, 92–93, 95–96
League Cup:	1988–89, 90–91, 92–93
Born:	Stirling, 26 January 1962

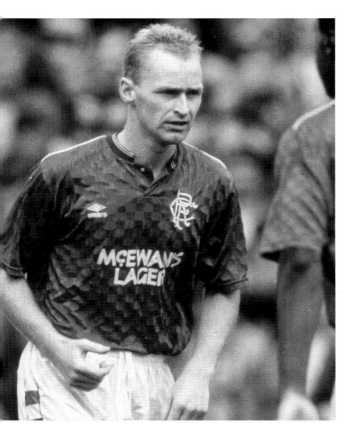

MICHAEL GARY STEVENS

1988-94

For six years, Gary Stevens was an outstanding defender for Rangers, a mature international player who came to Ibrox in the summer of 1988 already heavy with honours. His 285 games for Everton had brought him two English League Championships, an FA Cup victory over Watford and a European Cup Winners' Cup success against Rapid Vienna in 1985. There was also a confirmed place in the England national team which was to run to 46 appearances, 20 of them while with Rangers. Indeed his Ibrox career was compromised by an injury sustained on an England summer tour in 1992, on the eve of that year's European Championship finals, and 1992–93 was all but written off to recovery. Nevertheless, in his first four seasons with the club he had missed only three League games and played in 187 of a possible 240.

Gary Stevens, from Barrow-in-Furness, was an apprentice with Everton aged 16 and became a professional in July 1981. He was a critical member of the Everton team which had outstanding success in the mid-eighties. Stevens was a thorough success among Graeme Souness' signings, for £1.25 million in July 1988. For his money, Souness got an exceptional athlete, intelligent, tenacious, highly mobile, a full-back with speed on the overlap; a perceptive crosser of the ball and a long-throw expert, all of which gave a highly valuable attacking element to the team. He was a championship winner five times with Rangers. In his first season, 1988–89, he won both Championship and League Cup, and only his faulty pass back, completely out of character, let Celtic's Joe Miller in to score the only goal in the Scottish Cup Final, thus denying Rangers a treble success.

His versatility was clearly demonstrated in the Championship-deciding match of 1991, against Aberdeen at Ibrox when first he moved from right to left-back when Tom Cowan broke his leg, then to central defender when John Brown was carried off. That injury which kept Gary out for several months rather took the edge off his pace. He moved to Tranmere Rovers in 1994, for £350,000.

Games:	246
Goals:	9
League Championship:	1988–89, 89–90, 90–91, 91–92, 93–94
Scottish Cup	1992:
League Cup:	1988–89, 90–91, 93–94
Everton	
League Championship:	1984–85, 86–87
FA Cup:	1983–84
European Cup Winners' Cup:	1984–85
Honours:	46 England caps (20 with Rangers)
Born:	Barrow-in-Furness, 27 March 1963

TREVOR FRANCIS

1987-88

Trevor Francis joined Rangers late in his career from Atalanta in Italy, for £75,000. He had played in Italy with Graeme Souness, at Sampdoria of Genoa. Francis was an exceptional player, a vastly experienced England international footballer who played in a variety of forward positions. In his best years he had been a striker of killing pace and finish – witness the fact that he was the first £1 million footballer in Britain. From his native Plymouth he went to Birmingham City as a teenager, and Brian Clough paid that huge amount of money to take him to Nottingham Forest. At Ibrox he was used by Graeme Souness sparingly, always wide on the right, and judiciously, seldom being asked to play the full ninety minutes. His stunning first touch, his general ball control and close dribbling, and his accuracy with the ball delighted Rangers fans. His experience was invaluable to the club, but he left after his one-season contract to join Queen's Park Rangers where he became player-manager before moving on to Sheffield Wednesday; from there he became manager of Birmingham City.

Games:	25
Goals:	0
League Cup:	1987–88
Nottingham Forest	
European Champions Cup:	1978–79
European Super Cup:	1979–80
Honours:	52 England caps (none with Rangers)
Born:	Plymouth, 19 April 1954

IAN FERGUSON

1987–

Ian Ferguson, a powerful, hard-running midfield or forward player, was first noted at Clyde and was snapped up by St Mirren for £60,000 in 1986–87. He was noted even more when he scored a spectacular and, as it happened, winning goal for St Mirren against the more strongly fancied Dundee United in the 1987 Scottish Cup Final. This may have given Ferguson delusions of grandeur. In the following season, when it became known that Rangers wanted him, Ferguson reached a point when he could no longer play for St Mirren because, he said, of all the media pressure and speculation concerning his future. He also made it clear to St Mirren that he wanted to play for Rangers, despite the four-year contract he had with the Paisley club. He was bought by Rangers in February 1988 for £700,000. Many critics saw him as potentially one of the great players of the Scottish game. He was very successful in 1988–89, scoring in the League Cup final against Aberdeen, but his form slumped in 1989–90 as a result of injury and illness.

Games:	305
Goals:	45
League Championship:	1988–89, 89–90, 92–93, 93–94, 94–95, 95–96, 96–97
Scottish Cup:	1992–93, 95–96
League Cup:	1988–89, 90–91, 92–93, 93–94
St Mirren	
Scottish Cup:	1986–87
Honours:	9 Scotland caps
Born:	Glasgow, 15 March 1967

KEVIN DRINKELL

1988–89

Much missed by Rangers fans after he had left, Kevin Drinkell spent only fifteen months at Ibrox, from the summer of 1988 to October 1989. He was signed from Norwich City for £500,000, having previously been with his hometown team, Grimsby. He was sold to Coventry City for £800,000, this representing good business for Rangers if nothing else, and indeed his transfer may simply have been a question of profit and liquidity. A big striker, strong in the air, mobile and very active, he was a goalscorer who struck up a worthwhile finishing partnership with Alistair McCoist. In one sense he may have been a sacrifice, with the coming of Maurice Johnston. After a move to Coventry City, Kevin later returned to Scotland to become a player-manager, then an imaginative manager, with Stirling Albion, leaving the Forthbank club after their relegation at the end of the 1997–98 season.

Games:	54
Goals:	49
League Championship:	1988–89
League Cup:	1988–89
Born:	Grimsby, 18 June 1960

TOM COWAN

1988–91

A left-back, Tom was a young man of exceptional promise. His rise was somewhat meteoric – he had played only one season with Clyde when Rangers snapped him up for £100,000. He was clearly seen as a star and an investment for the future, but that never quite materialised. His career was compromised when he suffered a broken leg in the Championship decider, the last match of season 1990–91 against Aberdeen at Ibrox. He moved on, first to Sheffield United, then to Huddersfield Town.

Games:	15
Goals:	0
Born:	Bellshill, 28 August 1969

NEALE COOPER

1989–91

As a young player, Neale Cooper, with Scottish international selections at youth and Under-21 levels, was reckoned to be an outstanding prospect. Indeed, he was described by Franz Beckenbauer as the greatest prospect he had seen anywhere in the world at that age. His best position was clearly in central defence, but in his spell at Aberdeen in the early-eighties, manager Alex Ferguson, with Willie Miller and Alec McLeish established in the central positions, sought to make Cooper a ball-winning midfield player. He was a ball-winner with a vengeance, with a reputation as one of the fiercest tacklers in football. He had much success at Pittodrie – four Scottish Cup, two League Championship, one League Cup and one European Cup Winners' Cup medals. Rangers signed him in October 1988 from Aston Villa for £250,000, no doubt as cover for all defensive positions. Injury compromised much of his contribution through much of 1989. He left the club in the summer of 1991, and was recently manager of Ross County.

Games:	20
Goals:	1
League Cup:	1988–89
Aberdeen	
Scottish Cup:	1981–82, 82–83, 83–84, 85–86
League Championship:	1983–84, 84–85
League Cup:	1985–86
European Cup Winners' Cup:	1982–83
European Super Cup:	1983–84
Born:	Darjeeling, India, 24 November 1963

MEL STERLAND

1988–89

Mel arrived in March 1989 from Sheffield Wednesday, where he had been captain and where he had received a testimonial. A right full-back or midfield player, he cost Rangers £800,000. He was a burly figure who was never played in his best position, that of full-back. He went to Leeds United in the summer of 1989, but not before leaving the Ibrox crowd with good memories in the shape of two goals in what was virtually the Championship-winning game, against Hearts at Ibrox in April.

Games:	13
Goals:	3
Honours:	1 England cap (not with Rangers)
Born:	Sheffield, 1 October 1961
Leeds	
League Championship:	1992–93

ANDY GRAY

1988-89

Andrew Mullen Gray signed for Rangers in September 1988 for £25,000, surely bringing to an end a transfer trail that had involved him with half a dozen clubs and purchases worth a collective £2 million. He turned professional with Dundee United in May 1973, from schoolboy football. In September 1975 Aston Villa paid £110,000 for him, then in 1979 collected a then British record of a still-staggering £1.46 million from Wolverhampton Wanderers. Andy next moved to Everton, then Aston Villa again, and Rangers in fact signed him from West Bromwich Albion. With Everton he won English League, FA Cup and European Cup Winners' Cup honours. He played for Scotland at schoolboy, youth and Under-23 levels, and won twenty full caps. He was a big centre-forward, tall and very fast for his size and brave as could be, this quality taking him into the tightest of situations and bringing the inevitable series of injuries. He was particularly good and courageous in the air, and played the game with the enthusiasm of a McCoist. He was used by Rangers mainly as a substitute, but as a Rangers fan himself, rejoiced in his time at Ibrox. Andy became a lively, extrovert broadcaster on the game with SKY Television.

Games:	16
Goals:	5
Wolverhampton Wanderers	
League Cup:	1979–80
Everton	
League Championship:	1984–85
FA Cup:	1983–84
European Cup Winners' Cup:	1984–85
Honours:	20 Scotland caps (none with Rangers)
Born:	Glasgow, 30 November 1955

SANDY ROBERTSON

1987-94

The son of Malcolm, former Ayr United Morton and Dundee United winger, Sandy Robertson signed for Rangers on an 'S' Schoolboy form in June 1987 aged 16. He made his competitive debut in a 2–1 win over Dundee at Dens Park on 6 May 1989. He was a clever playmaker, of immense promise which was never fulfilled. In one respect, Sandy's experience at Ibrox may have been a consequence of the club's policy of recruiting expensive international stars. Others, such as Robert Fleck, Derek Ferguson, John Spencer and Gary McSwegan, may feel that their careers were compromised in the same way. Sandy Robertson was a player who deserved better than 36 games over six seasons. He was transferred to Coventry City in the summer of 1994 for £400,000, and was subsequently with Dundee United. His career at Tannadice was marred by a prison sentence, after which he attempted to rebuild his career with Airdrieonians.

Games:	30
Goals:	1
Born:	Edinburgh, 26 April 1971

TREVOR STEVEN

1989-91, 1992-97

The subject of a transfer tribunal ruling (Everton valued him at £4.5 million), Trevor came to Rangers in the summer of 1989 from the Liverpool club for £1.7 million. Formerly with Burnley, he had won English Championships, Cup and European Cup Winners' Cup prizes with Everton and become an established England international player as a right-winger or right midfield player. His partnership with Gary Stevens for Everton and England was resumed successfully for Rangers. Trevor took over the midfield role of Ray Wilkins and formed a telling combination with Nigel Spackman, Steven's calculated distribution marrying with Spackman's strength and exuberance.

He was one of many in an exodus of players from Ibrox in 1991, transferring to Marseille in August for a reported fee of around £5 million. He was back within a year – Marseille, it seemed, could not maintain the payments on such a transfer fee!

His second spell at Ibrox was dogged by injury problems and a player of his quality, when fully fit, would surely never have been out of the team. But he was certainly a regular in his first season back, 1992–93, a big season for the club in the Champions' League, and in winning the domestic treble. Alas, Steven missed the Scottish Cup Final win over Aberdeen – he seemed jinxed in this tournament. After all the honours with Everton, FA Cup, European Cup Winners' Cup and League Championship, he won everything in Scotland save the Scottish Cup. When Rangers won in 1992, he was with Marseille. He missed the 1993 and 1996 finals because of injury.

In season 1995–96, he started the season in the opening game against Kilmarnock, in August, but his next competitive appearance was as a substitute in the Scottish Cup semi-final match against Celtic in April 1996 – a full eight months later. Injuries again.

It was believed that manager Walter Smith saw Trevor Steven as the answer to his problems at right-back, even allowing for his signing of Stephen Wright. Steven could also play in an advanced right-back position, pushing forward, when Rangers played their three central defenders system. He was certainly highly thought of by the club management, but in the summer of 1997 he was forced to accept that his playing days were over.

Games:	184
Goals:	25
League Championship:	1989–90, 90–91, 92–93, 93–94
League Cup:	1990–91, 92–93, 93–94
Burnley	
3rd Division championship:	1982–82
Everton	
FA Cup:	1983–84
European Cup Winners' Cup:	1984–85
League Championship:	1984–85, 86–87
Olympique Marseille	
League Championship	1991–92
Honours:	36 England Caps (5 with Rangers)
Born:	Berwick, 21 October 1963

KEVIN MACDONALD

1988–89

Kevin came on a month's loan from Liverpool in the 1988–89 season. He was tall, slim, workmanlike, a midfield player who had previously been with Elgin City and Leicester City.

Games:	3
Goals:	0
Liverpool	
FA Cup:	1985–86
Born:	Dufftown, 7 September 1959

MAURICE JOHNSTON

1989–91

Maurice Johnston, centre-forward, joined Rangers on 10 July 1989 for £1.5 million from Nantes in France. An established Scottish international player, 'Mo' had previously played for Partick Thistle, Watford and Celtic. His signing may be considered the most sensational in Scottish football history, since he was widely, if mistakenly, assumed to be the first Roman Catholic player to play for Rangers. He was, in all probability, the first Catholic to be a first-team player since the Second World War. A possible exception to that would be Don Kitchenbrand, the big South African of the fifties, who confessed, long after his career at Ibrox was over, to being a Catholic.

As a player Johnston was a proven goal-scorer at all his clubs, his pace and sharp reflexes taking him into the striking places. Surprisingly good and imaginative in the air for his height (5' 9"), he was a tireless worker, a chaser of lost causes, unselfish in his distribution and totally fearless. Johnston took the knocks, and since he played in ankle socks, spurning any shin protection, there were more of these than need be. His physical movement was so intense, so concentrated that it sometimes appeared feverish, even desperate, and there was little relaxation in his game.

In his first 30 months at Ibrox, he scored a total of 51 goals in 110 games, an average not unreasonable in the intensity of the Premier Division and the exceptional circumstances of his stay there. But by the end of 1991 – he went to Everton on 18 November 1991 for a £1.5 million fee – he seemed to have lost some of his snap. He moved from Goodison, played for Falkirk for a small spell, and by the summer of 1997, was in the NASL, playing for the Kansas City team.

Under all the circumstances, signing for Rangers showed great courage and strength of character on the part of Maurice Johnston. Many doubted that anyone could cope with the pressures, in a city like Glasgow, or that the Rangers fans would allow him to cope, but from the beginning he was accepted by almost all the Rangers players and almost all the fans.

Games:	100
Goals:	46
League Championship:	1989–90, 90–91
Celtic	
League Championship:	1985–86
Scottish Cup:	1984–85
Honours:	38 Scotland caps (10 with Rangers)
Born:	Glasgow, 13 April 1963

DAVID DODDS
1989-91

Bought, no, doubt as cover for Alistair McCoist and Maurice Johnston, David Dodds brought with him a wealth of ex-perience when he joined Rangers from Aberdeen in September 1989 for £100,000. Capped as a schoolboy and later at youth and Under-21 levels, he began his professional career with Dundee United in 1975 where he won full Scotland caps. In the summer of 1986 he moved to Neuchatel Xamax in Switzerland for £180,000, a move which was unsuccessful and saw him back with Aberdeen that September for a fee of £215,000. While with Dundee United he made a habit of scoring against Rangers – nine goals in League games alone. A tall, rather awkward mover, nevertheless he is very mobile for his size, very clever in the air, and very adept at holding a forward line together and in laying off the ball. As his playing days came to a close in the mid-nineties, Davie became a coach at Ibrox, a post he relinquished in the summer of 1997.

Games:	21
Goals:	5
Dundee United	
League Championship:	1982–83
League Cup:	1980–81
Honours:	2 Scotland caps (none with Rangers)
Born:	Dundee, 23 September 1958

CHRIS VINNICOMBE
1988-94

At the same time as Sandy Robertson, and perhaps for the same reason, Chris Vinnicombe left Rangers for Burnley in the summer of 1994. He had signed from his home town team Exeter City, for sums variously reported as from £100,000 to £300,000, with the spread relating to a clause in the contract relating to the number of games he would play for Rangers. In the event, over four seasons, it was very few.

Chris was a talented left-back, or left wide midfield player, of slim build and of vision and accuracy in possession, so much so that at one time he was captain of both Rangers reserves and the England Under-21 team.

The UEFA policy of restricting the number of non-nationals, of whom technically Vinnicombe was one, discriminated against his long-term stay at Ibrox, in spite of him being happy with life in Scotland. Many felt that he was not given a fair chance to establish himself.

Games:	28
Goals:	0
Born:	Exeter, 20 October 1970

NIGEL SPACKMAN
1989-92

A bright articulate footballer with an outgoing personality, Nigel Spackman crossed paths with Ray Wilkins towards the end of 1989. As Wilkins left Ibrox for Queen's Park Rangers, Spackman left Queen's Park Rangers for the Glasgow club in a £500,000 transfer. Within days, he had a taste of Glasgow football. On 2 January 1990 at Celtic Park, his goal gave Rangers their first New Year win at Parkhead in 20 years. Spackman savoured the moment, newcomer or not.

Nigel was a dedicated footballer, positive, energetic, a ball-winner and a careful ball-user. Above all versatility was probably his principal asset, inspiring other players probably his principal pleasure. He added three Championships with Rangers to another won with Liverpool.

Probably his worst time during his stay in Scotland came when the SFA selected him to play for Scotland in 1991. Spackman has a Scottish grandmother and under UEFA and FIFA rules he was qualified to play for Scotland. But within 24 hours, the SFA had 'de-selected' him. It seemed that the four British associations had an agreement that only a parent would qualify a player in these circumstances. Rangers accepted this meekly and did nothing to pressurise the SFA into declaring Spackman a Scot for UEFA matches.

Nigel Spackman was transferred to Chelsea on 8 September 1992 for £485,000. His final appearance was on 2 September when he played very well in a 4–1 win at Motherwell. He and his family had seemed content in Scotland. His departure has never been explained. Following a spell at Chelsea, he moved to Sheffield United and when Howard Kendall left Bramall Lane, Spackman replaced him as manager. In March 1998, however, he resigned in controversial circumstances.

Games:	124
Goals:	3
League Championship:	1989–90, 90–91, 91–92
Scottish Cup:	1991–92
League Cup:	1990–91
Liverpool	
League Championship:	1987–88
Born:	Romney, 2 December 1960

BEN GINZBURG
1989-91

'Bonni' Ginzburg, came from Maccabi Tel Aviv for £200,000, as understudy to Chris Woods. He went straight into the fray in a League Cup match against Arbroath, then had a League baptism with matches against Hibs and Celtic, lost 2–0 and drawn 1–1 respectively. The goals lost against Hibs were considered 'soft' but Ginzburg was a capable substitute for Woods, when required. He was released in 1991 to make way for Alexei Mikhailichenko.

Games:	8
Shutouts:	4
Honours:	68 Israeli caps (2 with Rangers)
Born:	Tel Aviv, 12 December 1964

JOHN SPENCER

1986-93

John Spencer's career at Ibrox was greatly compromised by the presence of such contemporaries as Alistair McCoist, Maurice Johnston and Mark Hateley – formidable competition indeed for a striker.

John had signed in 1984 as a schoolboy and when he was called up from the Rangers Boys' Club, he had to serve a long apprenticeship in the reserves, where he formed a prolific scoring partnership with Gary McSwegan. In one Reserve League West match at Celtic Park they each had a hat-trick in a 7–4 win. In his last full season at Ibrox, he scored 30 goals in 29 competitive reserve matches. Spencer was capped at Under-21 level. He was short, strong, determined, tenacious, fast and fearless. His first-team debut came on 28 April 1987, a 1–1 draw with Clyde in a Glasgow Cup semi-final which Rangers won on penalties, and Spencer was in the team which nine days later beat Celtic in the final 1–0. But more than three years passed before he appeared in a major competitive fixture, a European Cup tie in which Rangers beat Valetta 6–0. Spencer scored. His League debut came, at last, versus St Mirren at Ibrox on 9 February 1991, a 1–0 win, and his first League goal was on 13 April in a win over St Johnstone, Graeme Souness's last game as manager of Rangers.

It had been a long, drawn-out overture to a career. In season 1988–89, he played four games for Morton on loan, and most of 1989–90 he spent with Lai Sun in Hong Kong, netting 20 goals. John's scoring ability was too good to be left languishing in reserve football and in 1992 he moved to Chelsea in a £500,000 transfer. He played successfully for the London club until the appointment of Ruud Gullit as player-manager. Shortly afterwards, John Spencer moved on to Queen's Park Rangers.

Games:	32
Goals:	11
Honours:	14 Scotland caps (none with Rangers)
Born:	Glasgow, 11 September 1970

COLIN SCOTT

1987-96

Colin 'Scooter' Scott, goalkeeper, joined Rangers from Dalry Thistle in 1987. Chris Woods was the man in possession. And in turn, when Woods left, the opposition remained international in the shape of Andy Goram and more recently Theo Snelders. It was never likely that Scooter would find fame and fortune within Rangers' League team.

He served a long apprenticeship in the Youth, Reserve League West and Premier Reserve Division teams, eventually appearing in the 'big' team in a League match at Kirkcaldy, replacing the injured Alistair Maxwell for the second half in a 1–1 draw with Raith Rovers on 2 October 1993. He started the game four days later, when Rangers went down 2–1 to Motherwell. Scooter played the last four League matches of the season – three lost, one drawn.

Happily the League Championship had been comfortably won. The draw was a 1–1 clash with Celtic before an all-blue audience of 47,018.

Colin did play on 26 December 1994 in a 2–0 win over Hibs, and over that entire holiday period, but on 7 January, Goram was in place against Partick Thistle at Firhill. He had to be replaced (and missed a good four months because of injury). When Scott, the substitute, was at fault for Thistle's late equalising goal, that was the end of his season.

Following an outstanding display at Kilmarnock in November 1995, his second consecutive winning shut-out, he was dropped for the next match, at home to Aberdeen, in favour of the veteran Billy Thomson. His final appearance was on 23 March 1996, a home 3–2 win over Falkirk and at the season's end, and the end of his contract, Colin 'Scooter' Scott left Rangers. He then played for a number of clubs, including Raith Rovers, without establishing himself.

Games:	13
Shut-outs:	4
Born:	Glasgow, 19 May 1970

JOHNNY MORROW
1988-96

An exciting attacking forward, essentially a winger, Johnny Morrow's game featured noticeable pace and no little skill. A Belfast boy, he signed as a teenager from Linfield in 1988, and his first-team debut came in the unlikely setting of the Borders, at Netherdale on 6 March 1989 in Rangers' 3–2 win over Gala Fairydean. The match inaugurated Gala's floodlights and was seen by over 5,000 spectators.

In the past decade at Ibrox, many players have had their careers interrupted by troublesome injuries. The names of Ian Durrant, Oleg Kuznetsov, Trevor Steven, Stephen Wright and more recently Gordon Durie, Stuart McCall and Sebastian Rozental come to mind. Johnny Morrow was hit as hard as any of them with a series of problems.

An attack of Morrow, McCoist and Spencer, when Mark Hateley, Maurice Johnston, Peter Huistra and Ian Ferguson among others were out, took Rangers to a thrilling 3–2 win over St Johnstone at Perth on 12 October 1991 and the Irishman played in the two following games. But the recovery of established players and the coming of Dale Gordon meant that the Belfast boy was pushed into the background. When his contract ended in June 1996, he moved to Oldham Athletic.

Games:	6
Goals:	0
Born:	Belfast, 20 November 1971

156 DAVID HAGEN
1989-94

David Hagen, an Edinburgh boy, was one of a group that included Steven Pressley, Neil Murray and Lee Robertson as precocious teenagers – virtually schoolboys – when they joined the club. He first signed as a thirteen-year-old and progressed through the club to make his debut in a competitive first-team match, as a substitute in the home 2–0 win over Hearts in September 1992. David played ten first-team games that season, scoring fine goals against Hibernian and Partick Thistle.

An old-style winger, or wide player, David was a strong, powerful runner, a space-maker rather than a goalscorer, one who could open the way for team-mates but in 1993–94 his career rather stalled. He was transferred to Hearts for £150,000. His final game for Rangers was the friendly at Huntly on 1 November 1994.

Games:	20
Goals:	3
Born:	Edinburgh, 5 May 1973

NEIL MURRAY
1989-97

One of three young players who took part in a memorable Champions' League match against Olympique Marseille at Ibrox in November 1992, Neil Murray, like Gary McSwegan and Steven Pressley, all products of the youth system, was seen as a highly promising player who would serve the senior team for many years.

When Neil moved on to Sion, the Swiss club, in January 1997, all three had left Rangers, victims perhaps of the tremendous pressure on places at Ibrox. In time, McSwegan and Pressley were to become clubmates at Dundee United.

Neil, principally a right-back, was used as often as not in midfield, where his energy, good balance, strength and courage belied a certain lack of pace. He joined the club in August 1989, and made his first-team debut at Kilmarnock, in Stuart McLean's testimonial match on 8 January 1990, Rangers winning 1–0 with a Johnny Morrow goal. His first competitive game, before 4500 at distant Stair Park, Stranraer, was in a 5–0 League Cup win for Rangers on 19 August 1992. His second competitive game, against Olympique Marseille, was something different, seen, apart from anything else, by ten times the number of spectators.

He was to win 10 caps at Under-21 level, the first against Portugal in 1993. In the mid-nineties he was a regular squad member although never quite commanding a regular first-team place. One of the highlights of his time at Ibrox was surely the opening goal against Aberdeen in the 1993 Scottish Cup Final, won 2–1. Another was the fact that he qualified in accountancy during his seven years with the club.

Games:	81
Goals:	2
League Championship:	1994–95
Scottish Cup:	1992–93
Born:	Bellshill, 21 February 1973

OLEG KUZNETSOV

1990-94

Signed from Dynamo Kiev for £1.4 million in October 1990 by Graeme Souness, after protracted negotiations, Oleg Kuznetsov came to Rangers with impressive credentials. And Ibrox had already had a sight of his talents. He had played against Rangers in the European Cup first round in September 1987 with team-mate Alexei Mikhailichenko, later to join him at Ibrox, and in a pre-season friendly which Dynamo won 3–1, with Oleg scoring their opening goal. It was to prove his only Ibrox goal.

Kuznetsov was a player of high quality, a world class player rock-solid in defence, quick, alert, confident in his accurate use of the ball. He was particularly good in the air and a player of marked versatility, evident in playing international football at full-back and midfield, as well as in his natural place in central defence.

Moulded to a large extent by the Kiev and Soviet coach, Valeri Lobanovski, he won three Championships with Dynamo, in 1984, 1985 and 1990, and three national cups, in 1984, 1986 and 1989. He was a European Cup Winners' Cup winner against Atletico Madrid (3–0) in Lyon, in 1985–86, and had collected 54 full caps for the USSR. Kuznetsov played in four of the five matches in the European Championship Finals of 1988, missing the final won by Holland, 2–0. He was prominent in the Soviet World Cup campaigns in Mexico 1986 and in Italy 1990. Perhaps the highlight of his international career was in winning the 1988 Olympic title in Seoul in a Soviet team captained by Mikhailichenko, with a 2–1 win over Brazil, after extra-time, in the final.

Thus when he first appeared, in a 5–0 win over St Mirren on 13 October 1990, his style and class and vision marked him, at the height of his maturity, as surely a core player for Rangers for the following four or five years. But just seven days later, Oleg Kuznetsov's world with Rangers disintegrated.

Only six minutes into a match against St Johnstone at Perth – Rangers' first appearance at the new McDiarmid Park – Kuznetsov was injured in a tackle with Harry Curran, one that had manager Graeme Souness referring, unfairly, to 'hammer throwers'. For the Ukrainian, the season was over – it had lasted ninety-six minutes. Even after he had recovered, in season 1991–92, he was used sparingly by the now-manager Walter Smith. In four seasons he managed only 35 competitive games and will be remembered as a tragic figure. His highly lucrative contract kept him at Ibrox, despite various enquiries, until July 1994, when he moved to Maccabi Haifa.

Games:	35
Goals:	1
Dinamo Kiev	
Soviet Supreme Championship:	1985, 1987, 1990
Soviet Cup:	1984, 1986, 1989
Honours:	58 USSR caps
	5 C.I.S caps
	1 Ukrane Cap
	Olympic Gold, Seoul, 1988
Born:	Kiev, 2 March 1963

LEE ROBERTSON

1990-96

From Salvesen Boys' club, Lee was a somewhat lightweight, fleet-of-foot midfield player or forward who made just three appearances for the club. However, many friends of Rangers will remember his penalty goal at Firhill in season 1991–92 which brought a 1–0 win over Celtic in the Glasgow Cup final. Lee made his first-team debut before 36,000 in a 1–1 draw with Hearts on 28 April 1992. He created an excellent impression but had to wait a year for his next senior game at Pittodrie. One substitute appearance in the next three seasons saw him move to Viking Stavanger of Norway in 1996.

Games:	3
Goals:	0
Born:	Edinburgh, 25 August 1973

TERRY HURLOCK

1990-91

In an Ibrox career that spanned all of one season, Terry Hurlock, a London boy, is remembered as a highly controversial character. He came from Millwall early in season 1990–91 and was quickly seen as the midfield ball-winner supreme. His tackling was ferocious by any standard and often took him close to the edge with referees. He managed a total of 35 games in the season and one of his two goals was of special importance – an equaliser against Celtic in the 1–1 Ibrox game in September. Hurlock was ordered off in the infamous Scottish Cup tie at Parkhead in March, when Rangers lost 2–0. They did get their money back on the player when Hurlock was transferred in the summer to Southampton, for £300,000.

Games:	35
Goals:	2
League Championship:	1990–91
League Cup:	1990–91
Born:	Hackney, 22 September 1958

PIETER HUISTRA

1990-95

Pieter Huistra was signed by Graeme Souness in the summer of 1990. He was transferred to San Frecce Hiroshima in Japan by Walter Smith early in 1995 at a time when many judged him to be showing his very best form.

A certain carelessness was seen by some in his crossing and inconsistency was another criticism laid at his door, as well as a certain lack of resolution, particularly in the matches against Celtic. The other side of this Dutch coin was that he was a player of fluent movement, delicate ball skills, poise and balance. A natural winger who could play in midfield and link effectively with Brian Laudrup. He came from Twente Enschede for £300,000 and went reluctantly to the Japanese club for £350,000. Many Rangers fans were saddened to see him go, but no doubt this and other transfers were influenced by the rules concerning the number of foreign players a club could employ.

Games:	158
Goals:	26
League Championship:	1990–91, 91–92, 92–93
Scottish Cup:	1993
League Cup:	1990–91, 93–94
Honours:	5 Holland Caps (3 with Rangers)
Born:	Goenga, Holland, 18 January 1967

STEVEN PRESSLEY

1990-94

Few Rangers players can boast of the career sequence that young Pressley enjoyed. Born in Elgin in the north of Scotland, hardly distinctive in itself as a recruitment area for footballers, he was 'spoken for' by Rangers at the age of 12. In the event, he signed from Inverkeithing Boys' Club on 2 August 1990, captained the Rangers youth team to success in the Glasgow Cup against Celtic in January 1992 and made his first-team debut that season, still in his teens, at Motherwell.

Pressley, a central defender of pace, mobility and courage, was seen by many as a natural and potential successor to Richard Gough. However, the signing of Basile Boli persuaded him to move to Coventry City, despite having been offered a new contract. After a season at Highfield Road, he returned to Scotland, with Dundee United, where he formed an outstanding partnership in the centre of defence with the vastly experienced Maurice Malpas.

Games:	44
Goals:	1
League Championship:	1993–94
Scottish Cup:	1992-93
Born:	Elgin, 11 October 1973

BRIAN REID

1991-95

Brian Reid from Greenock Morton was Graeme Souness' last signing as Rangers manager, a £300,000 transfer in March 1991 being the Reid climax to an outstanding season at Greenock for the big defender. He went straight into the Rangers team on 30 March in a crucial League fixture against Dunfermline, won 1–0 by a Gary Stevens goal. Ordered off, rather unluckily, in a home match, his third, against St Johnstone, he took no further part in that season, but better things were expected of him in 1991–92. Alas, in Campbell Money's testimonial match at Love Street, he suffered a cruciate ligament injury.

After a long absence, Brian was never the same player again – big, strong, powerful in the air and on the ground, he had seemed the ideal type of Rangers central defender. But he could never get beyond the reserve team and made a rather ill-considered transfer request early in season 1994–95. He was given what proved to be a last chance during a pre-season tour of Denmark in the summer of 1995, but a disastrous performance on 6 August at Ibrox, against Anorthosis Famagusta, saw him substituted. It was his last first-team match for the club. He eventually returned to Morton.

Games:	6
Goals:	0
Born:	Paisley, 15 June 1970

DAVID ROBERTSON

1991-97

Signed from Aberdeen for £970,000 when his contract there had expired, David Robertson came to Ibrox in July 1991 and over half a dozen years has clearly been one of Rangers' most valuable players. A left-back of burning pace, he is that rarity, a natural fully equipped left-back. As an attacking over-lapping full-back, he has a remarkable scoring rate for a defender and has linked up uniquely with Brian Laudrup. He was clearly the outstanding player in the position in Scotland. His meagre tally of three international caps would seem to belie this, but he has brought this on himself by declaring to the national team manager, Craig Brown, that he does not wish to be selected for Scotland if he is doomed to sit on the bench as a substitute, and is not guaranteed selection. Brown, not unreasonably, has taken the view that he cannot guarantee any player selection, and will not be dictated to in this respect. The loss would seem to be Scotland's, and Robertson is unlikely to add to his tally of international caps.

A staunch tackler, David is as fast in recovery as he is in attack. Out of contract at the end of season 1996–97, he signed for Leeds United in a £500,000 transfer. It seemed that in discussions with chairman David Murray and manager Walter Smith, David's estimate of his worth was rather more than they had in mind. However, his worth to Rangers was never more obvious than after his going. Walter Smith's failure to find an attacking left-back of similar standard cost Rangers dearly in season 1997–98.

Games:	250
Goals:	19
League Championship:	1991–92, 92–93, 93–94, 94–95, 95–96, 96–97
Scottish Cup:	1991–92, 92–93, 95–96
League Cup:	1992–93, 93–94, 96–97
Aberdeen	
Scottish Cup:	1989–90
League Cup:	1989–90
Honours:	3 Scotland caps
Born:	17 October 1968

MARK HATELEY

1990-95, 1996-97

On 7 November 1961 at Liverpool, Mark Wayne Hateley was born into the game. His father, Tony, had a long career with Aston Villa and other clubs and the young Hateley was to start his safari at Coventry City as a teenager in the summer of 1978. He moved to Portsmouth in the summer of 1983 and after a year there, he was signed by AC Milan for £915,000, a sizeable fee then. He had four years in Italy before a £1 million fee took him to Monaco, where he was to win a French championship. Thus Hateley was one of the now-commonplace 'multi-national' footballers.

He was brought to Ibrox in the summer of 1990, the price again around £1 million, a signing doubtless to displace Alistair McCoist with whom the Rangers player-manager had a rather gritty relationship. His arrival was not sensational. Rangers supporters, McCoist fans almost to a man, treated him severely and not entirely without reason. His ball control, particularly his first touch, seemed clumsy and he seemed less than fully fit as though the good life in the South of France had taken the edge off things. But Hateley buckled down and although his technique was never the most arresting aspect of his play, nevertheless it improved. It was his finishing power and strength in unsettling defences which became potent factors in his five years and five championships at Ibrox. Ironically, he was to form a lethal scoring partnership with McCoist. He scored 136 goals in 241 games in Rangers colours.

Many of his goals were memorable. Two against Aberdeen in the last and championship-winning match of the season against Aberdeen at Ibrox in May 1991 were critical – Aberdeen required only a draw to win that championship! There was a tremendous volley from distance against Leeds United at Elland Road in the European Champions' League of 1992, and the absolutely vintage Hateley goal at Pittodrie in February 1993. From Gary Stevens' perceptive cross from the right, Hateley beyond the far post soared above the big Aberdeen defenders to head the ball home with flashing power for the solitary goal of the match. He left the club rather suddenly in the autumn of 1995, apparently for domestic reasons, and joined Queen's Park Rangers where Ray Wilkins was manager.

But Hateley was to return to Ibrox just as suddenly as he had left, a return which, in the eventful month of March 1997, was dramatic in the extreme. Having lost a Scottish Cup quarter-final match at Parkhead, followed by a defeat by Dundee United, Rangers found themselves faced with the last of the four Old Firm League matches in which a win for Celtic would have thrown the Championship wide open by coming within two points of the defending champions, in crisis. They did not have one fit striker available, with Alistair McCoist perhaps no longer able to sustain a full 90 minutes play.

Desperate times demand desperate actions. Three days before the game, Walter Smith brought Mark Hateley back to Glasgow. Hateley had by no means been an ever-present with Queen's Park Rangers, but declared himself fit and insisted that his 'heart had remained with Rangers'. He played, unsettling the Celtic defence and playing a vital role in the one goal of the match. Rangers won one of the most remarkable victories in the history of the fixture. They had an eight-point lead over Celtic. The more emotional, of Rangers fans immediately declared the championship won. Having played a distinguished part in 'Nine-in-a-row', he moved south to become player-manager of Hull City.

Games:	222
Goals:	115
League Championship:	1990–91, 91–92, 92–93, 93–94, 94–95
Scottish Cup:	1991–92, 92–93
League Cup:	1990–91, 92–93, 93–94
Honours:	32 England Caps (1 with Rangers)
Born:	Wallasey, 7 November 1961

ANDREW LEWIS GORAM

1991-98

Born in Bury, in Lancashire on 13 April 1964, Andy Goram was an early starter. He was signed by nearby Oldham Athletic as a teenager, and spent several seasons with the club, gaining with Oldham the first of his many Scotland caps.

He moved to Hibernian in season 1987–88 and after four seasons there, he was signed by Rangers in June 1991, for £1 million, as the successor to Chris Woods. He was one of Walter Smith's first signings, the manager saying that the principal reason for it was that Goram had Scottish qualifications through a grandparent, whereas Chris Woods, under the regulations of the day, was a 'non-national', whose numbers had to be restricted.

Over the past half dozen seasons, Goram's work in the Rangers goal has been critical to the sustained success of the club. He has been a magnificent goalkeeper and despite the strong challenge of Jim Leighton of Hibernian, has maintained his place in the Scotland team when fit. A bad injury in December of 1994 kept him out for the rest of the season. Knee trouble was to plague him.

Goram has been quite outstanding in his anticipation and in his speed of movement, particularly at close range, on the ground in crowded areas. His greatest single talent probably emerges when he is left stranded on his own, facing an oncoming forward who has broken through the defensive lines. Then, decisiveness and courage are needed. In speed of thought and of action in such circumstances, in getting out fast, in confronting the forward, in closing off his angles and reducing his options, in dominating him and finally blocking the shot, Andy Goram has been the goalkeeper supreme.

He has not been much of a catching goalkeeper, seldom leaving his line for high crosses and when he does, he clearly prefers to punch. Some Rangers fans have been uneasy at his coping with high balls from the opposing right wing, and he was rigorously scrutinised in his first season and compared, not often kindly, with Chris Woods. But the fact is that he played in every Rangers competitive match that season – League, Scottish Cup, League Cup, European matches – a remarkable total of 55 in all.

Memorable performances were against Leeds United at Elland Road in Rangers' long European Champions' League run in 1992–93, and in the team's long unbeaten run, into double figures, against Celtic in 1995–96, 1996–97. It was a run which ended on 6 March 1997 in a Scottish Cup quarter-final match at Parkhead when Goram, with severe rib injuries, was obliged to play having had four painkilling injections. His unease and lack of mobility were major factors in Rangers' defeat. Goram was effectively out for the rest of the season, and manager Smith had to enlist Andy Dibble from Manchester City to see out the season in the Rangers goal. Indeed in April, Goram had specialist opinions on the condition of his knees and was likely to have surgery in the close season.

Off the field, Goram had been an adventurous lad, indulging in the odd scrape. He was once dropped by manager Smith for lack of fitness and in general not tending to Rangers business, and standards, as he should. Although Goram's performances throughout 1997–98 remained of a high standard, occasional lapses in concentration caused Rangers dearly. His contract expired at the end of that season and many felt that he should have been offered a new contract but the coming of Dick Advocaat, a renowned disciplinarian, resulted in a contract offer being withdrawn. In spite of all, he was one of only two Rangers players – Gordon Durie the other – to be included in the Scotland squad for the 1998 World Cup. However he walked out of the Scotland World Cup headquarters in New Jersey where the squad was training. In a letter which he handed to team coach Craig Brown, Goram explained that as the subject of tabloid newspaper allegations and fabrications concerning his rather turbulent private life, he felt persecuted. He felt also that the Scotland squad might be compromised by all of this when the players should be focused on preparing for France 98. He announced his retirement form international football. Goram left the training camp and returned to Scotland, saying, 'I am now clubless, and need to organise my future'. Andy Goram is a double international, having played cricket for Scotland.

Games:	260
Shut-outs:	107
League Championship:	1991–92, 92–93, 94–95, 95–96, 96–97
Scottish Cup:	1991–92, 92–93, 95–96
League Cup:	1992–93, 96–97
Honours:	43 Scotland caps (28 with Rangers)
Born:	Bury, 13 April 1964

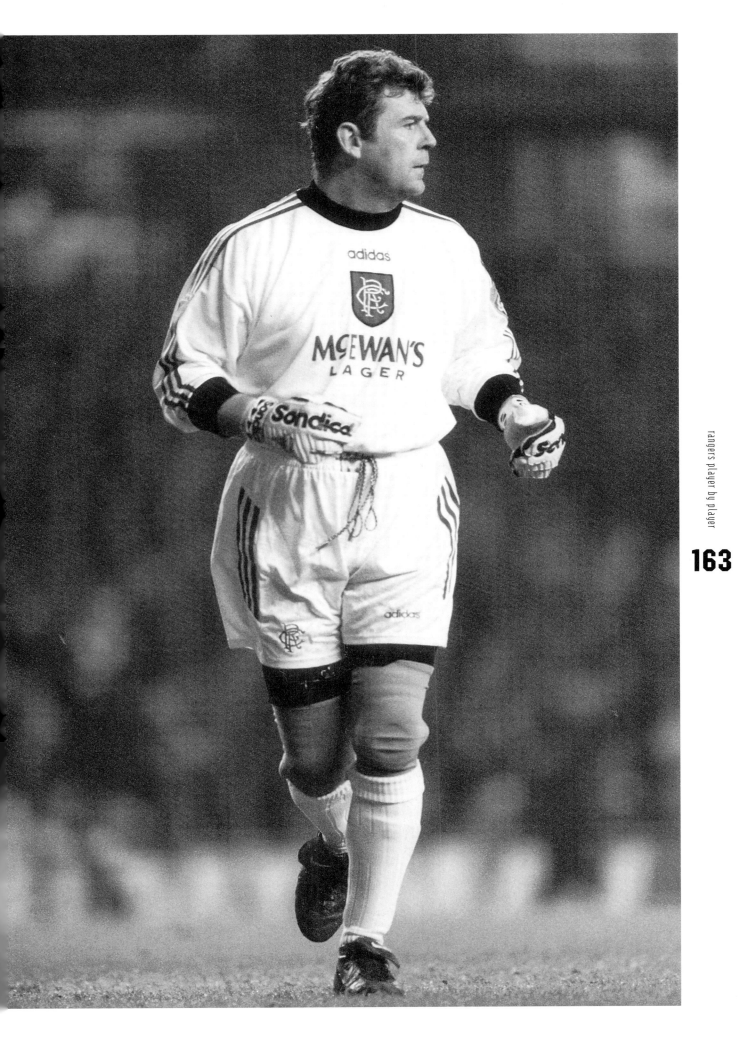

DALE GORDON

1991-93

Dale Gordon was bought for £1.2 million. It was not money well spent by the Rangers club. The fault was not entirely Dale's – he was caught up to a large extent by the UEFA ruling on 'non-nationals'.

Born in Great Yarmouth, he signed for Norwich City as an apprentice and played 206 League games, scoring 31 goals for the Canaries. Dale had played for England at schools, youth and Under-21 levels, and made an impressive start with Rangers, scoring two goals in a 5–0 win over Dunfermline on 9 November 1991. For the next six months he was a regular in the team. An industrious, wide player, he was skilful on the ball but his problem seemed to be inconsistency – his form away from home was much better than it was at Ibrox.

In his first season, he won both league and cup honours, and in 1992–93, a League Cup medal. He moved on to join West Ham United.

Games:	55
Goals:	8
Honours:	League Championship 1991–92
	Scottish Cup 1991–92
	League Cup 1992–93
Born:	Great Yarmouth, 9 January 1967

PAUL RIDEOUT

1991-93

Paul Rideout's stay was a short and, who can say, happy one. He was signed from Notts County in January 1992, probably as cover for Mark Hateley. He had been capped by England at schools, youth and Under-21 levels, and he first became something of a national figure by hitting three goals past Andy Bruce, a young Rangers goalkeeper, in the televised schoolboy international match at Wembley – Scotland won 5–4.

His senior career started at Swindon Town, moved along to Aston Villa, then three seasons with Bari in Italy where he scored 23 goals in 99 matches. Then came Southampton, a return to Swindon on loan, Notts County, then to Ibrox. Paul was a travelling man. His first match for Rangers was on 11 January 1992 in a 2–0 win over Hibernian. His first goal came in a 5–0 win over Airdrie on 29 February. He was an adaptable player and many Rangers fans thought he was best used in defence. His final game was as a substitute at Hampden in a League Cup tie, a 5–0 win over Dumbarton. Shortly afterwards he moved to Everton on a £650,000 transfer.

Games:	12
Goals:	1
Born:	Bournemouth, 14 August 1964

STUART McCALL

1991–

Signed by Rangers in August 1991, Stuart quickly made himself indispensable as a first-team player. He cost the Ibrox club £1.2 million and will surely be considered as one of manager Walter Smith's most successful buys. 'Midfield dynamo' might best describe Stuart's approach to the game. He has been a tenacious tackler, quick, positive and at the same time creative at the heart of the team, and was sorely missed throughout the second half of season 1996–97, twice needing surgery.

In three seasons with Everton, McCall's greatest memory will surely be the 1989 FA Cup Final when he scored two goals only for Liverpool to win 3–2.

Earlier, Stuart had been with Bradford City, and had been on the field when fire struck the old Valley Parade stadium. Born in nearby Leeds, he had revelled in the Rangers matches against Leeds United in the Champions' League of 1992–93. He scored the opening goal in Rangers' League Cup Final win over Aberdeen the same season.

Chosen for England at Under-21 level, McCall was a substitute at one match. When told to warm up, he realised that he preferred to play for Scotland – his father was a Scot – and went to the most distant part of the field and out of earshot, to warm up, and never did answer the call. With the departure of Walter Smith, the summer of 1998 clearly marked the end of an era and Stuart headed back to his native Yorkshire and his first club Bradford City.

Games:	264
Goals:	20
League Championship:	1991–92, 92–93, 93–94, 94–95, 95–96
League Cup:	1992–93, 93–94
Scottish Cup:	1991–92, 92–93, 95–96
Honours:	40 Scotland caps (29 with Rangers)
Bradford City	
Third Division Championship:	1984–85
Born:	Leeds, 10 June 1964

ALEXEI MIKHAILICHENKO

1991-96

When Alexei Mikhailichenko, affectionately known as 'Miko', appeared at Brockville of all places, Rangers were presenting to the Scottish public a player of the highest international category and one surely at the peak of an illustrious career. He had played 36 times for the USSR. He had captained the USSR to the final of the European Championship in 1988, a competition in which they had beaten England and Italy, losing only to Holland in Munich's Olympic Stadium to goals from Ruud Gullit and Marco van Basten. Later that year, Miko captained USSR to an Olympic Final win over Brazil in Seoul and was the Soviet Player of the Year.

But Rangers fans who had made the long trek to Kiev for the start of the European Champions' Cup campaign of 1987–88 had had an earlier introduction to Miko – on 15 September 1987, before a crowd of 100,000 in the Republic Stadium, he had hammered in a penalty shot which gave Dynamo Kiev a 1–0 win over Rangers. In the return at Ibrox, he figured in a bizarre goal when he was struck by the ball from behind, thrown by Victor Chanov, the freak incident which brought Marc Falco's opening goal, leading to the 2–0 win.

Dynamo Kiev won the Soviet Championships of 1985, 1986, and 1990 in his time and the Cup in 1985, 1987 and 1989. In 1990 he moved to Sampdoria for a £2.5 million fee. In his season there, Sampdoria won their first-ever Serie A championship. And at Ibrox, he was to win three Championships, one Scottish Cup and one League Cup – Championships in three different countries makes a fair boast. When he left Rangers, he left heavy with honours.

But Rangers fans will look back at his time at the club with a sense of what might have been. Miko was big, powerful, a commanding figure on the left side of the team. A long, searching stride could out-flank defences. Sharp technical skills could see him thread through close-knit defences. He was an accurate, perceptive finisher. In his first season, he rescued Rangers in a Scottish Cup fourth-round tie at Ibrox when they were trailing to a goal from Motherwell's Phil O'Donnell. His two goals turned the match, the second of them from an inspired dribbling run through the Motherwell defence. Rangers went on to win the Cup. And on New Year's Day 1994 at Celtic Park, he had two of the goals in Rangers' fulminating 4–2 win.

Like so many Rangers players in recent seasons, Miko had his share of injuries. Yet he never quite imposed himself on the game in Scotland in the way that Brian Laudrup, for instance, has done. He never sustained any form, sometimes seemed less than interested, was erratic and plainly lacked commitment. The fact that he refused all media interviews in English, despite being quite well equipped in the language, suggested that he never really sought to embrace the culture of his third country.

His first game had been at Falkirk on 7 September 1991. His last, ironically, was also against Falkirk, at Ibrox on 23 March 1996. Alexei returned to his native Kiev after a spell with Charlton Athletic.

Games:	134
Goals:	24
League Championship:	1991–92, 92–93, 93–94
Scottish Cup:	1991–92
Scottish League Cup:	1992–93
Soviet Player of the Year:	1988
Soviet Championship:	1985, 86, 90
Soviet Cup:	1985, 87, 90
Olympic Gold:	Seoul 1988
Sampdoria Championship:	1990–91
Honours:	USSR 36 (4 with Rangers)
	CIS 5 (all with Rangers)
	Ukraine 2 (both with Rangers)
Born:	Kiev, 30 March 1963

STEPHEN WATSON

1992–94

A young left-sided player, Stephen joined Rangers from Maudsley on 24 August 1990. He was essentially a full-back but also appeared in central defence and in midfield; his game was notable for a ferocious shot. He first played on 22 July 1992, a friendly 3–1 win over Queen's Park. His competitive debut came on 14 April 1993, in a 3–2 League win over Hearts. He played twice more that season, but the next campaign was blank and Stephen moved to St Mirren on 28 July 1994. His final first-team match had been on 24 July 1993 at Berwick.

Games:	3
Goals:	0
Born:	Liverpool, 4 April 1973

ALISTAIR MAXWELL

1992–95

'Ally' Maxwell was signed in the summer of 1992 for £300,000 from Motherwell, following a year-long contractual dispute there with the manager Tommy McLean. His career at Ibrox was not without drama.

The goalkeeper had been bought as cover for Andy Goram. Friends of Rangers welcomed him as one whose display in May 1991 had defied Rangers and brought them a crushing 3–0 defeat which almost cost them the championship. Maxwell's courage was not in question – despite internal injuries, he had played the entire match plus extra time for Motherwell in their 4–3 Cup Final win over Dundee United in 1991.

His competitive debut came in a comfortable 5–0 League Cup win over Dumbarton, but his league debut four days later was fraught – a 4–3 defeat at Dens Park. It was Rangers' only defeat from then, 15 August, until beaten by Celtic in the following March. Maxwell's first season was spent in the shadow of Goram and was no preparation for the visit of Celtic to Ibrox on 30 October 1993. Goalkeepers are traditionally remembered for their mistakes and Maxwell was almost unanimously damned for both Celtic goals in the 2–1 defeat. Worse was to come at the end of that season, in the Scottish Cup Final, lost 1–0 to Dundee United. But the fumble and the loss of the goal to United's Craig Brewster was more due to an errant back pass from David McPherson than by a routine goalkeeping error.

For all that, Alistair's 82 games over three seasons were rewarded with a League Championship medal and a League Cup winners' medal in 1993–94.

Games:	69
Shut-outs:	23
League Championship:	1993–94
League Cup:	1993–94
Motherwell	
Scottish Cup:	1990–91
Born:	Hamilton, 16 February 1965

CHARLIE MILLER

1992–

An immensely talented youth player, Miller won caps for Scotland at Under-21 level. He signed from Rangers Boys' Club in July 1992, and on 19 September 1993 made a surprise debut at Aberdeen in a match which Rangers lost 2–0. He was a near-regular in season 1994–95, playing in 21 of 36 League matches. Subsequently, such is the competition at Ibrox, he has found it difficult to sustain a place in the first-team, but Miller, midfielder of stocky build and fine ball skills, may yet prove to be a good long-term bet for the club.

Games:	96
Goals:	20
League Championship:	1994–95, 95–96
League Cup:	1996–97
Born:	Glasgow, 18 March 1976

DUNCAN FERGUSON

1993-94

Duncan Ferguson was transferred from Dundee United to Rangers in July 1993 for a transfer fee of £3.75 million, a record exchange between Scottish clubs. It made Ferguson the most expensive player in Scottish football history and, it was said, financed a complete new grandstand at United's Tannadice Park. There was to be an additional payment of £250,000 when the player completed 200 games for Rangers. The transfer involved controversial and protracted negotiations between the clubs, during which Rangers were fined £5000 for allegedly 'poaching' the player. And Ferguson became one of the most controversial players ever to play for the club. His off-the-field history included two criminal prosecutions for assault, with another pending at the time of his transfer to Rangers.

Duncan Ferguson was a very talented young player. That was beyond any dispute. A Stirling boy, he had signed for United as a teenager in February 1990 and was quickly seen as an exceptional striking forward. At 6' 3", his power in the air was intimidating. His first touch, for one so big, was deft. He had pace, and mobility. But in the event, his brief career at Ibrox against all expectation proved tawdry. To some extent it was beset by injury, but the fact was that in 23 appearances, he scored just five goals, hardly a return on the investment.

The roof fell in on Ferguson on 16 April 1994 at Ibrox, when he was alleged to have head-butted the Raith Rovers player John McStay. The referee merely spoke to Ferguson, but the SFA considered that the television evidence was sufficient to allow them to ban the player for 12 matches. And Glasgow's Procurator Fiscal brought a charge of assault against the player. A huge public outcry arose as to whether or not the SFA could sit in judgement on any player while a court case was pending. An independent appeals committee ruled that it could not.

A Sheriff Court sentenced Ferguson to three months imprisonment for head-butting the Rovers player McStay, who had not pressed charges against him. Ferguson failed in an appeal against the ruling (he had been on probation when he assaulted John McStay) and he served his time in Glasgow's Barlinnie Prison.

A Scottish Cup runners-up medal was all he had to show for his Ibrox career. It had lasted from 20 July 1993 to 11 September 1994. Then he went to Everton on loan, with the Liverpool club paying Rangers a hefty monthly 'rental'. A few months later, there was a full transfer to the Liverpool club. Rangers let it be known that they had recouped their investment in Duncan Ferguson.

Games:	23
Goals:	5
Honours:	7 Scotland Caps (none with Rangers)
Born:	Stirling, 27 December 1971

FRASER WISHART

1993–95

Fraser Wishart, released by Falkirk, signed for Rangers in July 1993. Initially on a two months' contract this was quickly extended to two years by manager Walter Smith in a compliment to a competent, responsible professional.

Fraser was born in Johnstone on 1 March 1965 and his road to Ibrox took in Pollok Juniors, Motherwell, St Mirren and Falkirk. In fact as a teenager he had played a trial in a Premier Reserve League game on 28 December 1983, which Rangers won 3–1 over Hibernian. Wishart was at home in either full-back position, with right-back perhaps his natural place. In his time at Ibrox that position was filled variously by Stuart McCall, Gary Stevens and Craig Moore, and Fraser certainly deserved more than his total of 18 appearances. He was transferred to Hearts for £50,000 in March 1995.

His work as chairman of the Scottish Professional Footballers' Association was testimony to the pride he had in the game and the seriousness with which he served that organisation.

Games:	14
Goals:	0
Born:	Johnstone, 1 March 1965

GREG SHIELDS

1993–1997

Greg, a Falkirk boy, is a product of the Ibrox youth system and joined the club on 1 July 1993 from Rangers Boys' Club. His first-team debut came on the last League game of the 1995–96 season, a 3–0 win at Kilmarnock. He played with distinction when called in season 1996–97, in European matches. A full-back or central-defender, he is an outstanding prospect. In the summer of 1997, Greg was transferred for £100,000 to Dunfermline Athletic, where he quickly established himself in the first-team.

Games:	11
Goals:	0
Born:	Falkirk, 21 August 1996

GORDON SCOTT DURIE

1993-

Formerly with East Fife, Hibernian and Chelsea, Gordon Durie from Paisley arrived at Ibrox in November 1993 from Tottenham Hotspur, Rangers having invested £1 million in him. For their money they got a fast, hard-running, powerful footballer who, in spite of several technical shortcomings, could score goals and carry much of the weight of the team, when needed, with great determination and courage. He was to take these talents to the national team many times over.

Durie was rather plagued by injury throughout his career, including his time at Ibrox, but over his four seasons contributed greatly to the successes of the team, and was a not inconsiderable goalscorer. One of his greatest distinctions is that he became the first Rangers player to score a hat-trick in a Scottish Cup Final, and only the third man in the history of the Cup to do it. As of the summer of 1996, Durie had more than 30 appearances with the national team.

In 1996–97, in the midst of Rangers' various injury problems when variously Gascoigne, McCall, Wright, Steven, Goram, McCoist and Durie were unavailable, manager Walter Smith was asked which player Rangers were missing most; he said immediately 'Gordon Durie'. It was a splendid compliment, if it surprised many people. He arrived in mid-season 1993–94 at a time when Rangers seemed to be wilting under the strain of many injuries – Durie scored several goals early in his time at Ibrox and contributed a great deal to the club's eventual success that season.

The loss of Gordon Durie following a serious head injury at Kilmarnock on 24 February 1998 cannot be underestimated in a barren Rangers season. The player was always an integral part of Walter Smith's squad. His quality was underlined when he was named as one of only two Rangers players selected for the Scotland squad for World Cup France 98. Andy Goram was the other.

Games:	155
Goals:	58
League Championship:	1993–94, 94–95, 95–96
Scottish Cup:	1995–96
Honours:	38 Scotland caps (13 with Rangers)
Born:	Paisley, 6 December 1965

BRIAN McGINTY

1993-1997

A big (6' 1"), powerful, strong-running forward, Brian is a product of the Ibrox youth system, and signed from the Rangers Boys' Club in July 1993. He made his debut on 7 January 1995 in a 1–1 draw against Partick Thistle at Firhill, and in the following season, played very well at Easter Road and Tynecastle in successive weeks (Rangers wins, 4–1 and 2–0 respectively). In 1997, McGinty joined his former colleague Mark Hateley at Hull City on a one-year contract.

Games:	4
Goals:	0
Born:	East Kilbride, 10 December

PAUL McKNIGHT

1993-

A Belfast boy, Paul joined from St Andrews Boys' Club in August 1993 and made his first-team debut as a substitute in the 1–1 draw with Partick Thistle on 13 May 1995. He impressed, and although he has been rather checked by injuries, Rangers have hopes that he will break through in time.

Games:	2
Goals:	0
Born:	Belfast, 8 February 1977

CRAIG MOORE

1993-

From the Australian Institute of Sport, Craig joined Rangers in September 1993 as a talented player of whom much was expected. Before coming to Ibrox, he had played in the World Youth Cup, and was a full Australian international. Central defender is probably his best position, although he has also played midfield, or full-back. Not exceptionally fast, his positional play compensates, and Walter Smith has used him tactically. When Smith, in the matches against Celtic, floods his midfield, tempting forward Celtic's temperamental flair players from Portugal and Italy, draws them into the web then counter-attacks quickly and strongly, he always finds a place for Moore. He made his debut on 5 April 1994 in a scoreless draw at Tannadice.

Games:	91
Goals:	4
Championship:	1994–95
League Cup:	1996–97
Honours:	5 Australia caps
Born:	Canterbury (Australia), 12 December 1975

BRIAN LAUDRUP

1994-98

Brian Laudrup was born into football, and fated to be famous. His father Finn had 21 caps for Denmark, including two appearances against Scotland, and Brian and older brother Michael played many times for the Danish national team – perhaps Brian's career summit in that respect came when Denmark won the European Championships in 1992 in Sweden.

The Laudrups have been football cosmopolitans. Michael in his time played for Juventus, Lazio, Real Madrid and Barcelona and Brian reached Ibrox in July of 1994 as an expensive (£3.5 million was the reported fee) 25-year-old who had followed an eventful trail. From the Brondby club in his homeland he had gone to Bayer Uerdingen for £650,000, then to the Bayern Munich, for £2 million before a move to Italy and Fiorentina for yet another £2 million fee.

The Italian club was relegated during his time there and Laudrup for a time was on loan to AC Milan. Apart from any other consideration, the fact that tactically Rangers would allow him to run free within the team pattern made Ibrox an irresistible attraction for the Dane.

This was never more manifest than on the stunning debut he made on 13 August 1994 against Motherwell at Ibrox. In the dying minutes, with the score set at 1–1, Laudrup set off from the right on a diagonal dribbling run which took him across the Motherwell defence and set up Duncan Ferguson for a match-winning shot. That made Laudrup an instant Ibrox darling and was the overture to an astonishing season for the Dane. Playing mainly in a No.11 shirt, he scored 10 goals in 33 League matches with a consistency that brought him Player of the Year awards from the Scottish Football Writers and the Scottish Professional Footballers associations.

Impressive ball control, acceleration and pace are the hallmarks of his game. His balance allows him to play on either wing. At 6ft tall and 13 stones, he is powerful enough to withstand the rudest challenges from defenders. Perhaps the greatest single characteristic of Laudrup's play is his poise in penetrating deep opposing defensive positions, right into the goal area. At that close range, he can still turn defenders, still unbalance goalkeepers with the deftness of his finishing.

The quality and precision of his crossing is exceptional in a modern game in which so much of this work is cheerfully aimless. With Paul Gascoigne, Laudrup forms a penetrative force for Rangers which opposing players and managers have recognised and fear, saying that it is impossible to contain both of them for an entire 90 minutes, that in any match, at least once either man will produce the thrust that destroys a defence and provides the scoring chance.

Some Rangers followers, who rejoice in watching these marvellous players, have sensed that there is a certain unspoken spice in their relationship, that each man is well aware of the other's achievement and point to Gascoigne's tour-de-force of scoring all three goals in Rangers' championship-winning match, that 3–1 win over Aberdeen on 28 April 1996. They are persuaded that it produced a marvellous tit-for-tat from Laudrup some three weeks later in the Scottish Cup Final. Then, he almost single-handedly destroyed Hearts, scoring two goals and setting up a hat-trick for Gordon Durie in the 5–1 win with a quite dazzling performance.

But no Laudrup goal was as thrilling, or as vital, as the courageous diving header which, with a 1–0 win over Dundee United at Tannadice on 7 May 1997, confirmed Rangers ninth successive League Championship triumph. It brought not only a Championship medal to the Dane, but underwrote his second Footballer of the Year award in three years from the Scottish football writers. Only two other players had won twice – both Rangers players, John Greig and Sandy Jardine.

In the summer of 1997, there were reports of a $4.5 million transfer to Ajax Amsterdam. Laudrup was persuaded to see out his contract but early in 1998, he signed a pre-contract agreement with Chelsea. His final season as a Rangers player was a great disappointment.

Games:	150
Goals:	45
League Championship:	1994–95, 95–96, 96–97
Scottish Cup:	1995–96
League Cup:	1996–97
Brondby	
League Championship:	1987, 88
Honours:	75 Denmark caps (27 with Rangers)
	1992 European Championship
Born:	Vienna, 22 February 1969

BILLY THOMSON

1994-96

Billy Thomson, a seasoned international goalkeeper of many clubs, made his debut for Rangers in Denmark. As cover for Andy Goram and Alistair Maxwell, he signed for the club in July 1994 when the team was on tour in Denmark and Germany, and was flown out to play in the little known Ikast, in Denmark, on 1 August 1994. In the 1–1 draw, one Basile Boli scored his first goal for Rangers.

Thomson had a long pre-Ibrox career. From Glasgow United, he joined Partick Thistle as a youngster and was understudy to Alan Rough the Scotland goalkeeper for three seasons. St Mirren spent a club record at the time, £50,000, for his services, which ran to six seasons and 166 games for the Buddies (and seven Scotland caps) between 1980 and 1984. Then came seven seasons under Jim McLean at Tannadice and runners-up medals with Dundee United in the 1986–87 UEFA Cup Final (winners IFK Gothenburg) and the Scottish Cup Finals of 1987 and 1988. Again, 155 League appearances were testimony to his durability.

When Alistair Maxwell was in dispute with Motherwell in 1991, Thomson moved to Motherwell, where his career seemed to be running down. Then came the call to Ibrox. He is now a goalkeeping coach for Dundee.

Games:	7
Shut-outs:	0
Honours:	7 Scotland caps (none with Rangers)
Born:	Linwood, 10 February 1958

174 ALAN JAMES McLAREN

1994-98

Signed from Hearts on 26 October 1994 for a fee of £2 million, Alan McLaren was seen by Rangers as a mainstay of defence for years to come, and, by many, as a successor to Richard Gough as captain of the club. Central defence was probably his preferred position, where he had been powerful, incisive, strong in the air, and not without talent in bringing the ball forward. He made an outstanding debut, against Celtic in a 3–1 win just four days after signing for the Ibrox club, in a match played at Hampden Park because of reconstruction at Parkhead.

McLaren's absence through injury for a long spell in season 1996–97 severely handicapped team performances. His loss to Rangers throughout the following season was as great as that of any of the other injured players. Alan played for some 30 minutes in the Ian Durrant testimonial match on 28 April against Sheffield Wednesday, but then had to accept that his playing career was over.

Games:	94
Goals:	5
League Championship:	1994–95, 95–96
Scottish Cup:	1995–96
League Cup:	1995–96
Honours:	24 Scotland caps (10 with Rangers)
Born:	Edinburgh, 4 January 1971

NEIL CALDWELL

1994-95

Full-back Neil Caldwell had a short career at Ibrox, but had one distinction during his spell there – he knew that he was to be released from his contract before he made a first-team debut, the game against Partick Thistle in the final League game of the 1994–95 season.

Neil came up from the ranks of Rangers Boys' Club and was a prominent player in the youth and reserve teams. A right-back of solid build, Billy Kirkwood, on leaving the Ibrox staff to become manager of Dundee United, thought sufficiently highly of Neil to take him to Tannadice, where he managed a couple of league games in 1995–96. Caldwell later went back to junior football with Petershill.

Games:	1
Goals:	0
Born:	Glasgow, 25 September 1975

BASILE BOLI

1994-95

Basile Boli, one of the most vibrant, not to say controversial, players in Rangers' long history, had come and gone in one season. For him, it was a season as eventful as any could be.

Boli was born on the Ivory Coast and had French citizenship and 45 appearances in the French national team. Following a transfer from Auxerre he won three French Championships with Marseille and scored the winning goal for the French club against AC Milan in the European Cup Final of 1993. He had been in a losing final with Marseille against Red Star Belgrade in 1991. Thus his credentials were of the highest order.

He was a sweeper par excellence, even if he could also thrill crowds with his surges up field which often brought goals, but Rangers, inexplicably, played him at either right-back or in central defence, partnering Richard Gough. They never did jell. Boli was often caught out of position, playing a system with which he was not familiar. Frustrated, he unburdened himself in a *France Football* magazine article, criticising Rangers' methods of training, of tactics, of discipline, match preparation and almost everything else.

Describing himself as 'black, catholic, republican, socialist', he was at a loss to understand why Rangers had signed him in the first place, since all that was the very antithesis of what the club represented. The fact that many people with Rangers sympathies agreed wholeheartedly with almost everything Boli was saying (except perhaps for the dress code) was somewhat lost in the controversy. The other question as to why he, therefore, had signed for Rangers was left unanswered but no doubt lay in the massive amount Rangers were paying him. Nevertheless, he played enough matches to add another Championship to his trophy collection. He moved on to Monaco.

Games:	31
Goals:	2
League Championship:	1994–95
Marseille	
European Champions Cup:	1992–93
Championship:	(three)
Honours:	45 France Caps (none with Rangers)
Born:	Adjame (Ivory Coast), 2 January 1967

GARY BOLLAN

1995-98

Transferred from Dundee United, with Alec Cleland, on 27 January 1995, former Celtic player Gary Bollan had been in a long-term dispute with the Tannadice club over the length of his contract. A capable left-side full-back or midfielder, Gary's career had been seriously compromised by injury. He made his debut against Aberdeen on 12 February, a few weeks after signing, in a match which Rangers lost 2–0, and played half a dozen League games that season. He managed only four the following season, 1995–96, all at left-back. Paradoxically, he played in three Champions League matches but sustained a bad injury on the frozen Westphalen Stadium in Dortmund on 6 December 1995, and after major surgery, he missed almost all of season 1996–97. His transfer to St Johnstone early in 1998 mystified many Rangers supporters, given that the club had struggled desperately to replace David Roberston. Gary's natrual position is left-back.

Games:	15
Goals:	0
Born:	Dundee, 24 March 1973

STEPHEN WRIGHT

1995-

A full Scottish international, and at age 23, having held down the right-back position for Aberdeen for a number of seasons, Stephen Wright was looked on as an ideal successor to Gary Stevens, and as someone who would solve a problem in defence for Rangers not solved since the departure of the Englishman. Wright, transferred for £1 million in July 1995, was seen as a player who might secure the position for as much as a decade, and a golden future was forecast for him.

But sadly, as with so many other Rangers players in the nineties, injury was to compromise his career. Just as he was bedding into the team and becoming a regular, an innocuous tackle in the game with Juventus at Ibrox on 1 November 1995 stopped him in his tracks. He was out for the rest of that season. At the start of season 1996–97, the injury recurred, and Stephen required further surgery. In season 1996–97, he played only one game. By the end of season 1997–98 Stephen had played a total of only 19 games and early in 1998 he went on loan to Wolverhamton Wanderers. His contract expired at the end of season 1997–98, and his future at Ibrox uncertain.

Games:	19
Goals:	0
Honours:	2 Scotland caps (none with Rangers)
Born:	Belldhill, 27 August 1971

DEREK JOHN McINNES

1995-

A Paisley boy, Derek was signed from Greenock Morton in November 1995, for £300,000. A midfield player, clever on the ball, he made his first-team debut on 9 November 1995 in a home 1–0 win over Partick Thistle, but played only six games that seasons. Injuries severely curtailed his seasons 1996–97 and 1997–98. He has been a regular squad player, rather on the fringe of the team, but many consider he will have a useful career at Ibrox.

Games:	40
Goals:	4
League Championship	1996–97
Born:	Paisley, 5 July 1971

OLEG SALENKO

1995-96

From August 1995 to January 1996, a brief spell of six months encapsulated the career of Oleg Salenko with Rangers. For a player of his eminence, it was a flirtation that left many Rangers fans puzzled as to why he had been signed. One answer offered to the first question was that he had been the next best thing when Rangers failed to get Florian Raducioiu, the Romanian, from Espanol, the Barcelona club.

Salenko burst onto the international scene by scoring five of Russia's goals in their 6–1 defeat of Cameroon in the 1992 World Cup Finals in the United States. He had opted to play for Russia after the dissolution of the Soviet empire. His career moved from Zenit Leningrad to Dynamo Kiev, where a dispute with the management cost him six months of inaction. He was eventually loaned to the Spanish club Logrones. The loan became a transfer and when 16 goals in 31 League appearances saved the club from relegation, he was snapped up by the Spanish club Valencia.

Oleg was physically slight, but he was highly skilled with the ball, a pensive player who could orchestrate attacks and penetrate defences and score goals almost by stealth. Eight in his 20 Rangers appearances was not an unreasonable return for his type of play. It may have been that Salenko never did quite accustom himself to Scottish ways, Rangers ways, but many Rangers fans regarded him as a ghost who flitted through the halls of Ibrox then, almost before they knew it, was off to haunt Istanbulspor, in Turkey.

Games:	20
Goals:	8
League Championship:	1995–96
Dynamo Kiev	
League Championship:	1990
Honours:	8 Russia caps (none with Rangers)
Born:	St Petersburg, 12 October 1969

PAUL GASCOIGNE

1995-98

When Paul Gascoigne joined Rangers in July 1995, many of the more responsible English football critics judged him to be their only world-class player of the nineties. His arrival at Ibrox brought an overwhelming welcome from Rangers fans.

Gascoigne at his best is the very best, but the question that was to vex Rangers, and the England international team was, 'How often is he at his best?' Injuries and suspensions compromised much of his career. A Gateshead boy, his career had embraced Newcastle United, Tottenham Hotspur and Lazio of Rome, and there was a certain element of unlikely romance in his joining Rangers – it appears that when the Rangers manager Walter Smith met him on a holiday beach in Florida, the possibility of him leaving Lazio for Rangers was first mooted. Having dominated the Scottish game for the previous half-dozen years, Rangers' ambitions now had them reaching out for success in Europe and to that end their policy was to make the world their oyster and sign players from wherever. Gascoigne was very much one such player.

Paul Gascoigne is a footballer of abundant, outrageous talent. He is a player of imagination and wide vision, his achievements based on an exceptional, instant ball control. From midfield, his instincts in attack are twofold – to penetrate defences with close-dribbling runs from deep, his quick feet taking him through densely-packed defensive mazes into the closest of menacing, finishing positions, or producing the same effect for the striking players with long precise passing penetrating the defensive lines. Gascoigne's use of the ball, his passing, long and short, is killingly accurate, and one of his most intriguing qualities is his capacity of materialising into spaces, ghosting into positions, unconsidered by opposing defences. With free kicks, he has been a scorer from unlikely positions, curving shots either way. He has been known to head goals. His finishing is subtle, a matter of placement rather than power.

In the first half of season 1996–97, before a January injury in a friendly game against Ajax in Amsterdam kept him out for three months, he was leading scorer with 13 goals, and he made critical scoring contributions to Rangers successes. In the 1995–96 Championship-clinching match against Aberdeen at Ibrox, he had all three goals in a 3–1 win after Rangers had gone behind. There was a stunning score against Celtic at Parkhead in the 2–0 September win, and two against Hearts in the Coca-Cola League Cup final of 1996.

But to this paragon, there was a converse. His disciplinary record on the field clearly compromised the club's reputation. When booked in the 1–1 draw with Celtic at Ibrox, it was his fifth in successive League matches, his 13th booking in domestic play and his 16th in 32 matches. He was ordered off in the European Champions League. Almost half of his infringements were for dissent – it seems he could not resist snarling at referees.

It seemed that Gascoigne was trouble-prone, accident-prone (15 operations before he was 30) and a 'primitive' who was only fulfilled when playing, in training or in the dressing room, with 'the lads', in a football community environment, a man who simply could not bear to be alone. Walter Smith, his manager, had defended him by saying that with Paul, one had to take 'the bad with the good'. In fairness, few footballers have been so hounded by the media, but what was clearly established after two years with the club was his vast talent, ranking him with the greatest players in Rangers' long history.

At the start of 1997–98, few Rangers fans could have imagined that this was to be Paul Gascoigne's final season at Ibrox. In October and November of that season, he was producing some superb performances for the club, being particularly outstanding in the 1–0 home win over Celtic on 8 November. 11 days later in the 1–1 draw at Celtic Park Gascoigne ran the show, in total command of the midfield until around the hour mark, when he was ordered off by referee John Rowbotham. It was a decision that in the view of many, including Walter Smith, was grossly unjust.

The ordering off arguably cost Rangers the match, the result of 1–1 coming with a very late equaliser from the Celtic player Alan Stubbs. Indeed many friends of Rangers felt that this was a turning point in the season. Had Rangers won, they would have been six points clear of Celtic, and the Parkhead club would have lost three successive matches, a severe psychological blow to them. Gascoigne was suspended for five games, during which time, Rangers lost four crucial points.

Perhaps the cutting edge had gone. Yet he was still one of the two world-class players at Ibrox (the other being Brian Laudrup), a player who, like Laudrup, could win matches for Rangers. Consequently, his transfer to Middlesbrough in March, for £3.5 million, was deemed by many as an act of surrender on the part of chairman David Murray, of an acceptance by him that the link was lost, and it was better to take the money and run.

Having played indecisively in England friendly matches against Belgium and Morocco, Gascoigne was one of six players to be dropped from the England squad for France 98. Glenn Hoddle declared that Gascoigne's omission was for tactical and fitness reasons and that the player was not prepared for what could possibly be a seven-game competition.

Gascoigne was devastated and enraged and flew back to London from La Manga in a fury bringing to an end a melancholy season for this immensely talented but persistently controversial footballer.

Games:	103
Goals:	39
League Championship:	1995–96, 96–97
Scottish Cup:	1995–96
League Cup:	1996–97
Tottenham Hotspur	
FA Cup:	1990–91
Honours:	54 England caps (22 with Rangers)
Born:	Gateshead, 27 May 1967

GORDAN PETRIC

1995–

Gordan Petric reached Rangers from Partizan Belgrade by way of Dundee United. He had been introduced to Scottish football by Ivan Golac, when he managed the Tannadice club, and was an established Yugoslav international when Rangers bought him for £1.5 million in the summer of 1995. A commanding central defender, he has headed important goals for Rangers, going forward for corner and free kicks. Highly skilled in possession, his rather languid attitude to things have had Rangers fans concerned at the lackadaisical element in his play, which has provoked a certain careless-ness. He is not alone in that. Playing for a team as successful as Rangers often sees players indulging themselves, and as with perhaps Albertz, Bjorklund, even Van Vossen.

With the arrivals in the summer of 1997 of Lorenzo Amoruso and Sergio Porrini, Petric struggled to maintain a place in the team. A succession of injuries also compromised his season.

Games:	94
Goals:	4
League Championship:	1995–96, 96–97
League Cup:	1996–97
Dundee United	
Scottish Cup:	1993–94
Partizan Belgrade	
League Championship:	1992–93
Born:	Belgrade, 30 July 1969

ALEC CLELAND

1995–

A Glasgow boy, Alec came from Dundee United in January 1995 for a fee of £750,000 as an attacking right sided full-back. His pace and attacking instincts rivalled those of David Robertson at left-back and made them a formidable wide partnership. With long-term injuries to Stephen Wright and Trevor Steven in 1996–97, Cleland filled a problem position for Rangers. His first goal for the club came on 30 September 1995 against Celtic, at Celtic Park in a 2–0 win.

Unusually for a defender, he scored a hat-trick, albeit against Keith in a 10–1 Scottish Cup win. Cleland was untypically ordered off in a European tie against Juventus in Turin. Alessandro del Piero, the hugely talented forward, teased and taunted Cleland all the evening, and the full-back eventually snapped, taking a wild swipe at the Italian.

The departure of David Robertson in 1997 meant that Cleland spent much of 1997–98 out of position at left-back. This did Cleland few favours and his form was clearly affected. Out of contract in the summer of 1998, he seemed certain to head for pastures new.

Games:	134
Goals:	7
League Championship:	1995–96, 96–97
Scottish Cup:	1995–96
League Cup:	1996–97
Dundee United	
Scottish Cup:	1993–94
Born:	Glasgow, 10 December 1970

THEO SNELDERS

1996–

Theo Snelders, the Aberdeen goalkeeper, joined Rangers on 27 March 1996 for £250,000 as reserve to Andy Goram. He made his debut three days later at Kircaldy in one of only two games that season. It seemed a reasonable signing for Rangers – Theodorus was an experienced Dutch international player at 33. But there was one shortcoming, one black mark. Whilst with Aberdeen he had been selected to play for Holland against Germany, and at short notice, apparently refused to play. Sadly the same scenario arose in the Scottish Cup quarter-final match at Parkhead on 6 March 1997. Snelders was called on to play and he reportedly refused leaving Rangers were in dire straits. Eventually Goram played but his clear lack of fitness was a major contributor to Rangers' defeat. It seemed unlikely that Snelders would play for the club again. Even the arrival of fellow-countryman Dick Advocaat to take charge of the team in the summer of 1998, might hold little hope for Theo. He had become very much third choice goalkeeper behind Andy Goram and Antti Niemi.

Games:	18
Shut-outs:	6
Aberdeen	
Scottish Cup:	1989–90
League Cup:	1989–90
Born:	Westervoort (Holland), 7 December 1963

JORG ALBERTZ

1996–

Albertz came from Hamburger SV in the summer of 1996 as an experienced player with two international caps for Germany, for a sum of £4 million. As a left-sided player in midfield, and occasionally at left-back, he is noted for an immensely powerful shot, in particular from dead-ball situations. He has been the scorer of spectacular goals with the club, one stunning strike against Celtic in the New Year game of 1997 coming to mind. He is tall at 6' 2", and powerful. There is also skill and composure in the play of the midfielder. In 1998 as the season's campaign boiled up, Albertz scored critical goals. On 21 February, a late winner at Easter Road was a shot of stunning power; a week later an injury-time equaliser from one of his dead ball speciality blasts against Hearts at Ibrox brought a 2–2 draw. But none were more critical or more spectacular than the goals he scored in successive games against Celtic. On 25 April 1998, in a critical game at Tynecastle he repeated the feat.

With the going of Gascoigne in March 1998, Albertz seemed to take on with relish – and much success – midfield creative responsibilities. His ordering off at Tannadice in the final League game of the season by referee Hugh Dallas seemed a most harsh decision by the official, one which robbed the German of a place in the Scottish Cup final against Hearts a week later, a loss which Rangers could ill afford.

Games:	89
Goals:	28
Honours:	2 Germany caps (none with Rangers)
League Championship:	1996–97
League Cup:	1996–97
Born:	Monchengladbach, 29 January 1971

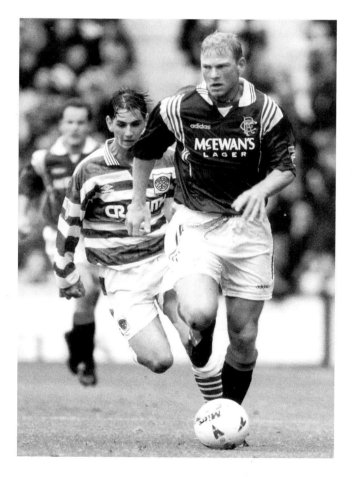

ERIK BO ANDERSEN

1996–97

Joining Rangers from the Aalborg club in Denmark, Erik Bo Andersen, at 6' 4" tall, simply had to be a striker. He was quickly seen as a player of some pace, of strong running power, good positional sense and movement, and determination in finishing. His lack of first touch suggested that he was not the most skilful forward, and it would be true to say that he was not quickly accepted by the fans. But the more discerning supporters noted that if Andersen's teammates played to his strengths and played the ball in front of him and not to his feet he could be a profitable player.

This was underlined early in his Ibrox career when he scored a hat-trick against Partick Thistle in a 5–0 league win on 13 April 1996. One goal came from his right foot, one from his left and one from his head. Season 1996–97 saw the Dane out of the team for long spells, partly due to injury, partly due to selection policies. He seemed to answer all criticism with two goals in the 3–1 win over Celtic in the hugely important Championship match. In the following League game against Hibs at Easter Road, he had another in the 2–1 win, but in the spring of 1997, he suffered a bad head injury which put him out of the last weeks of the season.

He left the club toward the end of 1997 to return to Denmark, joining Odense for £800,000. In going, he was critical of how he had been treated at Ibrox. This struck a chord with many friends of Rangers who certainly felt that this was one player who had received a raw deal from the club.

Games:	35
Goals:	18
Aalborg	
League Championship:	1994–95
Honours:	8 Denmark caps (4 with Rangers)
Born:	Randers (Denmark), 14 November 1970

JOACHIM BJORKLUND

1996–

Yet another import in Rangers' signing spree of spring and summer of 1996, Bjorklund came to Ibrox with impressive credentials – 44 caps for Sweden. He was signed from Vicenza, the Italian club, for £1.7 million and was quickly seen as a central defender of some pace. His first season with Rangers was of mixed quality, some of his games outstanding, others less so, but his strength of character was not in doubt, particularly after his performance in the hugely important win at Celtic Park, 1–0, in March, which tilted the Championship towards Rangers.

He was a player who had split the Rangers fans. Some admired his coolness and pace. Others simply did not rate him and were bewildered by the number of his Swedish caps. He was fielded, inexplicably, at right wing-back by Walter Smith for the Scottish Cup final of 1998, the first time he had ever played in the position. He may well blossom under Dick Advocaat.

Games:	83
Goals:	0
League Championship:	1996–97
League Cup:	1996–97
Honours:	58 Sweden caps (14 with Rangers)
Born:	Vaxjo (Sweden), 15 March 1971

PETER JACOBUS VAN VOSSEN

1996-

Peter Van Vossen, who had earlier been with Anderlecht and Ajax, arrived at Ibrox from Istanbulspor in Turkey in exchange for Oleg Salenko. There were Rangers fans quick to say that the Turks had the better of that particular deal. Peter's international career included a penalty goal against England at Wembley. A striker, or a wide midfield player, he has pace, stamina and considerable skill, but the one thing he does not have is a controlling first touch. It is fair to say that he did not make a sudden, stunning impact when he arrived at Ibrox for the second half of season 1995–96 – he signed in January. The rumour mongers had it that Walter Smith had believed, in signing Van Vossen, that he was getting an out-and-out striker.

Early in the 1996–97 season, Peter played well, scoring a memorable goal in the Richard Gough testimonial match against Arsenal. A change of strategy by manager Smith – using two forwards rather than three – told against Van Vossen. Sadly, many will remember him for the miss 'of the century' at Celtic Park in the November 1996 match when, unmarked and a few yards from an open goal, he scooped the ball high over the crossbar.

For Peter, 1997–98 was a miserable season in which he played only as a substitute in one League game, a defeat at Motherwell and in two League Cup games in which Rangers were fielding very much under-strength teams. The arrival of Dick Advocaat may give Van Vossen a new lease of life but as ever, it gets down to the business of how best his talents can be used for the team, and if a role can be found for him.

Games:	38
Goals:	10
Ajax	
League Championship:	1994–95
Anderlecht	
League Championship:	1992–93
Honours:	18 Holland caps (none with Rangers)
Born:	Zierikzee (Holland), 21 April 1968

SEBASTIAN ROZENTAL

1996-

The first South American player to play for Rangers, Sebastian is a striker, a goalscorer with a fine left-foot finish, handily built and an international for Chile. His signing was much protracted by work permit regulations, but he was eventually cleared in a $6 million (approximately £4 million) deal.

His debut was long awaited, and much acclaimed. He played the final 15 minutes of a 3–1 win in a League match at Motherwell, but his home debut was a Scottish Cup tie against St Johnstone. He scored, but played only 45 minutes. A cruciate ligament injury would keep him out of the game for more than a year. He returned to action for a Scottish Cup tie against Motherwell in February 1998, but after just four more appearances was sidelined once more. With further surgery required, it seemed unlikely that the Chilean would play first-team football until early 1999.

Games:	6
Goals:	1
Honours:	20 Chile caps (none with Rangers)
Born:	Chile, 1 September 1976

SCOTT WILSON

1996–

A central-defender who has progressed through the Ibrox youth ranks, signing from Rangers Boys' Club in 1995. A Baptism of fire against Ajax in the European Champions' League fixture at Ibrox on 30 October 1996 found the youngster acquitting himself so well that many friends of Rangers were unhappy at his substitution, but he had impressed Walter Smith enough to play in two more European ties that season.

Games:	4
Goals:	0
Born:	Edinburgh, 19 March 1977

DARREN FITZGERALD

1997–

Nicknamed 'mucker', the young Belfast-boy made his first-team breakthrough against Kilmarnock on 22 March 1997 as a substitute in Rangers' 1–2 home reversal. A phenomenal scoring rate at reserve and youth level ranks, the 5' 8" striker is one for the future.

Games:	1
Goals:	0
Born:	Belfast, 13 October 1978

BARRY FERGUSON

1996–

Younger brother of Derek, and likewise a midfield player of whom a great future is predicted. Signed from Rangers Boys' Club in July 1994, Barry's immense potential as a skilful footballer brought recognition in the final fixture of the season 1996–97 at Tynecastle. In season 1997–98, following the various absences of Paul Cascoigne through injury and suspension, and ultimately his transfer to Middlesbrough, many saw Ferguson as a replacement in the mid-field play-making spot , if not of the high quality of the Englishman.

A combination of circumstances, primarily injuries, loss of form and the idiosyncracies of team selections limited Ferguson's appearances to 11. These were good enough to bring him Scotland Under-21 selection. Let us hope the new regime at Ibrox will realise his great potential.

Games:	12
Goals:	0
Born:	Glasgow, 2 February 1978

ANDY DIBBLE

1997

A surprise short-term signing in March 1997 from Manchester City, the 6' 2" Welsh International goalkeeper was called up in an extreme emergency due to injury to Andy Goram and the absence of Theo Snelders. His debut at Celtic Park on 16 March 1997 being in the League fixture which all but clinched Rangers' ninth successive title.

Dibble did not let Rangers down that day and played seven games in all in the Championship run-in, his Ibrox stint being the latest port of call in a career that has encompassed Cardiff City, Luton Town, Sunderland, Huddersfield Town, Manchester City, Aberdeen, Middlesbrough, Bolton Wanderers, West Bromwich Albion and Oldham Athletic. Capped at every level by his country, Andy Dibble was the first Welshman to play for Rangers in the post-war era and will surely regard his 'old firm' debut as a highlight of his career alongside that of his outstanding display for Luton Town in their Littlewoods cup victory.

Games:	7
Shut outs:	4
Honours:	3 Welsh caps (none with Rangers)
Born:	Cwmbran, 8 May 1965

STEVEN BOYACK

1996–

A product of Rangers Boys' Club and a player of immensepromise, Steven Boyack won every honour at youth level with Rangers. A midfield/forward player, his first-team debut as a substitute arrived at Hibernian on 18 September 1996. In season 1997–98, he joined former teammate Mark Hately at Hull City on loan.

Games:	1
Goals:	0
Born:	Edinburgh, 4 September 1976

MARCO NEGRI

1997–

Marco Negri took Scottish football by storm with his scoring exploits in the first half of his first season. He had scored no fewer than 33 goals by the turn of the year, 30 of them in the Scottish League. His scoring rate was such that all records for both club and Scottish football in a single season, seemed at risk. He had been signed in the summer of 1997 in a £3.75 million transfer from Perugia, a club with which he had scored 35 goals in two seasons, including 15 in 27 games in Italy's Serie A. However an eye injury while playing squash with Sergio Porrini, together with a slump in form, limited his scoring to four goals in the second half of the season. Towards its end, he was not even a member of the squad for Rangers games.

This was a state of affairs with which he was none too happy, and it appeared he would not be at Ibrox for the start of season 1998–99. That apart, a season's total of 37 goals in 40 games is remarkable for any player.

A player of considerable technical ability, Marco was perhaps a late developer, having played in the lower divisions in Italy for several seasons before finding success with Perugia. His style on the field seemed laid back, distant, almost lazy and his lack of emotion and celebration after scoring the most spectacular of goals puzzled Rangers fans and contrasted hugely with the reactions of his contender for the position, one Ally McCoist. Early in the season he scored one of the great goals of the year, against Dundee United at Ibrox, when he flicked the ball over several defenders, including the seasoned Maurice Malpas before lobbing the astonished goalkeeper, Sieb Dijkstra. Negri turned away, matter of fact about the whole thing.

185

Games:	40
Goals:	37
Born:	Milan, 27 October 1970

SERGIO PORRINI

1997–

A £2.75 million signing from Juventus in the summer of 1997, Porrini is a player of vast experience having been with AC Milan, Atalanta, Bergamo as well as Juventus during his career in Italy. In that time, he won two Italian international caps, and won two championships with Juventus. He also has the distinction of having played, less successfully, with Juventus in two European finals – the 1994–95 UEFA Cup final against Parma, which Parma won, and the 1996–97 European Champions' League final against Borussia Dortmund, which Borussia won! However he did play, more successfully, in the 1994–95 Italian Cup final, a two-legged affair to give Juventus a 3–0 win.

Porrini signed for AC Milan at the age of 18 and prospered at the San Siro until he fell out with coach Arrigo Sacchi, who described him as 'a little strange'. He subsequently moved to Atalanta. Strong in defence, right-back is probably his preferred position, but mainly because of injuries to others, Rangers have used him mainly in central defence in his first season. With a sound tactical brain, Sergio is an experienced player, believed to be a disciple of Marcello Lippi's creed of serious and extreme physical conditioning. He was perhaps surprised at a more relaxed training regime at Ibrox, but has sought to stay true to his own principles of preparation.

Games:	37
Goals:	4
Juventus	
League Championships:	1996–97, 1994–95
Italy Cup:	1994–95
Honours:	2 Italy caps (0 with Rangers)
Born:	Milan, 8 November 1968

GENNARO GATTUSO

1997–

'Reno' Gattuso was signed in the summer of 1997, aged 19, an amateur with the Perugia club. His signing caused something of a rumpus between Italy and Scotland. Italian regulations demand that a player must play a given number of Serie A games before he can sign a professional contract, and Rangers were able to sign him before he did that – in fact he was signed before the end of the Italian season 1996–97. Perugia complained to FIFA, the world governing body, which found in favour of Rangers.

Young Reno is a player of immense energy, a midfield dynamo who seems to cover every inch of the field. Walter Smith's intention had been to use him sparingly throughout 1997–98, believing that he was one for the future, but injuries and other circumstances meant that he played 38 games. During the season he was capped by Italy at Under-21 level. Some critics have suggested that he expends a great deal of energy to comparatively little effect, but he is not without skill – for example his pass which set up Alistair McCoist's goal in the 1998 Scottish Cup final was quite perfect.

Not surprising for such a young player, he has been homesick from time to time, and that as much as anything may drive him back to Italy prematurely. Time will tell.

Games: 38
Goals: 4
Born: Corigliano Calabro (Italy), 9 January 1978

JONAS THERN

1997–

Jonas Thern has played at the highest levels of the European game – with Malmo, Benfica, Napoli and Roma, from whom Rangers signed him in July 1997. He has captained his country, and played in a European final, for Benfica against AC Milan in 1990. In 1992 he was transferred from Benfica to Napoli for £3.5 million, a huge fee then, and evidence of his qualities, as were his national championship successes with Malmo and Benfica.

A strong, aggressive, busy midfield player, Jonas seldom wastes possession and prefers to do the simple thing – when he played in midfield beside Paul Gascoigne, he tended to collect from defence, then move the ball to Gascoigne and let him get on with it, a role rather like that of Paul Lambert at Borussia Dortmund. With Gascoigne gone, Thern adopted a more dominant role in midfield. He scored some excellent goals with power shooting, important goals among them. There was a winner at Dunfermline in March 1998, and an equaliser at Kilmarnock. His opening goal against Celtic at Ibrox on Easter Sunday was a stunner, volleyed from 25 yards.

His absence from the last few games of the season proved a crippling blow to Rangers. He missed the last home game – the second last league game – which Rangers lost in the last few minutes to Kilmarnock and which had they won, as things turned out, they would have been champions. Critical too was his absence from that season's Scottish Cup final.

Articulate, intelligent and dignified – Thern is a fine ambassador for club and country, keeping himself very fit at 31. His reason for coming to Rangers – he had a very good offer from IFK Gothenburg – raised many questions. He said they had made him an offer he could not refuse, better than his combined salaries from Roma, Napoli and Benfica!

Thern had played for local team Varnano before joining Malmo. His first cap for Sweden was in 1987 against West Germany at Gelsenkirchen. In the match he formed the midfield with Robert Prytz, the former Rangers player.

Games:	29
Goals:	4
League Championship:	1985–86, 1987–88 (Malmo)
Swedish Cup:	1985–6 (Malmo)
League Championship:	1990–91 (Benfica)
Honours:	75 Sweden caps (4 with Rangers)
Born:	Falkoping (Sweden), 20 March 1967

STAALE STENSAAS

1997–

From Rosenberg Trondheim in Norway, in the summer of 1997, and for a £1.75 million fee, Staale joined Rangers on the same day as Lorenzo Amoruso. He was to become perhaps Walter Smith's most disappointing signing. In his defence, it can be said that he plays in the one position in the modern game which is difficult for any club to fill satisfactorily – that of left wing-back. Yet when Rangers signed him, he had never been capped by Norway and it was said that he had been offered around English Premiership clubs for £500,000!

He was signed as a replacement for David Robertson, but made no real impression at Ibrox. He won three Norwegian championships with Rosenberg and in 1995–96 and 1996–97, played in 18 European Champions' League games, including a sequence when AC Milan was eliminated and Rosenberg got to the quarter-final stage before losing to Juventus. A natural athlete, Staale has never been inhibited about making forward runs.

Games:	28
Goals:	2
Rosenberg	
League Championship:	1994–95, 1995–96, 1996–97
Born:	Trondheim (Norway), 7 July 1971

TONY VIDMAR

1997–

Tony Vidmar was the first player to join Rangers in the new era of freedom of contract following the 'Bosman' ruling. He came from the Dutch club NAC Breda as a defender on either side, but basically a left-back. He is a skilful player going forward but has still to establish himself at Ibrox. He played in the Australian national team, with Craig Moore incidentally, in the fateful match against Iran which saw them fail to qualify for France 98, under the management of Terry Venables.

Games:	19
Goals:	0
Honours:	8 Australia caps (8 with Rangers)
Born:	Adelaide, 4 July 1970

LORENZO AMORUSO

1997–

During the summer of 1997 Lorenzo was the first of Rangers' Italian signings, from Fiorentina for a fee of £4 million. He reputedly rejected an offer from Manchester United in joining Rangers. Considered by many Italians as 'their best uncapped defender', he was to be plagued by injury from the moment he joined Rangers. Indeed the Ibrox club signed him in the knowledge that he had to undergo Achilles tendon surgery. In the event, after two operations, he had missed virtually the entire season. His competitive debut came only in April 1998, some nine months after he joined the club.

He is a central defender of not inconsiderable skill, a combative player, strong, powerful, of enormous presence on the field, enjoying a thunderous shot with free kicks from outside the penalty area. Walter Smith must ponder what might have been had Amoruso been fully fit throughout the season. Amoruso was the defensive linchpin of the fine Fiorentinan side which went to the semi-finals of the European Cup Winners' Cup in 1996–97. In both semi-final legs, against Barcelona, although Fiorentina lost, Amoruso effectively blotted out the great Ronaldo.

His entry into the Scottish Cup semi-final match against Celtic was dramatic indeed. He replaced the injured Petric after only 20 minutes, then made an immediate impact on the game. A very impressive player, he won an Italian Cup with Fiorentina, when they beat Atalanta 3–0 over two games in the 1995–96 competition.

Games:	6
Goals:	0
Italian Cup:	1995–96 (Fiorentina)
Born:	Bari, 28 June 1971

ANTTI NIEMI

1997–

Finnish international goalkeeper signed from FK Copenhagen for £700,000, Antti found his appearances restricted by not one but two hand injuries. He has been a mainstay in goal for Finland but no doubt tries to forget the game in which his country was freakishly eliminated from France 98 by Hungary, by an own goal in the fourth minute of injury time.

Previously with HJK Helsinki, Antti also had to contend with Andy Goram, and probably, in season 1998–99, with Charbonnier. Inevitably, he has made it known that he will not be content with being number three. He has never let Rangers down, and has looked an entirely competent goalkeeper. He must have been desperately disappointed to have missed the Scottish Cup final of 1998, having played in the three preceeding league games.

Games:	7
Shutouts:	4
Finland League Championship:	1991–92
Finland Cup:	1993 (with HTK Helsinki)
Honours:	25 Finland caps (4 with Rangers)
Born:	Oulu (Finland), 31 May 1972

JONATAN JOHANNSON

1997–

This young Finnish player and attacking left side midfielder, scored for Finland against Scotland at Easter Road in April 1998. Born in Stockholm, he was in fact signed from Estonian club Flora Tallin, for whom he had registered nine goals in nine games. He had played a trial for Chelsea before joining Rangers. Slim and skilful he is clearly one for the future. He had earlier played for TPS Turku, in his home country.

Games:	10
Goals:	0
Honours:	11 Finland caps (5 with Rangers)
Born:	Stockholm, 16 August 1975

THE MANAGERS

William Struth

William Struth, manager of Rangers from 1920 to 1954, was born in Edinburgh. He was a stonemason by trade, which no doubt helped to make him physically strong. As a young man he was a 'pedestrian', a professional runner who did the rounds of the tracks up and down the country, running for money as and where it was available. He became trainer of Clyde FC in 1908, then of Rangers in 1914.

On the death of the club's secretary-manager William Wilton – by drowning at Gourock in 1920 – Struth became secretary-manager. In the thirty-four years that followed, until he retired at the end of season 1953–54 and became vice-chairman of the club, Rangers won eighteen League Championships, ten Scottish Cup Finals and two League Cup Finals; the club won the Glasgow Cup eighteen times, the Glasgow Charity Cup twenty times. In season 1929–30 Rangers won every competition entered – Scottish Cup, League Championship, Reserve Cup, Reserve Championship, Glasgow and Glasgow Charity Cups.

Struth's record speaks for itself. If it is rivalled in any way, that would surely be by the Celtic successes of Jock Stein – nine Championships, seven Scottish Cups and six League Cups from 1965–75. And for longevity in the manager's chair, Struth can be spoken of only alongside his contemporaries, Willie Maley of Celtic and John Hunter of Motherwell.

He was a disciplinarian and a dandy – both elements of his character which were impressed upon the club. Struth never had much to say about the playing of the game, about tactics, about how to handle peculiarities in the opposition from week to week. That was left to his senior players and captains, players such as Tommy Muirhead, David Meiklejohn and George Young, who would guide the younger men. But behaviour and appearances were paramount. Struth had a network of informer friends of the club all over the country, and few Rangers players misbehaved without being discovered. Few avoided the consequences, which were an invitation to go 'up the stair' to Struth's office and a session in which the offender was (metaphorically) pinned to the wall. And the extremists who didn't listen closely enough would one way or another presently leave the club.

Struth kept half a dozen or more suits – all of them double-breasted – in his office at Ibrox, and might change two or three times a day. And he saw to it that Rangers players were all properly turned out, from the bowler hat and spats of the twenties to the club blazer and slacks.

William Struth became director-manager of the club in 1947, retired as manager in the summer of 1954, and died on 21 September 1956 at the age of eighty-one. He was buried in Craigton Cemetery in Glasgow, a stone's throw from the club and the stadium which had been his life's work.

Scot Symon

By any reasonable standards, Scot Symon was an outstanding success as a football club manager. When he retired from playing at the end of season 1946–47, he became manager of East Fife. In his first season they were promoted to the First Division, or Division A as it was then called. In 1949–50 this little provincial club won the League Cup. Also in 1949–50 they reached the final of the Scottish Cup and faced Rangers, losing 3–0 to an outstanding display by the winners, who scored in seconds. Symon moved to Preston North End in March 1953, saw that team into an FA Cup Final at Wembley, where they lost to West Bromwich Albion, then was invited back to Ibrox in June 1954 when Bill Struth vacated the managerial chair.

At Ibrox his success continued. The Championship was won in 1956, '57, '59, '61, '63, '64; the Scottish Cup was won in 1960, '62, '63, '64, '66; and the League Cup in 1961, '62, '64 and '65. The early sixties saw an exceptional Rangers team including Baxter and McMillan, Greig and McKinnon. Rangers were twice finalists in the European Cup Winners' Cup, in 1961 and 1967.

Scot Symon was the last of the lounge-suit managers, the waistcoat managers. He was never a track-suit man, never a man for working much on tactics. He let playing systems emerge from the talents of his players rather than imposing tactical systems on them. And he signed some extremely good players, excellent buys for the club. Scot was a shy man, by no means a media performer, essentially a man of his time, a man of the thirties. And, of course, Rangers do not operate simply to 'reasonable standards'. Scot Symon left Rangers on 1 November 1967, when they were top of the League, having won six and drawn two of the eight matches played. On that very day Celtic, European Cup holders, were playing in South America for the World Club Championship with the team that was to dominate the rest of the decade.

Perhaps it was the correct decision by the club to change managers. Perhaps they needed a more contemporary figure – Symon was an old-school gentleman, and he was 58. More and more, football club management was being seen as a young man's game. But the manner of his going brought no credit to the board of directors. Clearly John Lawrence, the chairman, should have spoken to Symon personally, informally, perhaps seeking his counsel in the first place on the appointment of a team man-ager, suggesting that he, Symon, should become general manager with a seat on the board. After all, the man had been a tremendous servant to the club, both on and off the field. Instead, Lawrence sent a business associate who had no involvement with football nor with the club to do it for him. Symon, a proud man, not surprisingly 'took the huff' in the time-honoured phrase and would have none of it. He quit. He was briefly a director of Dumbarton, then manager of Partick Thistle. He died on 30 April 1985.

David White

David White played wing-half for Clyde and, a Glasgow boy, spent his entire career with the Shawfield club. He became player-coach, then in 1966 manager of Clyde, and in 1967, when both Rangers and Celtic were in the finals of European competitions, Davie travelled with both clubs on observer, 'educational' trips. Perhaps he impressed the Rangers people. On their return from their Nuremberg final he was appointed assistant manager by Scot Symon. Five months later, with the departure of Symon, Davie White was manager of Rangers.

He had virtually no success in his two years at Ibrox – one Glasgow Cup victory amounted to nothing in the eyes of the faithful. He was perhaps desperately unlucky to have to contend with the astonishing Celtic team of Jock Stein, and the disappearance from the team of Baxter and McMillan. In season 1967–68, for example, Rangers were unbeaten going into their thirty-fourth and final League game against Aberdeen at Ibrox. They lost a League match for the only time that season, finished with 61 points, yet had to cede the Championship to Celtic, by two points.

In European football, White's Rangers in successive seasons reached the quarter-finals and the semi-finals of the Inter Cities Fairs Cup, but lost to Leeds United and Newcastle United respectively. White had the team playing quite well, even stylishly at times, but when it came to the clinching of a championship or a cup, bad luck always seemed to be on hand. In the 1969 Scottish Cup Final, scarcely credible defensive mistakes by experienced players invited Celtic to run all over them, which Celtic did 4–0. It was Rangers' heaviest Cup Final defeat. A goalkeeping fumble by Gerry Neef cost them a 1–0 defeat by Celtic at Parkhead and dismissal from the League Cup the follow-ing season.

White was perhaps not a disciplinarian. The players' dress was often sloppy, training sessions were missed and feeble excuses accepted. The end came for Davie White with the double defeat by Gornik Zabrze in November 1969, in the European Cup Winners' Cup. In the first match in Poland it was immediately obvious that the young manager had underestimated Gornik, saying in advance that Rangers would go all out in attack. They did – they were two goals down in twelve minutes and lost 3–1. In the second match at Ibrox, two goals in twelve minutes were again lost – this time the closing twelve minutes – and it was Gornik again, 3–1 again. That evening the Rangers board met, and the next day David White was a former Rangers manager. He later managed Dundee to a League Cup victory. It may well be that Davie lacked the years, the maturity, the tactical and international experience for a job which is unlike any other in football.

Willie Waddell

Willie Waddell finished playing in the summer of 1956 and a year later was manager of Kilmarnock. In eight years there he brought surprising success to the provincial club – a Championship victory of all things, in 1964–65; a Scottish Cup Final (0–2 v Rangers in 1960) and two League Cup Finals (0–2 v Rangers in 1960–61 and 0–1 v Hearts in 1962–63). He became manager of Rangers on 3 December 1969. 13 months later, he faced what he may have come to believe was the greatest challenge of his public life.

On 2 January 1971, Rangers drew 1–1 with Celtic at Ibrox before a crowd of 80,000 people. In a match without any unruly incident, on the field or on the terraces, Jimmy Johnstone had scored for Celtic in the very last minute, only to see Colin Stein equalise with just 15 seconds left to play. Rangers fans, spilling down Stairway 13 from the huge terraces, met disaster. One fan, riding on another's shoulders, toppled forward near the top of the exit staircase. The domino effect sent the huge crowd sprawling down the stairway. The result was that 66 people were crushed to death and 145 injured in one of football's worst disasters.

With a board of directors that seemed so stunned as to be ineffectual, Waddell took command. Two days later Rangers contributed £50,000 to the Lord Provost's Appeal Fund for the relatives. Waddell saw to it that the club was represented at each of the sixty-six funerals. The players, and many former players, were summoned and ordered to take part. But most of all, Waddell was haunted by the thought that the same thing might easily happen again.

It was time to make changes to an Ibrox which was huge, aged and in fact obsolete. He researched the modern grounds in Germany and elsewhere throughout Europe and beyond, and within the decade Waddell had transformed Ibrox into probably the most attractive and sophisticated football stadium in Britain. It is a magnificent monument to the man. True, he was aided by Rangers Pools, which provided some of the £10 million funding (it invariably produces a seven-figure gift to the club each year). But Willie Waddell had done it – crabbit or not, he had done it. He was an achiever. He got things done – on the field, at Kilmarnock, in journalism, as a Rangers player, as a Rangers executive. And he was a visionary. He brought in Jock Wallace as coach, and in June of 1972 made him team manager. It was the beginning of better days for the Light Blues.

Willie Waddell died on 14 October 1992. He was 71. In the long history of this great club, it has had no greater servant. He has been player, manager, general manager, managing director, vice-chairman and finally an honorary director and in each of these capacities over a span of some 56 years he brought a massive achievement and distinction to the club. He will rank with the greatest names in the club's history. His memory is preserved at Ibrox Stadium, most prominently in the members' Waddell Suite.

Jock Wallace

Jock Wallace, from Wallyford in Midlothian, was a hard man, often called 'Rock' Wallace if seldom to his face, and he had a remarkable, far-travelled career in the old game. Not many men could envisage being manager of Rangers. Wallace was, twice. Not many managers in Scotland can envisage winning the treble of League, Scottish Cup and League Cup. Wallace did it, twice.

A goalkeeper, he played first for Airdrie and was transferred to West Bromwich Albion for £8000 in 1959. From there he moved to Bedford, Hereford and Berwick. Indeed, on that most fateful of all days in Rangers' history, 28 January 1967, Jock Wallace was in the Berwick goal in their first-round Scottish Cup tie, when the Rangers of Berwick beat the Rangers of Glasgow 1–0. There were many consequences of that result. As player-manager of the border club, he made them promotion chasers within a couple of years. In 1968 he went to Hearts as assistant to manager John Harvey, and in June 1970 Willie Waddell, a good judge of abrasive characters, took him to Ibrox as coach. In June 1972 he was appointed team manager. He resigned in May 1978 and joined Leicester City. In 1982 he was back in Scotland to manage and help consolidate the promoted Motherwell. he succeeded John Greig at Ibrox in November 1983 and was sacked in April 1986 by David Holmes, chief executive, no doubt to make way for Graeme Souness. Jock then went to the Seville club in Spain, later returning to manage Colchester United. These are the bare bones of his career.

Jock Wallace was a hard man, a hard taskmaster, a motivator supreme who, in his time in National Service with the King's Own Scottish Borderers, had served in Northern Ireland, and had fought Communist insurgents in the jungles of Malaysia. His training methods were sometimes controversial – at one time he had Rangers players running up and down the huge sand dunes at Gullane. Yet this brought them bursting fitness and was probably a foundation for the long careers which players such as Sandy Jardine, Alex Macdonald, Tommy McLean, Alex Miller, John Greig, Colin Jackson and others enjoyed. And he brought on young players in the seventies such as Derek Johnstone, Bobby Russell and Alistair Dawson, all of whom had long careers. A further testament to the Wallace teaching methods was the number of these players who went into management.

He was tactically shrewd. As coach in 1970–71, his League Cup win over Celtic, even if a narrow 1–0, dented if it did not end the dominance of Jock Stein's team. As manager he won the Centenary Scottish Cup in 1973, against Celtic again, this time by 3–2. There was the European Cup Winners' Cup success in 1972, and then came the winning of the Championship in 1974–75, for the first time in 11 years.

With this impetus came the winning of the treble of League, Scottish Cup and League Cup, in 1975–76 and again in 1977–78. It was the first time in Scottish football history that any manager had done this. But only a matter of days after completing the second treble, with a 2–1 Scottish Cup Final win over Aberdeen on 23 May 1978, Jock Wallace shocked Scottish football by resigning. John Greig was named manager the next day.

The reasons for Wallace's departure from Ibrox have never been publicly explained, but a clash of personality with Willie Waddell, even amid all that success, is usually accepted as the cause. Waddell had brought Wallace to Ibrox as coach. He had made him team manager on 7 June 1972 when he, Waddell, became general manager. The general opinion seems to be that Waddell would not release money that Wallace had decided was necessary to reinforce the team. Waddell, it should be said, was very much involved in the design, construction and funding of the new stadium at this time.

Wallace took off for Leicester City and took them to the Championship of the Second Division of the Football League, and to a place in the FA Cup semi-finals. There was no doubt that this man knew the business of running a football team. He was back north in the summer of 1982 with Motherwell, and eighteen months later, following the resignation of John Greig, returned to Ibrox. Jock brought new life to what was an ailing team, with a long, unbeaten run. Rangers won the League Cup in March of 1984, beating Celtic in the final 3–2, and the 1984–85 final against Dundee United, 1–0. But the team never did challenge for the Championship. Aberdeen and Dundee United had become powers in the land. Indeed, season 1985–86 could be said to have been the worst in Rangers' League Championship history. It was the only season in its existence in which the club failed to average at least one point per match.

When the John Lawrence organisation bought out enough of the Rangers shareholdings to give them control of the club, changes may have been inevitable and extra pressure would have fallen on Wallace. As it was, an abysmal 2–0 defeat by Tottenham Hotspur in April 1986 saw Wallace sacked by David Holmes, a John Lawrence appointee and chief executive of the Rangers club. Jock Wallace, undaunted, took himself off to Seville to manage the Spanish club, then returned first to manage Colchester United, then to become a director of the Essex club.

It was at Colchester that Wallace's ill-health was diagnosed as Parkinson's disease. He bore it with the bravery and determination that had characterised his life. He was often seen at Ibrox, and at away matches, paying his own admissions, making no demands on the club. At his funeral service in St Michael's Church, Inveresk, Midlothian, he was described as 'the epitome of a Ranger'.

John Greig

There is an old football saw which insists that promoting a player directly from the dressing room to the manager's chair, as it were, never quite works. More often than not, that is true, and the experience of Kenny Dalglish and the Liverpool club may simply be the exception which proves the rule. Alas, it was certainly true in the case of John Greig, one of the greatest of all Rangers players.

John was appointed manager of Rangers on 24 May 1978, the day after Jock Wallace left Ibrox, first time round. He inherited the 'Treble Team' of 1977–78, Wallace's second treble as a manager, Greig's unprecedented third as a player. John had played a total of 41 matches that season.

With a squad of experienced and successful players to hand, with his knowledge of the club, its ways and its history, there was no reason to suppose that John Greig the manager might not maintain this success. The team won the League Cup and the Scottish Cup, the final of which required three games against Hibernian, and in the European Champions Cup disposed of Juventus and PSV Eindhoven before going down to Cologne in the quarter-final. The Championship was lost to Celtic at Parkhead in a decisive game by 4–2. Five minutes from the end, Colin Jackson inadvertently headed into his own goal, and in the very last minute Murdo MacLeod whacked in the fourth. Celtic took the title by three points. In hindsight, it was an ominous failure by Greig's team.

His second season, 1979–80, was something of a near-disaster. Rangers finished fifth in the Championship. All season long they failed to beat Celtic in any competitive game. They went out of the League Cup at the third round, beaten home and away by Aberdeen. Greig indulged in a flurry of buying and selling. Ian Redford came from Dundee for £210,000, Gregor Stevens from Leicester City for £150,000; Derek Parlane went to Leeds United for £160,000. The team did get to the Scottish Cup Final, the one hope of salvaging something from the season, and faced Celtic in another critical match. A good open game ran true to what was becoming the Greig form – seventeen minutes into extra time, George McCluskey diverted a Danny McGrain shot which McCloy had covered, and Celtic had won, 1–0. Gordon Smith's move to Brighton brought in £400,000; Colin MacAdam cost a 'tribunal' fee of £165,000 from Partick Thistle, Jim Bett £180,000 from the Lokeren club in Belgium.

The next season, 1980–81, saw Rangers make a bright opening of an unbeaten run over the first fifteen matches. Aberdeen again dumped them out of the League Cup, and in the Scottish Cup they overcame Dundee United 4–1 in a replayed final. But still the League was beyond them – they finished third.

At the end of season 1981–82, experienced players such as Sandy Jardine, Colin Jackson and Tommy McLean left the club. Rangers won the League Cup again, reached the Scottish Cup final for the seventh successive year, yet lost to Aberdeen after extra time, and yet again could do no better than third in the Championship. This continuing failure in the League was beginning to irk the many friends of Rangers – which was reflected in Ibrox attendances. In

1982–83 Greig paid Hibs a record £225,000 for Craig Paterson, but Rangers finished fourth in the Championship, no fewer than eighteen points behind the champions, Dundee United. John Greig resigned on 28 October 1983, saying 'I've finished with the game!' – exactly what many men would say in a moment of pique, a time of frustration. In early 1990 he did come back to the game, back to the club, as manager of public relations for Rangers, a rather less fearsome post than that of manager.

A certain amount of detachment is needed by football managers. When a man has spent some eighteen years as one of the boys in the dressing room downstairs, and is pitched upstairs at a day's notice, he must find it difficult to establish a code of discipline to apply to his friends. Failure to do that may have been the fate that befell John Greig.

Graeme Souness

As Rangers' very first player-manager, Graeme James Souness has made a greater contribution to Scottish football than he ever did on the field despite fifty-four caps and captaincy of his country. When he took control of the management of the Rangers team in April 1986, he revolutionised the Scottish game. By spending vast amounts, by Scottish standards, on buying players and importing high-quality English players, enticing them no doubt with huge salaries and the prospect of playing in European competitions from which English clubs were banned, Souness reversed the trend of a century or more, when the norm was that Scottish players went to England to seek greater reward.

Thanks to an earlier manager, and managing director, of Rangers, Willie Waddell, Rangers already had a modern, magnificent stadium in the mid-eighties. The Souness ambition was clearly to make the team match the stadium, and if it took a cosmopolitan recruiting policy to do that, so be it. His avowed aim was for Rangers to win a European competition. When the call came from David Holmes, then chairman of the club, in the late spring of 1986, Graeme Souness was ready. He had a mass of international experience and playing achievement behind him with Scotland, of national and European experience with Liverpool, and the direct personal experience of playing at the highest level of Italian football, perhaps the most sophisticated footballing atmosphere in the world.

But before settling into the new job came the World Cup Finals in Mexico that summer. Souness, the captain, was left out of the team for the final critical group match against Uruguay, an error of judgement on the part of Alex Ferguson, the international team ma-nager, to which he later confessed at a huge charity lunch in Glasgow, apologising publicly to Souness, who was present.

To complete a remarkable story in the remarkable fortunes of this Rangers club, Graeme Souness and a friend, David Murray, bought control of the club from the Lawrence organisation in 1989. Murray was a self-made millionaire with interests in metal stockholding and property, and one of a new wave of young Scottish entrepreneurs. Souness was thus into the wider management of the club and may have made a potential contender for Bill Struth's record of service as a manager. Although still registered as a player, he became preoccupied more and more with management.

Yet only six weeks after saying 'I'll never leave Ibrox', Souness resigned, on 16 April 1991, and took himself off to manage Liverpool, where his former team-mate Kenny Dalglish, had resigned. Souness spent a couple of years at Anfield, spent huge amounts as he had done at Ibrox in buying players, suffered massive heart surgery, won the FA Cup, but not the League Championship, Liverpool's abiding concern. He spent two seasons managing Galatasary in Turkey – they won the Cup but not the Championship – and by season 1995–96, he was back in England, in the Premiership, as manager of Southampton.

Walter Smith

When Brian Laudrup headed that dramatic goal at Tannadice, on 7 May 1997, which gave Rangers a 1–0 win over Dundee United and clinched their ninth successive League Championship to equal the Celtic record, it brought Walter Smith, the Rangers chieftain, a certain immortality. It was the 12th major honour he had brought the club since succeeding Graeme Souness as manager in April 1991, an average of one title every six months! It made Smith surely one of the greatest of Rangers' managers and a potential challenger to the career achievements of the famous William Struth. Indeed embracing his years at Ibrox as assistant to Souness, it brings a total of 20 honours to which he has contributed.

Smith was born in Glasgow to a Rangers 'family' and was a dyed-in-the-blue fan of the club in boyhood. His youthful ambition was to play for the club, and he had hoped that the call from Ibrox would come when he played for Ashfield, the Glasgow junior team. Instead, the summons came from Tannadice, where he had a solid career over nine years. He spent 18 months with Dumbarton, then returned to Dundee United to play out his career as a thoroughly dependable wing-half. The Dundee United manager, Jim McLean, interested him in coaching and appointed him assistant manager in 1982. Smith contributed greatly to the United successes in the eighties, and became a director of the club. Within a few weeks of his appointment to the United board came the belated call from Ibrox – in April 1986, Graeme Souness invited him to become his assistant. It was a call that could not be refused. And when Souness decided to leave, suddenly, in April 1991 to manage Liverpool, it took David Murray, chairman, only two days to appoint Walter Smith as Rangers manager. In time he became a director of the club. Walter Smith thus has an impressive background in football management at the highest level.

Early in season 1997–98 the disappointment at Rangers elimination from two European tournaments by IFK Gothenburg in the Champions League and RC Strasbourg in the UEFA Cup brought severe pressure on chairman David Murray following several years of unacceptable results in Europe. Despite all his considerable domestic success, manager Walter Smith knew that the club's ambitions lay in success in European competition. He announced at the club's A.G.M. in October 1997, that he would leave the club at the end of the season.

Smith received standing ovations from the packed hall, not just in respect of his outstanding domestic record, but also in recognition of the fact that here was a Rangers supporter, born and bred. No matter what shortcomings, if any, Walter Smith may have had, he had given his all for the club. His record of trophies won was second only to those of Bill Struth (34 years in the job) and Scot Symon (13 years). Smith had seven years as manager. But European success is now the yardstick. By staying with the club for the rest of the season, Smith clearly hoped to see it set a historic 'ten-in-a-row' of League Championship wins. Alas, his swan-song saw the Ibrox club complete the season without a single trophy won, for the first time in 12 years. With £34M spent in the previous three seasons, this was a substantial failure – perhaps no Scottish club, perhaps no British club, has so under-achieved. But Walter Smith himself could say, hand on heart, 'I was born a Rangers supporter. I remain a Rangers supporter. I will die a Rangers supporter'.

Dick Advocaat

On 1st June 1998, Dick Advocaat joined Rangers as head coach, succeeding Walter Smith. His playing career in his native Holland started in 1971 at the relatively late age of 23, when he signed for Den Haage. He was there for three years before joining Breda Kekrod, moving on to Berlo. In 1980, he joined the National Soccer League in USA, playing for Chicago Stings.

In 1982 he returned to Holland to begin a coaching career with amateur side DVSP and two years later, in a move that startled Dutch football, he became assistant coach to Runus Michels, the national team manager. In 1987 he was appointed manager of the Haarlem club, then in 1989 became coach at Dordrecht where the director of football was former Celtic coach Wim Jansen. In their first season, the pair won promotion to the top league. In 1992, Advocaat replaced Michels as national team coach and led the Dutch team to a quarter-final place in the 1994 World Cup finals.

After the World Cup, he became coach at PSV Eindhoven. In 1996, he won the Dutch championship, ending the dominance of Ajax – indeed Eindhoven won the Dutch double of league and cup that season. Upon joining Rangers, Advocaat said that he had 'discussed the way ahead for Rangers Football Club with David Murray, the chairman on several occasions.' He continued, 'I had a very clear vision of the direction in which I wish to take the club, and I look forward to working with everyone at Ibrox to ensure that this direction brings even more success for this great club.'

Advocaat is without doubt one of the most highly rated coaches in world football. His former colleague Wim Jansen regards him as one of the most acute tacticians in the game, meticulous in his forward planning. He is also a strict disciplinarian, but it remains to be seen how he copes with the relaxed culture enjoyed by Scottish footballers.

STATISTICS

		LEAGUE App Gl	SCOTTISH CUP App Gl	LEAGUE CUP App Gl	EUROPE App Gl	TOTAL App Gl
Albertz, J	96–	63–20	8–3	6–3	12–2	89–28
Alexander, T.	70–71	2–0	0–0	0–0	0–0	2–0
Amoruso, L.	97–	4–0	2–0	0–0	0–0	6–0
Andersen, Erik Bo	95–98	24–15	3–1	2–2	6–0	35–18
Anderson, S.	59–60	1–0	0–0	0–0	0–0	1–0
Armour, D.	74–79	3–0	0–0	1–0	0–0	4–0
Arnison, Norman	55–57	0–0	0–0	2–2	0–0	2–2
Arnison, Billy	46–47	7–1	1–0	2–3	0–0	10–4
Austin, A.	57–58	1–0	0–0	0–0	0–0	1–0
Baillie, D.	60–64	31–0	4–0	3–0	2–0	40–0
Baird, S.	55–61	121–39	16–2	26–6	16–5	179–52
Bartram, J.	87–88	11–3	3–0	0–0	0–0	14–3
Baxter, J.	60–65, 69–70	150–19	21–0	54–2	29–3	254–24
Beattie, S.	85–87	5–0	0–0	0–0	0–0	5–0
Beck, T.	64–66	11–2	2–0	1–0	0–0	14–2
Beckett, W.	50–51	1–0	0–0	0–0	0–0	1–0
Bell, D.	85–87	35–1	0–0	4–0	5–0	44–1
Bett, J.	80–83	104–21	18–2	24–6	6–1	152–30
Bjorklund, J.	96–	59–0	8–0	4–0	12–0	83–0
Black, K.	81–84	24–1	3–0	7–1	0–0	34–2
Boli, B.	94–95	28–2	1–0	1–0	1–0	31–2
Bollan, G.	94–98	11–0	0–0	1–0	3–0	15–0
Bonnyman, P.	72–73	0–0	0–0	1–0	0–0	1–0
Boyack, S.	96–	1–0	0–0	0–0	0–0	1–0
Boyd, Gordon	75–76	1–0	0–0	0–0	0–0	1–0
Boyd, Willie	51–52	2–0	0–0	0–0	0–0	2–0
Brand, R.	54–65	206–127	33–29	54–38	24–12	317–206
Brown, Bobby	46–56	211–0	33–0	52–0	0–0	296–0
Brown, John	87–96	207–14	33–4	18–0	20–0	278–18
Bruce, A.	81–86	2–0	0–0	0–0	0–0	2–0
Burns, H.	83–87	52–4	1–0	8–0	2–0	63–4
Butcher, T.	86–91	127–8	11–0	21–1	17–2	176–11
Caldow, E.	53–66	265–17	39–4	68–1	35–3	407–25
Caldwell, N.	94–95	1–0	0–0	0–0	0–0	1–0
Caskie, J.	46–49	26–3	4–0	9–2	0–0	39–5
Christie, J.	61–62	3–3	0–0	4–3	1–2	8–8
Clarke, Robert	80–82	1–0	0–0	0–0	0–0	1–0
Clark, Sandy	82–85	41–14	7–2	10–S	4–1	62–22
Cleland, A.	94–98	96–4	14–3	10–0	14–0	134–7
Cohen, A.	86–88	7–0	0–0	2–0	3–0	12–0
Conn, A.	68–74	93–23	13–3	31–11	12–2	149–39
Cooper, David	77–89	376–49	49–7	77–18	38–1	540–75
Cooper, Neale	88–91	17–1	2–0	1–0	0–0	20–1
Cowan, T.	88–91	12–0	1–0	0–0	2–0	15–0
Cox, S.	46–55	207–14	40–3	63–3	0–0	310–20
Cunning, R.	54–55	3–0	0–0	2–0	0–0	5–0
Dalziel, G.	78–84	34–9	8–1	6–1	0–0	48–11
Davies, W.	80–86	13–1	3–0	5–0	2–1	23–2
Davis, H.	56–64	168–8	23–0	42–3	28–2	261–13
Dawson, A.	75–87	218–6	36–0	39–1	23–1	316–8
Denny, J.	70–79	37–0	3–0	21–0	5–0	66–0
Dibble, A.	97–	7–0	0–0	0–0	0–0	7–0
Dodds, D.	89–91	17–4	2–0	0–0	2–1	21–5
Donaldson, G.	72–74	5–0	0–0	5–0	0–0	10–0
Drinkell, K.	88–89	36–11	8–5	6–2	4–1	54–19
Duncan, G.	57–60	12–5	2–0	1–0	0–0	15–5
Duncanson, J.	46–51	93–41	17–7	30–11	0–0	140–59
Dunlop, R.	50–53	3–0	0–0	0–0	0–0	3–0
Durie, G. S.	93–	113–43	17–9	7–1	18–5	155–58
Durrant, I.	84–98	249–26	19–3	40–8	39–8	347–45
Elliott, A.	55–56	2–0	0–0	0–0	0–0	2–0
Falco, M.	87–88	14–5	0–0	3–3	2–2	19–10
Ferguson, Alex	67–69	41–25	6–0	10–4	9–6	66–35
Ferguson, Derek	82–90	111–7	8–0	11–1	15–1	145–9
Ferguson, Eric	83–86	14–1	0–0	0–0	0–0	14–1
Ferguson, Duncan	93–94	14–2	3–0	4–3	2–0	23–5
Ferguson, Iain	84–86	32–6	1–0	8–3	4–2	45–11
Ferguson, Ian	87–	222–28	26–6	27–7	30–4	305–45
Ferguson, Barry	96–	8–0	4–0	0–0	0–0	12–0
Findlay, W.	47–54	70–37	11–7	33–21	0–0	114–65
Fitzgerald, D.	97–	1–0	0–0	0–0	0–0	1–0
Fleck, R.	83–88	85–29	3–0	8–2	8–3	104–34
Forrest, J.	62–67	105–83	10–6	37–50	11–6	163–145
Forsyth, Alex	78–81	25–5	1–0	8–0	7–0	41–5
Forsyth, Tom	72–82	218–2	36–2	50–2	22–0	326–6
Frame, J.	48–52	1–0	0–0	0–0	0–0	1–0
Francis, T.	87–88	18–0	1–0	2–0	4–0	25–0
Franks, A.	59–60	3–0	0–0	0–0	0–0	3–0
Fraser, Cammy	84–87	52–6	3–1	12–2	8–0	75–9

		LEAGUE App Gl	SCOTTISH CUP App Gl	LEAGUE CUP App Gl	EUROPE App Gl	TOTAL App Gl
Fraser, Scott	83–85	9–0	1–0	0–0	0–0	10–0
Fyfe, G.	69–76	64–22	1–0	20–8	6–1	91–31
Gardiner, W.	51–55	25–16	3–2	3–1	0–0	31–19
Gascoigne P.	95–98	73–30	8–3	7–4	15–2	103–39
Gattuso, G.	97–	29–3	4–0	3–0	2–1	38–4
Gillick, T.	46–50	104–49	16–5	20–8	0–0	140–62
Ginzberg, B.	89–91	4–0	0–0	3–0	1–0	8–0
Goram, A. I.	91–98	184–0	26–0	19–0	31–0	260–0
Gordon, D.	91–93	45–6	7–1	2–1	1–0	55–8
Gough, R.	87–98	318–25	37–2	37–3	36–4	428–34
Grant, B.	59–60	1–0	0–0	0–0	0–0	1–0
Gray, Andy	88–89	14–5	1–0	1–0	0–0	16–5
Gray, David	46–47	9–0	0–0	3–0	0–0	12–0
Greig, J.	61–78	498–87	72–9	121–17	64–7	755–120
Grierson, D.	52–57	72–42	13–6	21–11	0–0	106–59
Hagen, D.	89–94	16–3	1–0	1–0	2–0	20–3
Hamilton, J.	73–78	59–5	11–2	6–1	1–0	77–8
Hateley, M.	90–95, 97–	169–88	17–10	19–11	17–6	222–115
Henderson, Martin	74–78	33–10	5–3	6–1	3–0	47–14
Henderson, Willie	60–72	276–36	44–5	60–11	46–10	426–62
Heron, B.	69–70	7–0	0–0	0–0	2–0	9–0
Hogg, B.	57–59	2–1	0–0	0–0	0–0	2–1
Houston, D.	73–74	10–0	0–0	4–0	3–0	17–0
Hubbard, J.	49–59	172–77	19–5	41–23	6–1	238–106
Huistra, P.	90–95	125–22	9–1	15–1	9–2	158–26
Hume, R.	59–62	17–3	3–0	0–0	3–0	23–3
Hunter, Donald	73–75	3–0	1–0	0–0	0–0	4–0
Hunter, Willie	62–64	1–0	0–0	0–0	0–0	1–0
Hurlock, T.	90–91	29–2	2–0	4–0	0–0	35–2
Hynd, R.	63–69	31–4	4–1	6–0	7–0	48–5
Jackson, C.	63–82	341–23	53–8	75–8	36–1	505–40
Jardine, W.	65–82	451–42	64–8	107–25	52–2	674–77
Johannson, J.	97–	6–0	3–0	0–0	1–0	10–0
Johansen, K.	65–70	158–4	21–2	32–2	27–1	238–9
Johnstone, Derek	70–83, 84–86	369–132	57–30	85–39	35–9	546–210
Johnson, Joe	47–52	32–8	2–2	2–1	0–0	36–11
Johnston, Maurice	89–92	76–31	5–1	13–9	6–5	100–46
Johnston, Willie	64–73,80–82	246–91	42–10	65–16	40–8	393–125
Kennedy, Andy	82–84	15–3	3–1	2–0	0–0	20–4
Kennedy, Stewart	73–80	99–0	10–0	19–0	3–0	131–0
King, R.	61–62	2–0	0–0	0–0	1–0	3–0
Kirkwood, D.	86–89	7–0	0–0	1–0	2–0	10–0
Kitchenbrand, D.	56–58	29–26	3–2	3–1	2–1	37–30
Kuznetsov, O.	90–94	34–1	0–0	0–0	1–0	35–1
Laudrup, B.	94–98	116–34	13–5	4–3	17–3	150–45
Liddell, C.	51–55	35–8	6–2	11–2	0–0	52–12
Lindsay, J.	46–52	17–0	1–0	4–0	0–0	22–0
Little, Adam	47–51	6–0	0–0	0–0	0–0	6–0
Little, John	50–61	178–1	32–0	55–0	10–0	275–1
Logie, W.	56–57	16–0	0–0	0–0	3–0	19–0
Lyall, K.	81–84	9–0	1–0	2–0	0–0	12–0
Macdonald, Alex	68–81	336–51	50–15	79–18	38–10	503–94
MacDonald, Iain	69–73	11–2	1–0	2–0	0–0	14–2
MacDonald, John	78–86	163–44	24–13	34–15	9–5	230–77
MacDonald, Kevin	88–89	3–0	0–0	0–0	0–0	3–0
MacFarlane, D.	84–89	7–0	1–0	1–0	0–0	9–0
MacKay, W.	75–85	24–1	3–0	7–2	3–1	37–4
MacKinnon, D.	82–86	102–1	7–0	23–1	9–0	141–2
Marshall, D.	46–53	14–7	9–0	6–2	9–0	20–9
Martin, N.	58–70	75–0	6–0	14–0	15–0	110–0
Mason, J.	72–74	16–2	1–0	2–0	0–0	19–2
Mathieson, W.	64–75	174–2	36–0	38–0	28–1	276–3
Matthew, A.	58–60	28–7	3–2	4–1	2–2	37–12
Maxwell, A.	92–95	53–0	7–0	7–0	2–0	69–0
McAdam, C.	80–85	65–15	12–8	19–9	3–0	99–32
McCall, Ian	87–90	21–2	1–0	1–0	1–0	24–2
McCall, Stuart	91–	193–15	27–0	16–3	28–2	264–20
McCallum, A.	70–71	1–0	0–0	0–0	0–0	1–0
McClelland, J.	81–85	96–4	13–1	30–2	14–1	153–8
McCloy, P.	70–86	351–0	55–0	86–0	43–0	535–0
McCoist, A.	83–	418–251	47–29	62–54	54–21	581–355
McColl, I.	46–61	360–11	59–1	100–2	7–0	526–14
McCulloch, W.	49–55	49–9	14–5	5–1	0–0	68–15
McDougall, I.	73–77	31–3	2–0	3–0	1–0	37–3
McEwan, A.	58–59	1–0	0–0	0–0	0–0	1–0
McGinty, B.	93	3–0	0–0	1–0	0–0	4–0
McGregor, J.	87–92	26–0	0–0	4–0	4–0	34–0
McInnes, D. J.	95	27–1	1–0	5–2	7–1	40–4
McIntyre, Jim	81–82	1–0	0–0	0–0	0–0	1–0